LIVING HEADSHIP

Living Headship
voices, values and vision

Edited by

Harry Tomlinson, Helen Gunter and Pauline Smith

P·C·P
Paul Chapman
Publishing Ltd

First published 1999

P·CP
Paul Chapman
Publishing Ltd

Paul Chapman Publishing Ltd
A SAGE Publications Company
6 Bonhill Street
London EC2A 4PU

SAGE Publications Inc
2455 Teller Road
Thousand Oaks, California 91320

SAGE Publications India Pvt Ltd
32, M-Block Market
Greater Kailash - I
New Delhi 110 048

British Library Cataloguing in Publication data

A catalogue record for this book is available from the British Library

ISBN 0-7619-6381-2
ISBN 0-7619-6382-0 (pbk)

Library of Congress catalog card number available

Typeset by Dorwyn Ltd, Rowlands Castle, Hants
Printed and bound in Great Britain

Contents

Contributors

Helen Gunter is a lecturer in the Department of Education at Keele University. She is particularly interested in the rapid growth of entrepreneurial and technicist managerialism, and its impact on teacher professionalism. This is demonstrated in her recent book, *Rethinking Education: The Consequences of Jurassic Management*, which uses chaos theory to evaluate critically the current orthodoxy of visioning and heroic leadership in education.

Pauline Smith is head of CPD at Crewe School of Education, Manchester Metropolitan University. She is particularly interested in developing effective partnership with LEAs and other agencies to provide continuity of support for teachers in management professional development. She is Lead Assessor with NW Regional Assessment Centre for NPQH and closely involved in the HEADLAMP programme design and delivery.

Harry Tomlinson is a professor at Leeds Metropolitan University where he was responsible for the MBA in Educational Leadership. He is Centre Manager for the Yorkshire and the Humber Region Training and Development Centre where he is responsible for the National Professional Qualification for Headship (NPQH) and is Project Director for one of the seven consortia delivering the Leaderships Programme for Serving Headteachers (LPSH). After 18 years of headship his main interest is school and headteacher performance as evidenced in books *The Search for Standards* and *Performance Related Pay in Education*.

Bernard Barker was educated at Cambridge and York Universities and was the first comprehensive school student to become a comprehensive headteacher. After 17 years at Stanground College in Peterborough, he now combines the leadership of Rowley Fields Community College in the city of Leicester with tutoring at the University School of Education.

Yvonne Bates began her career in London and worked as Head of Maths and Deputy Head in Hertfordshire. In 1997 she was seconded to the Headship of Lilian Baylis School in Lambeth with a brief to remove the school from special measures and affect a change in its reputation as one of the worst schools in the country. Her work at Lilian Baylis was the subject of a Carlton TV documentary and was featured extensively in the national and international press. Having fulfilled her brief in Lambeth she was appointed to the Headship of Sir Frederic Osborn School in Hertfordshire which was also in special measures.

Les Bell is Professor of Educational Management and Director of the School of Education and Community Studies at Liverpool John Moores University. His latest book, published by Routledge, is *The Skills of Primary School Management* (with Chris Rhodes).

Angela Bird has been a teacher for 27 years, 11 of which she spent in a socially deprived area on the outskirts of Birmingham. She has been headteacher at Woodlands Infant School for 14 years during which time she has played an active role in developing in-service support for primary heads and deputies throughout her local education authority. She is currently a member of the LEA's Literacy Strategy Group, Early Years Planning Task Force and the lead teacher representative on the University of Warwick Institute of Education Board.

Gwenn Brockley has been headteacher of Gwaenygog Infants School since September 1995. Gwenn specialised in the vision-making process while working for her master's degree in education and management at Manchester Metropolitan University (1997). She has led presentations regarding the process of 'setting the vision' and how the vision impacts on the target-setting process to headteachers across North Wales.

John Cain started teaching with the former ILEA as a teacher of business studies and economics in 1975. Three years later he moved to Surrey becoming a deputy head in 1988. He was co-author of *Investigating Business* which was published in 1989. He was appointed headteacher of Reigate School in 1993 and gained an MBA from Leeds Metropolitan University in educational management in 1997. A substantial part of his work was to explore the relationships between school culture and performance.

Carolyn Clarke was educated in Coventry and completed her teacher training at Sheffield in 1976. Her first teaching post was at Henry Bellairs Middle School, Bedworth, Warwickshire; after 7 years she moved to a post in Wiltshire and then on to schools in Southampton, rising to Deputy Headteacher at Heathfield Junior School. She believes in the importance of developing quality learning and was significantly influenced by the learning network developed in Wiltshire under the guidance of the Wiltshire English Inspector Pat D'Arcy.

Elizabeth Duffy   After University in Liverpool and South Carolina, Elizabeth took a temporary job as a supply teacher in Worcester and enjoyed it so much she has been teaching every since! After 8 years in Portsmouth (including a sabbatical year to do an MA at the London Institute of Education) she became Head of Department then Senior Teacher in Kent, followed by deputy headships, first in Kent and then in Lewisham. In 1993 she became head of a comprehensive school in Cheshire and in 1997 gained an MBA from Keele University. In September 1998 she began her second headship in Buckinghamshire.

David Gower   When he started teaching, David developed a strong interest in how children learn science. He subsequently completed his MEd in science education before combining the development of 'Science for All' courses in a Kent comprehensive school with research for a PhD in learning psychology. He became a deputy head in Bedfordshire before taking up his present post in Chester in 1989.

Frances Hardy is headteacher of the Sacred Heart RC Primary School in Roehampton. She has spent most of her teaching life within the Catholic sector and has been head of her present school for 15 years. As part of her MA in school management at Kingston University she focused on how she introduced appraisal into the school. She is at present engaged in research into the role of headship in a Catholic primary school.

John Loftus is headteacher of a primary school plus nursery in an outer London borough. Originally the school was built as a first school (pupils 3–8 years) and remained so for 20 years. Then, due to borough reorganization John had the task of bringing the school through to full primary school status.

Terry Martin is a lecturer in the Education and Social Science Division at the University of Southampton. His teaching and research interests are in the area of counselling management and professional development. The course which forms the basis of the work described in his chapter utilises case-study presentations to explore and resolve management problems. He has worked with the Health Education Division on another course, 'Bereavement and Loss Education', and has co-edited and contributed two chapters to a book entitled *Loss and Bereavement: Managing Change* (Blackwell Science).

Ray Moorcroft is Course Leader for the MA at Manchester Metropolitan University, Programme Manager for the NPQH in the North West Region and is currently working with the first cohort on the Leadership Programme for Serving Heads (LPSH). He has held senior positions in both industry and education, and has extensive national and international experience in organisational improvement initiatives.

Nick Selley is a Senior Lecturer and Tutor for the MA and other research degrees in education at Kingston University. His main interest is in the primary school curriculum and methodology, and he has recently published *The art of constructivist teaching in the primary school*.

Eric Tope has been head of St Thomas the Apostle since January 1983. He has been head of mathematics at both grammar and county secondary schools and Deputy Head Curriculum and Pastoral at his present school. More recently he gained a MBA in educational leadership from the Leeds Metropolitan University and is currently working towards his doctorate at the International Leadership Centre, Lincoln.

Tony Tuckwell is by origin a Wiltshireman and read modern history at St Peter's College, Oxford. He taught in Hampshire and was deputy head in Trafford before taking up the headship of King Edward VI Grammar School, Chelmsford in 1984. Since 1991 he has worked for the National Educational Assessment Centre at Oxford Brookes University and is now a senior assessor and Centre Director. In 1996 Ofsted classified him as an outstanding leader. In 1997 he published 'Managing learning and teaching' in *School Leadership for the 21st Century* (Routledge) edited by Brent Davies and Linda Ellison. He retired from Headship in 1999.

Mark Wasserberg has worked in five schools, including his current appointment as Head of School at Poynton County High School in Cheshire. Mark is an English teacher and spent five years as Head of English at King Edward VI High School in Stafford, before becoming a deputy at The Westwood High School in Leek, Staffordshire. His case study is based on the four and a half years he spent as headteacher at Dane Valley High School.

Mo Williams has been involved in education for almost 30 years, working mainly in inner-city schools. She took an eight-year career break when she had a family but in that time was involved in community work and adult education. The notion of 'the learning school', and the place of staff development within that, has been central to her management roles in both middle and junior schools. Her prime role as headteacher is to ensure quality learning experiences for pupils through the work of a motivated, professionally skilled and competent staff team. Accessing quality development opportunities for the staff and enabling staff to manage change are central.

Introduction: constructing headship – today and yesterday

HELEN GUNTER, PAULINE SMITH and HARRY TOMLINSON

This Introduction begins with an analysis of the construction of headship and of the professional development and training of headteachers in England and Wales over the past century, in order to provide a historical context in which the voices of the present-day headteachers in this book have been spoken, heard and shaped. Such professional accounts have a role in illuminating the connection between the microcontext of lived experience and the macropolitical, ideological and structural dimensions in the construction of the headteacher's practice and identity.

This book is about 'voices' – and 'values' and not simply 'visions'. It presents the stories and struggles of headteachers today as being both a legitimate methodology and an alternative, richer understanding than the essentially conservative and debilitating notion of the all-powerful visionary leader. The position we take in putting this collection of chapters together, in which headteachers talk about their work and research, is one which takes inspiration from Hall and Southworth's (1997, p. 164) review of the literature on headship:

> the central importance of the headteacher is a longstanding theme. It appears in a number of guises, but most compellingly in the school effectiveness research which claims to show that heads make a difference to the schools they lead. The idea that powerful and visionary heads enhance the school's effectiveness is thus a continuing belief in the research and the teacher profession generally. Yet beyond this assertion surprisingly little else is known. School effectiveness studies and more recently school improvement commentaries have offered some broad ideas about the nature of effective leadership, but these are relatively generalised and superficial. Longitudinal and observational studies of heads increasing the effectiveness of schools they lead are presently lacking.

This book aims to make a contribution to the foregrounding of the perceived realities and professional practice of headteachers through their own observations of their professional context. In doing this we do not aim to present an objective analysis in which these headteachers are under our gaze, but to enable the reader to engage with texts which focus on the inter-relationship of the headteacher and the structural context in which they are trying to understand their work.

This inter-relationship between agency and structure is the conceptual framework in which the voices, values and visions of the headteachers are located. We reflect critically on the rise and persistence of the agency of the headteacher as a charismatic and visionary leader; and explore the more recent centrally defined programmes of headship training, in terms of what Bush (1998) has identified as appropriate and sufficient preparation. Headship often seems to be presented in the form of dichotomies: weak–strong, manager–managed, empowered–disempowered, masculine–feminine, leader–follower, transactor–transformer. This to a certain extent is constructed by those who seek to relegate one form of headship in favour of a new one, rather than seeking to understand the knowledge claims on which their prescriptions are based. Questions of whether any real change has occurred to the dominant autocratic-independent model of headship, within an apparent shift of role and culture towards entrepreneurship, rationality and technical efficiency, in the late twentieth century, provide an alternative framework and permeate this Introduction.

CONSTRUCTING HEADSHIP YESTERDAY

It can be argued that the myth of the 'Great' Victorian headmaster became all pervasive in the political context of the late nineteenth century which saw the resurgence of the public schools and the emergence of a maintained system of secondary schools. Thomas Arnold's influence extended far beyond Rugby and, as Bamford (1967) records, twice as many men were promoted to headship from Rugby as from any other public school. Arnold's authoritarian and paternalistic construct of headship was also evident in the newly constituted HMI of that period who favoured the appointment of heads in the Arnoldien mould to the new grammar schools. This same view of headship is depicted also in the images and documents relating to the growing number of elementary school headteachers in the nineteenth century.

This legitimacy of the 'traditional', 'charismatic' authority of the headteacher is easily understood within the *laissez-faire* political economy of the mid to late nineteenth century and also in Morant's 1902 Act where the delicate balance of power between central and local bureaucratic control was seen to be protected by the relative independence of the role of headmaster. During these periods a series of practical handbooks of school management and teaching were the only major source of training and support for the headteacher (Taylor, 1968). The Headmasters' Conference and Association, set up by 1890, brought headmasters of secondary schools

in touch with the great figures of the day, heard them declare with passion their determination to defend their independence against central authority and local authorities proposed by the Royal Commission on Education and was strengthened in his own resolve to assert his authority over his school and its destiny.

(Baron, 1956, in Musgrove, 1970, p. 188)

Where the headteacher's 'independent' power and authority are rationally and traditionally legitimated by an élite, it is perhaps unsurprising to find that there is a dearth of guidance and training for the role. The dominant values and expectations of our class-based society during the late nineteenth and early twentieth centuries inevitably supported the independent, authoritarian and disciplinarian position of the headteacher, whose object like Arnold's was 'to form Christian men'. As Buckley (1985, p. 8) has noted, a powerful and distinctive role concept of headship thus emerged of 'the benevolent autocrat, feared and loved by staff and pupils'.

However, the dominant values of this earlier period cannot surely explain why, as late as the 1960s, Taylor (1968, p. 140) was writing of the lack of specific guidance on school administration for headteachers. He starts his chapter on 'Training the head' with the words that 'any aspirant or serving Head in England who wanted a text or book of guidelines about his job would be unlikely to find anything published in this country that would be much help to him'. It would seem that society had to experience two world wars, the growing emancipation of women and the shattering of a paternalistic pattern before the independence and authority of the headteacher were even questioned and notions of professional development and training addressed. However, as this Introduction goes on to discuss, any 'real' change or challenge to the 'traditional' concept of headship as described above is to be sensibly questioned.

An examination of *Headship in the 1970s* (Allen, 1968) reveals both continuity and some change in the dominant ideology surrounding the power and authority of headship during the late sixties and early seventies. Allen writes that 'Headteachers hold one of the most powerful jobs left in a democracy. The sudden onset of comprehensive reorganisation has made even the Department of Education and Science realise that the days of the amateur head, muddling through are over' (*ibid.*, frontispiece). These political imperatives for the government and its agencies to respond to a period of changed attitudes towards schooling are evident throughout texts of this period. Questions such as 'what does society expect of a headmaster in one of the new, reorganised schools?'; 'what authority is wielded by the head?'; 'what are the special relationships of the head with his staff, pupils and parents?'; and 'can headteachers be trained for the job?' were starting to be framed. It would appear from the literature that the traditional concept of 'headmastership' (*sic*) was starting to be examined critically in the late sixties and seventies; and the notion that a single charismatic personality at the centre of the school, who could give 'cohesion and moral purpose to the school's activity', was starting to be questioned.

From an optimist's standpoint, it could be agreed that the popular concept of the headmaster as the 'captain of the ship' possessing authority by virtue of position and personal qualities thus started to shift at this point, and the notion of professional competence and a wider understanding of the environment of the school entered the forum. New forms of delegation and a sharing of authority can be identified within the espoused theories of the seventies and the need for the training of heads proposed due to 'the contemporary pace and complexities of curriculum change' (Taylor, 1968, p. 144). However, the existence of very little systematic information about 'what Heads do' and little systematic thought given to 'what they should do' at this point in time meant that courses were 'relatively unstructured' or focused on the problems defined by the participants.

Lord James (DES, 1972) in his influential report crystallised the lack of specific preparation for headship since the time of his own headship in the 1940s. He referred to the fact that he was 'fortunate enough' to serve under a man who was himself 'a great headmaster'; who regarded it as a duty to prepare James for headship 'by discussion' and by writing 'a remarkable document' for him. Despite his good fortune James (p. 15) felt that 'we should not leave this kind of preparation to the chance that a future headmaster may be working under a great man'. He proposed the design of courses which would help headmasters 'to face new problems and wider responsibilities, even if they are less inspiring than the informal help that I was fortunate enough to receive' (p. 15). James was clearly an advocate of in-service education and training as a means of bridging the gulf between advancing knowledge and classroom practice. However, the potential narrowness or conservatism of 'training' as opposed to 'education' was also starting to be debated in the seventies, with claims that the 'training' approach tends to overemphasise the development in heads of purely managerial skills that should be more widely diffused across the staff (Allen, 1968). Instead writers wished to encourage the kinds of research and study outside the context of training that would help to bring the changes in leadership as a shared responsibility, with new patterns of school organisation and new relationships between personnel in school. To be trained, it was argued, is to have 'achieved competence in certain instrumental skills and fields of knowledge' (p. 147). Whereas to be educated implies a much lengthier process, involving being 'initiated into a language of discourse . . . and inducted into a culture' (Taylor, 1968, p. 147).

It is interesting, now, to contrast these explicit in-service proposals of the late sixties and early seventies for 'maximum opportunities for personal and professional growth within their roles' with an analysis of the ideology of in-service provision for aspiring headteachers and teachers over the last 30 years. The history of headship education and training provision cannot of course be fully separated from the INSET provision of the teaching profession as a whole. Writers from the 1960s onwards called for a 'continuum' of career-long development for all teachers; however, during the 1970s a structured continuum could not be seen in the variety of training programmes that had developed 'in a somewhat haphazard way and in an uneven fashion', throughout England and Wales (Buckley, 1985, p. 86). Whilst the DES had begun to play a more interventionist role in training since 1977, nevertheless the traditional autonomy of more than a hundred LEAs, together with the historically significant tradition of the powerful and independent 'headmaster', can be seen to have still dominated the scene. Meredydd Hughes (1985) in the early 1980s illustrated how slowly the traditional view of the headteacher with its strong emphasis on the morality of 'pastoral care' was to change. However, the pressure for a national initiative on 'professional development provision for senior staff in schools and colleges' grew during the 1980s as a result of DES-sponsored research projects and the like. A more 'managerial approach' to headship was discussed during this period and King's (1968) analysis of the head's role as chief executive was elaborated by Hughes (1985) into the re-nowned 'leading professional' and 'chief executive' roles – without any diminution of power and authority.

By 1983, a new national scheme was in operation 'to develop the expertise needed to organise schools and their curriculum, and to handle resources'. Sir Keith Joseph stated 'at the moment there is insufficient management training for headteachers and we, together with the LEAs, want to increase it' (Buckley, 1985, p. 89). The three elements of the initiative identified in Circular 3/83 (DES, 1983) were: the creation of a national development centre; the secondment of experienced heads; and senior staff for one-term secondments and regional 20-day short courses.

The 1980s witnessed a concerted effort on the part of central government to increase the provision of management training for heads and to address the irregular pattern of professional development for senior staff that had developed over a decade with the minimum of co-ordination or conscious planning. James' (DES, 1972) proposal for a one-term secondment and more co-ordinated in-service provision was thus partially enacted at this point, albeit in a climate of accountability, efficiency and possibly an instrumental view of schooling in terms of 'the needs of industry'. However, as Wallace (1991, p. 7) reported: 'valuable though this effort has been, the majority of current heads and senior staff are likely to have received little or none of this training.' Nevertheless, the conditions of service for teachers imposed by the government in 1987 inevitably increased in-service training for management and staff development and contributed to the drive during the early 1990s for the increasing use of management development activities which did not require staff to be released from their regular teaching commitment, thus avoiding disruption for pupils. The DES School Management Task Force, reporting in 1990, emphasized this school-centred management development approach where learning support is founded on 'self help, backed by a range of opportunities to stimulate and enhance what may be learned simply by doing the job' (Wallace, 1991, p. 10).

It is interesting to compare this early nineties' view of the headteacher's role as being concerned with school-based staff development and the importance of creating conditions conducive to learning for those staff aspiring towards greater management responsibility with the traditional 'pastoral' and 'charismatic' headteacher image persisting from earlier decades. This 'brief historical analysis' of the preparation of headteachers thus confirms Grace's (1995, p. 26) argument that

> concepts of leadership and management do not float freely in the discourse of textbooks of educational administration or in the prescriptions of technical primers of school management. Such concepts have a history, a politics and a set of complex and changing cultural and ideological relations with the wider society of which they are a part.

The most recent leadership and management development initiatives and activities of the 1990s provide a political and structural backdrop to the voices of our headteachers as they describe and analyse school-based developments into strategic management and the implementation of goals. Several questions relating to 'continuity' and 'effectiveness' of professional development are raised at this point. For example, are the management development initiatives introduced by the Teacher Training Agency, such as HEADLAMP for the new headteacher and National Professional Qualification for Headteachers (NPQH) for the aspiring headteacher, both of which stress the importance of 'strategic direction' and of 'communicating the vision', still imbued with the values of the 'heroic' headteacher whose prime role is to steer his ship to improvement in terms of academic achievement? Does the 'technical' language of competency within the National Standards for Headship (TTA, 1997) lead towards a more rational and bureaucratic view of the headteacher's role to the detriment of the inspirational artist or moral leader of previous decades? Furthermore, if the values of 'pastoral care' and 'educating the whole child' had become so deep seated in the UK, as this historical analysis supports, how might these recent TTA initiatives have started to impact on these dominant values? Do our headteachers' voices still reflect the importance to them of the spiritual, aesthetic and ethical dimensions of their jobs? Or do they find themselves in conflict with a more dominant entrepreneurial marketing culture linked to measuring pupil achievement? More fundamentally, is the headteacher's traditional power and authority seriously challenged or just repackaged by the more recent leadership and management development training courses of the 1990s?

The emergence of the HEADLAMP programme for new headteachers, in 1994, can be seen to be a culmination of the considerable development activity of the late 1980s and early 1990s in relation to headteacher training. It followed the recommendations of the School Management Task Force (DES, 1990) for LEAs to promote partnerships with schools and external bodies, including higher education, in order to develop high-quality management provision. The report (*ibid.*) had stressed the importance of helping managers analyse their needs; setting targets for their training and development requirements; and examining the most appropriate modes of delivery both on and off-site and monitoring and evaluating the effectiveness of the management development in the workplace. The HEADLAMP programme introduced by the

TTA followed those proposals in its format and legitimised training and development for new headteachers and the time needed for it at a point when headteachers across the country were neglecting their own professional development or 'looking for a quick fix' (Baker, 1996). In 1994 the DfEE, OFSTED and CBI/UBI supported a research project into the training and development needs of headteachers, their deputies and chairs of governors in secondary schools (DfE, 1995). It is noteworthy that 'strategic management' was identified highly as a training priority and that this 'task' appears strongly in the list of HEADLAMP tasks and abilities used for headteacher needs assessment within the context of school development. Our own experiences of the HEADLAMP scheme, now undergoing a review by TTA, concurs with that of Busher and Paxton (1997, p. 123) of a scheme 'permitting a holistic approach to headteachers' professional enrichment and institutional improvement, leaving control of the process in the hands of the headteacher encouraging autonomy based on sound knowledge and ethical guidelines for professional practice rather than dependency based externally validated and presented frameworks of action'.

It is interesting to note that the TTA consultation document on HEADLAMP referred to headteacher 'competencies', whereas the final scheme detailed a range of 'tasks and abilities'. In 1998, the more detailed National Standards for Headship (TTA, 1997) replaced the existing HEADLAMP tasks and abilities and the debate about competency-driven management development programmes became more controversial. Certainly, the 'old' HEADLAMP programme could be designed to support the development of 'autonomous decision-making' by the headteacher in partnership with a skilled mentor or critical friend. In Cheshire LEA, for example, it has led to very effective 'action learning sets' of headteachers being formed, providing peer support, visits and bespoke training to the group, facilitated by LEA/HEI mentor-tutors.

The HEADLAMP programme and its holistic partnership approach based on trust and mutual respect (Smith, 1997) contrasts sharply in certain important respects with the NPQH programme for aspiring headteachers introduced from 1996. The HEADLAMP programme can be seen to continue to support the concept of the 'independent' headteacher who in a culture of collegiality is simply 'empowered', through time, money and mentoring to engage in a process of professional and institutional development in partnership with academics and officers, based on a validated self-audit of needs in context. In contrast the National Professional Qualification for Headteachers (NPQH) launched in 1997 and the emergent national Leadership Programme for Serving Headteachers (LPSH) (1998) can be seen to be far less flexible in their procedures for needs assessment and training provision. The question addressed here is whether this increased prescription fundamentally challenges the traditional concept of the 'all-powerful' headteacher – or simply adds legitimation and certification.

The NPQH operates solely through the 22 regional centres who bid successfully for the contract to deliver assessment or training and represents an externally validated and heavily prescribed framework of professional development for aspiring headteachers. Despite the earlier withdrawal of the term 'competency' from the TTA lists of headteacher tasks and abilities, the use of neocompetency-based assessment processes, based on trained observers and interviewers analysing participants performing in simulated situations, are techniques which are used in the NPQH and they are clearly akin to those used in US competence programmes for selection and promotion. Unlike the 'best' competency-based approaches to management development and training, there is no evidence to suppose that the NPQH with its prescribed assessment and training packages is likely to 'foster personal responsibility for, and control over, development and training' (Jirasinghe and Lyons, 1996, p. 108).

The present fragmentation of support for the NPQH candidate, with the separation of assessment from training and development at a structural level, mitigates against a planned and co-ordinated management development programme for headteachers; or one that relates closely to the contextually based assessment of needs and is designed to address particular school development issues in a continuous policy of improvement. Smith (1998) has argued for greater coherence and effectiveness of the NPQH programme and the value of a continuous mentoring approach to professional development for aspiring and in-service headteachers in order to support their 'double-loop learning' (Kolb, 1984) and the development of 'meta-competences' (Eraut, 1994). The present heavy emphasis on off-site course delivery of the Strategic Management Compulsory Module, together with the barriers to accrediting teachers' prior learning into the NPQH and the cumbersome assessment procedures using ambiguous national standards and 'hidden' criteria for assessment, all lead us (and others – Bush, 1998; Ouston, 1998) to question the efficacy of the change of management development culture evident between the processes of HEADLAMP and NPQH. More particularly, the NPQH is questioned for its ability to develop a critical consciousness, or simply high-order analytical skills that could lead to personal and professional development in the role of the headteacher (Gunter, 1999).

The collaborative culture of personal and professional learning incorporating a school-based action research process and use of critical friend or mentor cannot easily be seen in the present NPQH programme. Instead of equality of access to high-quality training and assessment in a soon-to-be mandatory qualification, there are instead inconsistencies in the provision itself. Equal opportunities issues relating to gender and variations in the context-specific opportunities for leadership experience and confidence building (Cubillo, 1998) are clearly in evidence. It will be interesting to see whether the Leadership Programme for Serving Headteachers (starting in 1998) reflects the values and beliefs of leadership training evident in the NPQH programme or hearkens back to a culture of greater autonomy and power for the individual headteacher to self-assess and to design an appropriate programme of learning for him or herself.

However, the reality of headship might be somewhat different from what is presented to teachers undergoing this type of national training. While we have seen the endurance of the dominance and authority of the headteacher, in different guises, over time, nevertheless accounts of our headteachers illustrate what Grace (1995) has identified as an equally strong theme of professional collegiality. Throughout their accounts the heads speak of trust and mutual respect, a culture of collegiality, even a 'culture of counselling' to promote learning and personal development and thereby whole-school development. Several headteachers use the tool of writing the school mission statement or the school development planning process as a means of culture building or promoting a 'community school climate'. Most of the headteachers demonstrate the importance they attach to building relationships and effective clusters of teachers across the school. What is interesting here and worth knowing more about is how headteachers engage with the models of headship which are presented to them in texts and training courses, and how they translate them into their own practice.

What in-post and aspiring headteachers are being presented with as effective professional practice has a past as well as a present. White papers, circulars, government agency reports, training curriculum, legislation are all texts which encode a particular meaning of headship. The purpose of the next section of this Introduction is to describe the particular model of leadership which has been encoded in official documentation from the 1980s as a means of structuring the professional practice of educational professionals.

CONSTRUCTING HEADSHIP TODAY

Opportunities to reflect on the current construction of headship are rare. Either you are in-post or aspiring to it, or working on the best system for appointment. However, if we actively read what is being presented as 'effective headship' then we will see a clear and consistent story. Consider the following requirements and exhortations for educational professionals. *Excellence in Schools* (DfEE, 1997, p. 46) tells us:

> The vision for learning set out in this White Paper will demand the highest qualities of leadership and management from headteachers. The quality of the head often makes the difference between the success or failure of a school. Good heads can transform a school; poor heads can block progress and achievement. It is essential that we have measures in place to strengthen the skills of all new and serving heads.

The National Standards for Headteachers (TTA, 1997, p. 4) state that

> The headteacher is the leading professional in the school. Working with the governing body, the headteacher provides vision, leadership and direction for the school and ensures that it is managed and organised to meet its aims and targets. With the governing body, the headteacher is responsible for the continuous improvement in

the quality of education; for raising standards; for ensuring equality of opportunity for all; for the development of policies and practices; and for ensuring that resources are efficiently and effectively used to achieve the school's aims and objectives. The headteacher also secures the commitment of the wider community to the school, by developing and maintaining effective networks with, for example, other local schools, the LEA (where appropriate), higher education institutions, employers, careers services and others. The headteacher is responsible for creating a productive, disciplined learning environment and for the day-to-day management, organisation and administration of the school, and is accountable to the governing body.

Headship is leadership, and a particular type of leadership. Such an approach is being consecrated through the celebration and honouring of heads who rescue and revive schools labelled as 'failing'. Resistance to the seduction of this charismatic and visionary headship is not easy. This is especially the case when we look around at the abundance of recent literature and centralised professional development which as Ball (1995) observes is located in entrepreneurial strategies and is designed to make policy happen to professionals rather than enable professionals to challenge policy. Consider the following strategy presented in management literature to in-post and aspiring headteachers:

> It would seem that emphasis should be given to transforming rather than transactional leadership, with the intent being to change attitudes and bring about commitment to a 'better state' which is embodied in a vision of excellence for the school. We know that outstanding school leaders have such a vision and that they succeed in communicating it in a way that secures the commitment of others in the school and its community. The most important aspect of communication is the meaning it conveys. So it is important for the school leader to decide on the meanings which are intended and then to choose acts which will ensure the intended outcome. Leadership is concerned with gaining commitment to a set of values, statements of 'what ought to be', which then become the heart of the culture of the school. Gaining this commitment can be achieved in a number of ways, especially with collaborative approaches to decision-making and with placing at school level high responsibility and authority for making decisions related to the allocation of resources in the school.
>
> (Beare *et al.*, 1993, p. 160)

We can identify that what is being sold to educational professionals as leadership through centralised training and literature tends to be underpinned by the following characteristics:

- The emphasis is on leadership which seems to float free of educational values, and professionalism is being reconstructed as management processes rather than an ethical commitment to children and their development.
- Leadership is presented as a consensus and unitary-focused process in which the culture is managed, rather than a professional relationship in which the realities of dilemmas and contradictions are revealed.
- Effective leadership is strongly normative and tends to be based on a construction of what ought to be rather than what we know about the day-to-day experiences of headship.

- Leadership methodology is often ahistorical (the past seems to begin in 1988) and the biographies and narrative stories of headteachers tend to be marginalised as being deficit to the acceptable model of effective leadership.
- The agency of headteachers is emphasised at the expense of the structural context in which their work is located. It seems that generic headteachers can bring their vision and mission to the school in which an insistence on the right to manage is legitimised as the means of marginalising the structural injustices within the community.
- Children and teachers are constructed as objects to be managed; they are relegated to follower status. It seems that children and teachers are to be dazzled by the heroism of the leader in taking them to a better future, while simultaneously they are integrated into accountability mechanisms for educational standards which are under-resourced.

Transformational leadership, in contrast to transactional leadership (Burns, 1978), is central to this. We are told, and told repeatedly, that headteachers should have a vision of where the school is moving towards. This vision is embodied within headteachers, it is rooted in their values and manifest in their language and behaviour. Engagement with 'followers' is through neutral processes which either transmit the vision or ensure a triumph over competing visions. It is not really clear what the status is of competing or alternative visions, their existence is recognised (and encouraged) by some writers, but ultimately the headteacher needs to use a combination of personal charisma and/or organisational levers to ensure compliance.

History quite rightly is being problematicised but futuring is almost sacred, and there is considerable evidence that a critical perspective is absent from the prescriptions of leadership models, as can be seen in the largely descriptive assessment tasks set for the NPQH. The future appears to be a comfortable and safe place for headteachers, as they are given the script and props to enable the predicted challenges to be dealt with – whilst the future is an uncomfortable and unsafe place for teachers to be unless they accept the role of technical implementer, and become the audience, of the future. Perhaps teacher experiences of implementing other people's visions, combined with the intensification of work (Hargreaves, 1994), are making a good case for futuring to be seen as both practically and morally unsustainable.

Important work is taking place within educational studies both to chart our knowledge of headship and to keep alternative versions alive. What we know about headship so far has been well presented and analysed by Hall and Southworth (1997) and it is not our intention to repeat this analysis. However, Hall and Southworth (*ibid.*) do present a series of themes from their extensive literature search which is very helpful in presenting an understanding of what we don't know about headship and a possible agenda for further work.

Theme 1 While the ascendancy of the headteacher is an enduring feature,

... we do not have a sophisticated understanding of how heads make a difference and how this might vary according to the school's context, size, development needs and the head's professional background, experience, skills and knowledge. Although the centrality of the head is widely acknowledged, it has not been examined in very much depth.

(Ibid., p. 165)

The connection between leadership and school performance is widely promoted. However, Gronn (1996, p. 21) has very powerfully argued that 'a causal relationship between school-based management and improved student outcomes is yet to be demonstrated. Perhaps ... leadership under self-management is not making a difference or is not the difference to be made'. In fact, putting the theory, practice and research about headship into a historical context enables us to confirm Grace's (1995, p. 41) argument that the current 'market mission' for headteachers is a part of a central theme within the autocratic traditions of schooling in England and Wales. Grace (1997, p. 65) has argued the following about the location of education and schools within the democratic project:

English schooling culture in the twentieth century has always had, at its heart, a major paradox and contradiction. Formally designated as the cultural agency for 'making democracy work' and involved, at specific periods, with explicit pedagogical projects to enhance education for citizenship, its own practice has remained largely undemocratic. Among a complex of reasons for this lack of democratic practice in school like, the influence of the hierarchical 'headmaster tradition' has been significant. While this tradition may have modified over time into more consultative forms, the fact remains that most headteachers are the operative school leaders and that few examples exist of serious organisational democracy involving major decision making by headteachers in association with teachers, pupils and other school staff.

Transformational leadership draws a veil over the realities of how enduring power relations operate. Gronn (1996) argues that heads have learned the 'officially sanctioned language', and he demonstrates that far from being the visionary leader the realities, as we currently know them, are that heads continue to do what they have always done, and that is to bargain and negotiate, but since 1988 with a larger number of interest groups. Perhaps we ought to be asking a different question about headship: why is autocratic leadership continuing to be promoted through a repackaging and relabelling process?

Theme 2   Leadership seems to be less connected with functional role and more with an entitlement to enable teachers to participate effectively in management decisions: ' . . . the use of management teams reflects heads' attempts to improve the effectiveness of their schools by increasing the power of colleagues' contributions. Such heads may be seeking to empower colleagues by transforming the nature of leadership in the school' (Hall and Southworth, 1997, p. 165).

Grace's (1995) work has revealed that in tension with the headmaster tradition is the professional collegiality of the postwar world in which subject and pedagogic knowledge dominated. From the 1980s this has been marginalised as a result of the colonisation of teacher professionalism by process collegiality in which teachers speak the language of teams and consensus cultures. The work of Jenkins (1997, pp. 207–8) demonstrates this:

> The research has confirmed that many heads are committed to changing the culture of their schools into collaborative learning cultures. Any residual belief that ideas of empowerment, collaborative decision making, improving performance and responding to stakeholders are alien imports from industry and commerce has now disappeared. The building of collaborative cultures is increasingly seen as the most creative way of coping with the unpredictability of postmodern organisations and the rapidly changing context in which they operate . . . Interestingly, the idea of a 'strong' and 'weak' leader has been turned on its head. The 'strong' leader is now perceived as the person who has the skills and abilities to create a collaborative culture which, in effect, diminishes autocracy and extends leadership to others in the organisation. The 'weak' leader is the person who is unable to create the culture which stakeholders are looking for, although these leaders often give the appearance of being 'strong' through their autocratic stances. Heads are judged on their ability to create the culture which draws all the stakeholders into a coherent integrated organisational process where all have their part in promoting the organisational vision.

It seems that the authentic professional empowerment in the form of teachers being able to determine their work and exercise judgement about pupil progress and standards has been reviled and confiscated by external agencies. Instead teachers are being given process empowerment labelled as 'leadership' to implement externally determined change and to support the surveillance functions of an externally accountable senior management team. We could ask why teachers are being characterised as waiting to be led, almost as if they are holding hands in awe of the leader as parent and moral guardian. A hearkening back, perhaps, to the Arnoldian culture described earlier in this Introduction.

Theme 3   Headteachers are taking a more strategic role in school performance and are losing their connection with the classroom:

> . . . as heads begin to take a harder and increasingly evidence-based view of the school the character of their professional leadership changes. Some studies suggest that heads in the 1990s are finding it more difficult to teach, because of demands on their time. These heads do not see themselves as leading by classroom example, rather, they are now acting as the school's resident inspector and leading school reviews. In effect, their professional leadership has been recast. They are apparently taking a stronger interest in outcomes and the school's 'product'.
>
> (Hall and Southworth, 1997, p. 166)

Grace's (1995) analysis puts this assessment into a historical perspective by arguing that ongoing tensions between exclusive and inclusive headship are being resolved within the current policy context in favour of the former. So-called data-rich schools are locating learning within a positivist and objectivist tradition in which knowledge is narrowly defined according to performance measures. The collection, organisation and presentation of information for external agencies mean that professional identities are under pressure. There is the separation of managers from the managed (Al-Khalifa, 1989) and the decision-maker from the technician (Ball, 1990a; 1990b). We could ask how can teachers articulate this lack of respect for their traditional teaching territory and resist generic leadership imperatives.

Theme 4   Discontinuous change is a central part of the headteacher's work: ' . . . heads have become accustomed to policy developments disturbing established structures and creating turbulence in schools (e.g. the introduction of school performance league tables; the advent of school inspections). Moreover, such changes powerfully affect how teachers' and headteachers' work is organised' (Hall and Southworth, 1997, p. 166). The management of change is endemic throughout educational literature, and is based on a view of the world, and more specifically the policy context, which makes change appear inevitable and desirable. Teachers are often presented as conservative incrementalists who are barriers to change and hence in danger of becoming failing stakeholders. The tragedy in all this is that any claim to be able to manage change tends to be based on rational linear processes (Gunter, 1997), and perhaps it is this mindset which results in failing schools, teachers and children. When set within the policy context we can see that the reality of change management is more about the implementation of punitive centrally determined policy than a school-based development agenda. Perhaps we could ask different questions about how we seek to understand the interaction and tension of agency and structure in how headteachers' work is conceptualised and organised.

Theme 5   Headship is complex but studies tend not to enable a differentiated approach, and

> . . . using a gender perspective creates new possibilities for exploring the lives of men and women who teach, manage and lead in education . . . educational leadership is firmly rooted in professional identity. Gender, in turn, is a crucial component of that identity. Future research that fails to take this and the gendered nature of schools and colleges into account is likely to be incomplete.
> (Hall and Southworth, 1997, p. 167)

The gendered nature of headship and leadership is now well chronicled (Adler *et al.*, 1993; Ozga, 1993; Hall, 1996) and research into gendered racism and sexuality is enriching our understanding of organisational life (de Lyon and Migniuolo, 1989; Davidson, 1997). While we can expose writings on school leadership which ignore these issues, we have to decide whether structural injustices are to be ameliorated through an 'and women' approach or policy adjustments, or whether theory and practice will be focused on underlying power relations and cultural norms. Perhaps the question we could ask is whether leadership studies can and do enable teachers to challenge existing power structures. There appears to be little evidence of this in the TTA NPQH leadership and management programmes.

Theme 6   Headteacher development is not fully understood, and there is a

. . . need to map what are the critical incidents and epiphanies in their professional development and understanding. If it is true that heads are central players in their schools' success, then we urgently need to embark on studies which illuminate how they can be supported, challenged and developed into highly effective headteachers.

(Hall and Southworth, 1997, p. 167)

The lack of knowledge about the realities of headship and the need for more ethnographic studies is increasingly becoming an important part of the literature on headship (Gronn, 1996). The control of headteachers over this process will depend on the ethical stance taken by researchers. There remains the possibility that such research could be used to distil generic truths as a means of disciplining educational professionals and retaining undemocratic power structures. Alternatively the situated voices of headteachers could tell a different story which could enable teachers to resist training and induction into the TTA-sponsored model of headship. Perhaps the question we could ask is how do we enable and support teachers to analyse and share their professional biographies as a creative rather than domesticating process?

Hall and Southworth (1997, pp. 167–8) conclude with a seventh theme, in which they argue that what we know remains partial: 'in terms of research into headship in the UK, we are probably, at best, only approaching the end of the beginning in our understanding of headship.' They argue in favour of 'more research into the topic, new methodologies and more sophisticated reflections and understandings'. The powerful nature of Hall and Southworth's work is in both generating questions and in the stimulation of new questions.

UNDERSTANDING HEADSHIP TODAY

The origins of this book lie within our own professional biographies as practitioners and more recently as members of university departments of education. We have both participated in and taught on the award-bearing and non-award-bearing courses identified by Hughes *et al.* (1981) and more recently reminded of by Fidler (1998, p. 309): 'what became clear in the research was the complementary nature of the outcomes of the two forms of study – headteachers needed a comprehensive and sustained understanding of principles and they also needed knowledge of practical ways forward on specific issues.'

What has increasingly become clear to us in our grand total of 75 years as educational professionals is that both 'theory for understanding' and 'theory for action' (Hoyle, 1986) provided this complementary preparation. What has also resonated with us is the everyday engagement with the professional concerns of teachers which has increasingly been in tension with the strongly normative strategies from the post-1988 era. Our work has confirmed Møller's (1997, p. 99) research and analysis of two types of dilemmas faced in both day-to-day and strategic thinking:

The *dilemmas of loyalty* were expressed in actions where the principals found it difficult to decide with whom their loyalty should lie in times of conflict. Which groups were most important? Was it possible to discover a pattern of decisions? Should they owe loyalty to students and parents, teachers, superiors, to a common curriculum, to personal pedagogic values? The *dilemmas of steering* were expressed in actions where there was a tension between: administrative control *versus* professional autonomy; challenge *versus* support; change *versus* stability.

While many teachers have been researchers for a long time and have had this validated not only through positive changes in school but also through a formal award such as a Master's degree, we would agree with Maguire and Ball (1994) that much of this remains invisible. There are indeed problems with the work of the lone researcher but as Maguire and Ball (*ibid.*) go on to argue this type of work is one possible area where issues of 'social justice and social critique' can continue to be researched at a time when funding is drying up. Furthermore, facilitating dissemination through this type of book means that we are responding positively to the concern that 'university bookshelves are crowded with dissertations and theses whose contents are rarely known or read beyond a very small circle' (*ibid.*, p. 271). At the same time we are very much aware that even though these type of collections are becoming more prevalent on the bookshelves (Preedy, 1989; Crawford *et al.*, 1994), there can be two main concerns: first, we do not always know the connection between the individual chapter and the publication process (Gunter, 1997); and, secondly, as Ozga (1990) has argued, the theoretical context which links the particular story to the 'bigger picture' can remain obscured. The rest of this section presents our response to how we have handled our representation of the professional accounts in this collection.

In foregrounding the first issue we decided to approach headteachers who had undertaken postgraduate work to ask if they were interested in turning their research projects into a chapter for this book. This approach was both personal as we contacted our own students who had recently graduated, but we also contacted our colleagues in other university departments of education to see if they had someone who might be interested. The brief given to the chapter authors was to write about an aspect of their research in which they drew on the literature and presented their observations from a personal point of view. We were interested in the headteacher accounts of how the rhetoric of a strategic vision for the school looked like in practical day-to-day activities. For the authors this process has been one of describing a process of change and development within their own school. In this sense the authors are very much describing their lived experience with an emphasis on the 'I' and how they have struggled with their own agency.

In compiling this book we are very much aware of the issue of whom these accounts are for. They are very much for the people who have written them, as well as their colleagues who are actively encoded into the narratives, as a means of wanting to describe the realities of the job as they have experienced it. They are also for others who are interested in the lived experiences of professional practice within an educational setting. We are very much aware that these accounts could be seen to be privileged as they are written by people who have the status to be able to tell the story in this or that particular way, and have been selected as a means of being included in the collection. Furthermore, while voices may be heard, the structures which previously generated meaning through 'contextual and theoretical discourse' could be silenced, and so the 'general patterns, social contexts, and critical theories will be replaced by local stories and personal anecdotes' (Goodson, 1995, p. 90). While the structural issues to do with gender, age, class, race and sexuality are central to understanding the interaction between the headteacher and their context, perhaps we need to begin to understand how this may be revealed through seeking to understand how the professional self is and has been constructed. Goodson (*ibid.*) sees these interactions as 'trading points' in which the issues of understanding and identity are negotiated and worked through.

We do not deny the problematic nature of this, and we are highlighting these issues to enable the reader to be aware of these structural factors in a way which is often not made explicit in edited collections. We are not promoting the authors as somehow having knowledge which the reader must accept or absorb; there are no quick fixes here. We present these chapters from a range of headteachers, who have some interesting things to say. We do not present the illusion of coherence, but instead we promote the telling of stories in which you as reader will work and rework it: the telling and retelling of stories is a central part of human lives and cultural practice.

The connection with the bigger picture is one which enables us to problematise the link between making noise and having a voice, and we would like to present a theoretical lens through which we can develop an understanding of the relationship between the agency of the individual and the structural context in which they are located. As we have shown, headteachers (along with other educational professionals) have been and currently are in receipt of official texts which contain particular assumptions and value systems regarding their professional practice. These texts are often mediated through the construction of other texts such as training courses, reports from research projects and 'management by ringbinder' (Halpin, 1990) publications. This process of translation, interpretation and engagement can be sensitised through the theoretical lens of 'readerly' and 'writerly' texts. Bowe *et al.* (1992, p. 13) have used the work of Barthes to provide a conceptual understanding of the policy process as discourse in which 'we would want to approach legislation as but one aspect of a *continual* process in which the loci of power are constantly shifting as the various resources implicit and explicit in texts are recontextualised and employed in the struggle to maintain or change views of schooling'. The spaces in which we can be creative are not available in a 'readerly' text where there is strong direction and prescriptive outcomes. However, in 'writerly' texts we can see 'through to something beyond' (*ibid.*, p. 10) in which we can decide the position we intend to take and the possibilities for alternative outcomes. The rational and linear cause-and-effect policy process is substituted by a more humane knowledge claim about what it is we do when we engage in professional practice, and this supports the view of Bowe *et al.* (*ibid.*, p. 22) that

> practitioners do not confront policy texts as naive readers, they come with histories, with experience, with values and purposes of their own, they have vested interests in the meaning of policy. Policies will be interpreted differently as the histories, experiences, values, purposes and interests which make up any arena differ. The simple point is that policy writers cannot control the meanings of their texts. Parts of texts will be rejected, selected out, ignored, deliberately misunderstood, responses may be frivolous, etc.

This is the complex and contradictory setting in which we present these chapters written by headteachers. We do not see headteachers as neutral implementors of macropolicy, and neither do we see them as leaders of micropolicy. These chapters are a contribution to developing the more sophisticated understanding of the work of headteachers which Hall and Southworth (1997) have identified is a gap in our knowledge. This understanding comes from seeing the headteacher as a part of a complex and organic network of influences in which the operation of agency (practice, emotion, intellect) is mediated by the structural factors within the local and national context. Power struggles and contests regarding legitimacy are central to the policy process (Bowe *et al.*, 1992), but it is illuminative that only the headteachers who are sacked from, or who save, 'failing' schools appear to grab the headlines.

The headteacher accounts and our organisation of them are themselves a text, and are 'interpretations of interpretations' (*ibid.*). We have placed them in alphabetical order in two sections which separate primary headteachers and secondary headteachers. Each section is offered to all readers, but we felt it would help the busy professional to have this basic structural support. The following is a brief overview of the chapters and is itself, we hope, presented as a 'writerly' text.

Angela Bird, with Les Bell, explores strategic management in an infant school. Angela has been headteacher for 14 years and her analysis traces her own understanding of the head's role over this period. There have been three phases: before the Education Reform Act 1988; implementing the reforms with the stress surrounding the implementation of the National Curriculum; and, more recently, the development of strategic leadership and the complexities that this implies. There is a concern about the excessive focus on the headteacher's leadership and the apparent rebirth of the myth of the hero-innovator. Angela prefers to develop the capacity to manage change so that schools are made positive by design, based on a genuine collective view of a creative and talented group who have confidence in themselves. The head is the focal point of a network of human relationships. Strategic planning is a journey to cultural transformation with a wider involvement of parents and

Investors in People as a means. Despite an excellent OFSTED report Angela wishes to move on from a reductionist focus on targets which 'makes simplistic assumption about the nature and purposes of education and suffers from an impoverished, mechanistic and narrow view of what counts as achievement'.

Gwenn Brockley, with Ray Moorcroft, has used total quality management for 'Building the vision: a TQM approach'. A number of schools have used different-quality systems to provide a basis for school development. This chapter provides an opportunity to evaluate the appropriateness of TQM in this particular school. For Gwenn this must be about long-term improvement based on true commitment. She is particularly sceptical about mission statements which are inspiring messages of hope, well thought-out by the head and/or senior managment team only. TQM is interpreted as a philosophy offering a chance to break the chains which restrict school improvement. She decided to use the theory implicit in TQM to structure the development of the school's vision statement using an interesting strategic environmental analysis. The working party/focus group was representative of the school stakeholders. Gwenn recognises and resists the overwhelming temptation for heads to do it all, as staff react to pressing concerns. The process is to empower the community to find a voice.

'The culture of counselling as an engine for change' (Chapter 3) explores an alternative approach. Carolyn Clarke inherited a school in 1992 with a traditional culture where the micropolitics were challenging. The ground rules for the MA (Ed) group led by Terry Martin which Carolyn joined became the basis for the process by which the group in school similarly defined the ways in which members would relate and the climate they wished to encourage. The analysis then concentrates on three processes significant to the counselling culture: teams and team-building, enhancing self-esteem, and problem-solving techniques. The teams have created calmness and support, evidenced in the lack of anxiety or tension normally associated with end-of-term fatigue. The development of self-esteem is central to the counselling process and is built into the school system for teachers and pupils, with a practical consequence, for example, in the anti-bullying policy. The use of transactional analysis and the development of listening skills both help improve problem-solving and in creating a climate where staff and children work productively. A culture of counselling has been created using soundly based techniques, such as solution-focused therapy, to improve learning.

In Chapter 4, Frances Hardy explores her action research project which considered the headteacher's role in relation to spiritual development. She argues that the action research process enabled her to lead the team as collaborators and fellow researchers, and that the quality of this process has been validated by the process of developing the mission statement and two inspections. This inevitably focused on what was the heart of Catholicism. The quality of the process and the learning are evident in the analysis presented, as is the evidence that the mission statement developed is a unique living document. The OFSTED and Diocesan inspections have different perspectives on spirituality, but what the head wants is that the children 'have begun to know and love the God who made them'.

Headteachers have responded in different ways to the market-place they find themselves in. John Loftus in Chapter 5 deals with the issues head on. A reorganisation one year after his appointment involved a change from first to primary school status in a particularly difficult context, resulting in John being constrained in his priorities to enable the school to survive. The living contradiction involved in seeking to sustain values and being an active participator in carrying through the government's policy is central. The response is to become clear about marketing and his values, and then working out how to live those values in practice through a solitary struggle. The tension is resolved through a focusing on marketing with a professional commitment to avoid the competitive even in the continuous cycle of relentless change. The chapter illustrates the commitment to values that is required of headteachers.

Mo Williams concentrates on trust, education, achievement, motivation and security (TEAMS). If all teachers are managers then working in teams and empowering individuals provide elements of potential contradiction. Few heads share their letter of application with their colleagues, but this interpretation of the leading professional is based on openness and on an insistent emphasis on teams. The concentration on learning through purposeful teaching and high expectations sustains this. An effective use of assertive discipline provides a framework for learning and teaching, and learning for all through staff development. TEAMS has worked. The OFSTED report agrees that 'The team spirit in this school is of an exceptionally high order'.

Bernard Barker has been an eloquent voice supporting and questioning comprehensive education for 40 years. 'Double vision: 40 years on' takes us on his journey from school where he was 'inspired by the potential, troubled by the reality'. The vision presented here is profound because it avoids the simplicities which still characterise debates about comprehensive schools and their organisation. The focus on teachers who challenge was exciting and Stanground developed a national reputation. The central issue of 17 years of headship has been challenging the Callaghan and Kenneth Baker agendas which undermined the vision the author shared with Aneurin Bevan: 'These boys and girls are to be asked to wield the royal sceptre: we must therefore give them the souls of kings and queens.' One senses that this has sustained Bernard Barker, even after he returned to Stanground 11 years into his headship after a year as inspector. There is an anger about OFSTED, after his own 'complicity in the intensification of work' in which all have become creatures of OFSTED's 'ultra-regulated world'. Barker recognised the need to move on. However his energy was revived to rise to the challenge to take on a school heavily criticised by OFSTED. His sustained vision took them out of special measures.

In 'A vision for Lilian Baylis', one of the worst schools in the country according to the Secretary of State, and with four years in special measures, Yvonne Bates describes how she transformed one of the most socially deprived schools in the country within a year so that 'we were not about to limp out of special measures but to emerge with a flourish'. This was achieved by the powerful shared vision that has driven the school. A school where 84% are entitled to free school meals and almost 20% are excluded from other schools because of behavioural difficulties presented a challenge. Yvonne recognised the vision that was necessary and that it had to focus on good-quality teaching in a disciplined environment with a concentration on learning. There is a devastating simplicity in the process of fostering pride and then communicating that confidently, even to the local trader on the Lambeth Walk, who took her hand pityingly when she introduced herself as the new headteacher, looked sad and said 'You poor cow'. The power to communicate belief in the future, rebuild confidence and to realise the vision included a hard-nosed concentration on performance targets because the school was not so bad. Good-quality teaching and learning led to the local press running stories of success and achievement.

John Cain has completed his first five years of headship and is now looking to build on this. Chapter 9 challenges some of the assumptions about vision-making. The start was to build on the strong discipline and financial situation and the governors had made an excellent choice for their school. The week after appointment the intake fell from 100 to 75 with a planned admission of 150. John Cain saw his role as almost obvious though this may be because he applied sharp intelligence to the analysis. There was therefore no vision thing but recruitment was the priority. There was a communication through individual parents with the headteacher taking all parents on a tour of the school. Setting was introduced and the next double intake, after a reorganisation, produced two year groups of 140, and therefore the capacity to make a more strategic vision statement with simple strong targets. The values seem to the author, and as presented, self-evident. That may be their strength. The school will have virtually doubled its size in seven years, but there is no complacency. There is an acceptance of the reality that performance will be measured in absolute and value-added terms. It is important to accept the reality of the current environment as a headteacher and to succeed within the current policy framework.

The application of the concept of creativity in leadership is the focus of Elizabeth Duffy's chapter. After recently completing five years in her first headship this chapter provides Elizabeth with an opportunity to reflect on past experience and to anticipate the next headship. The career path to headship was clearly unplanned, though it was the emergent big issues which made headship feel like a philosophical, analytical and intellectual pursuit – but also simply an extension of good exciting teaching. The professional and personal are clearly one. Thomas Jefferson's 'Timid men prefer the calm of despotism to the boisterous sea of liberty' informs this boisterous leadership. This chapter is derived from Elizabeth's research on the kind of leadership that might support creativity. If teaching is to be a creative passionate profession it requires creative passionate leadership. The second headship is in a school which might expect to be similarly creative.

In 'Modelling development alternatives', David Gower provides a more technical analysis of the application of new forecasting techniques in schools. Some schools are more systematic in using tools for analysing complex school management problems using computer-based solutions. What is significant in the process here, however, is the management of the cultural issues as the decision support systems were developed. The apparent contradictions between such rational processes and the assertion that education is about people are seen as oversimplifications. However the tensions need to be managed. This will be of interest to headteachers with an interest in applying communications and information technology to school leadership and management. This process described here is a decision support system, and is hard edged and technical. It is argued that this complements and supports strategy formulation. The decision support system modelled provides a means of forecasting the outcomes of continuous predictable change.

Eric Tope provides 'A quality approach to school improvement', this time in a secondary-school context. He is conscious of the danger of an overemphasis on vision but also proud of a culture which combines a number of elements including south London street wisdom, outrageous nerve and pastoral care rooted in the Catholic ethos. A satisfactory OFSTED inspection in 1993 led, indirectly, to a positive response through action planning, using a TQM model. The process of implementation is followed through with a focus on what the school did, how changing the culture requires energy and how the head needs to create an appropriate climate for change. Here there is a very clear focus on teaching styles and sharing development collegially. The new Centre for Research, Development and Teacher Training in the school demonstrates the commitment to professional development and the school as a learning community.

Tony Tuckwell, in exploring 'Teacher Participation in Decision-Making', recognises that, in theory, the participation of teachers in the shaping and implementation of policy is central. He explores the practicalities of this recognising that teachers need freedom of action to be creative and inspirational. There is a concern that teacher participation does not, in practice, lead to improvements in teaching strategies. The psychological contract with teachers is central but must be genuine. There is an interesting commentary on the uneven engagement pattern with decision-making over a teacher's career. The costs of participation need to be recognised as do the variations in time between individuals within the same institution. His research in the school led to changed practice with the maximum presentation of information reducing the need for involvement in decision-making of restricted professionals, extended professionals, coasters and no-hopers. If the vision is to liberate the visions that dance within each teacher's head there will be little sense of decision deprivation.

Mark Wasserberg reflects on his experience in his first headship, considering how the vision can genuinely be shared in large secondary schools. Chapter 14 shows how it is possible to use OFSTED to create a focus for development. Leadership is interpreted as being about changing the culture and having the skills to uncover the assumptions blocking change. The commitment of the head can be demonstrated in playing in the school band and refereeing football matches, whilst at the same time the underlying personal professional development can be painful. These symbolic activities are about personal involvement as is talking to the pupils and knowing most of them by name. A particularly significant element of leadership is encouraging others to see themselves as leaders. The commitment to the quality of learning as central in the culture is the focus of this leadership.

REFERENCES

Adler, S., Laney, J. and Packer, M. (1993) *Managing Women*, Buckingham, Open University Press.

Al-Khalifa, E. (1989) Management by halves: women teachers and school management, in de Lyon, H. and Migniuolo, F., eds, *Women Teachers*, Buckingham, Open University Press.

Allen, B. ed. (1968) *Headship in the 1970s*, Oxford, Blackwell.

Baker, L (1996) *The Professional Development of Headteachers: LEA Provision for Management Development and Training of Headteachers Beyond Induction*, Slough, EMEI/NFER.

Ball, S.J. (1990a) *Politics and Policymaking in Education: Explorations in Policy Sociology*, London, Routledge.

Ball, S.J. (1990b) Management as moral technology: a luddite analysis, in Ball, S.J., ed., *Foucault and Education*, London, Routledge.

Ball, S.J. (1995) Intellectuals or technicians? The urgent role of theory in educational studies, *British Journal of Educational Studies*, Vol. XXXXIII, no.3, pp. 255–71.

Bamford, T.W. (1967) *The Rise of the Public Schools*, London, Nelson.

Baron, G. (1956) Some aspects of the headmaster tradition, in Musgrave, P.W., ed., *Sociology, History and Education*, London, Methuen.

Beare, H., Caldwell, B. and Millikan, R. (1993) Leadership, in Preedy, M., ed., *Managing the Effective School*, Buckingham, Open University Press.

Board of Education (1928) *Handbook of Suggestions for Teachers*, London, HMSO.

Bowe, R., Ball, S.J. with Gold, A. (1992) *Reforming Education and Changing Schools*, London, Routledge.

Buckley, J. (1985) *The Training of Secondary School Heads in Western Europe*, Windsor, NFER.

Burns, J.M. (1978) *Leadership*, New York, Harper & Row.

Bush, T. (1998) The national professional qualification for headship: the key to effective leadership? *School Leadership and Management*, Vol.3, 18, pp. 321–33.

Busher, H. and Paxton, L. (1997) HEADLAMP – a local experience in partnership, in Tomlinson, H., ed., *Managing Continuing Professional Development in Schools*, London, Paul Chapman.

Crawford, M., Kydd, L. and Parker, S. (1994) *Educational Management in Action*, London, Paul Chapman.

Cubillo, L. (1998) Women and NPQH – an appropriate leadership model? Paper presented to the British Educational Research Association Conference, Queen's University, Belfast, 27–30 August.

Davidson, M.J. (1997) *The Black and Ethnic Minority Woman Manager*, London, Paul Chapman.

de Lyon, H. and Migniuolo, F. eds (1989) *Women Teachers*, Milton Keynes, Open University Press.

DES (1972) *Teacher Education and Training (the James Report)*, London, HMSO.

DES (1983) *Circular 3/83, the In-Service Teacher Training Grants Scheme*, London, DES.

DES (1990) *Developing School Management: The Way Forward* (report of the School Management Task Force), London, HMSO.

DfE (1995) *Developing Senior Managers in Schools*, London, HMSO.

DfEE (1997) *Excellence in Schools* (Cm 3681), London, HMSO.

Eraut, M. (1994) *Developing Professional Knowledge and Competence*, London, Falmer.

Fidler, B. (1998) Editorial, *School Leadership and Management*, Vol.3, 18, pp. 309–15.

Goodson, I.F. (1995) The story so far: personal knowledge and the political, in Amos Hatch, J. and Wisniewski, R., eds, *Life History and Narrative*, London, Falmer Press.

Grace, G. (1995) *School Leadership: Beyond Educational Management. An Essay in Policy Scholarship*, London, Falmer Press.

Grace, G. (1997) Critical leadership studies, in Crawford, M., Kydd, L. and Riches, C., eds, *Leadership and Teams in Educational Management*, Buckingham, Open University Press.

Gronn, P. (1996) From transactions to transformations: a new world order in the study of leadership? *Educational Management and Administration*, Vol. 24, no. 1, pp. 7–30.

Gunter, H. (1997) *Rethinking Education: The Consequences of Jurassic Management*, London, Cassell.

Gunter, H. (1999) Contracting Headteachers as Leaders: an analysis of the NPQH, *Cambridge Journal of Education*, Vol. 29, no. 2, pp. 249-62.

Hall, V. (1996) *Dancing on the Ceiling: A Study of Women Managers in Education*, London, Paul Chapman.

Hall, V. and Southworth, G. (1997) Headship, *School Leadership and Management*, Vol. 17, no. 2, pp. 151–70.

Halpin, D. (1990) Review symposium, *British Journal of Sociology of Education*, Vol. 11, no. 4, pp. 473–6.

Hargreaves, A. (1994) *Changing Teachers, Changing Times: Teacher's Work and Culture in the Postmodern Age*, London, Cassell.

Hargreaves, A. and Evans, R. (1997) Teachers and educational reform, in Hargreaves, A. and Evans, R., eds, *Beyond Educational Reform: Bringing Teachers Back In*, Buckingham, Open University Press.

Hoyle, E. (1986) The management of schools: theory and practice, in Hoyle, E. and McMahon, A., eds, *World Yearbook of Education 1986: The Management of Schools*, London, Kogan Page.

Hughes, M. (1985) Leadership in professionally staffed organizations, in Hughes, M., Ribbins, P. and Thomas, H., eds, *Managing Education: The System and the Institution*, London, Holt, Rinehart & Winston.

Hughes, M., Carter, J. and Fidler, B. (1981) *Professional Development Provision for Senior Staff in Schools and Colleges: A DES Supported Research Project*, Birmingham, University Faculty of Education.

James, Lord (1973) 'The James Report's third cycle,' in Watkins, R. (ed.) *In-service training: structure and content*, London, Ward Lock.

Jenkins, H. (1997) Leadership: a model of cultural change, in Fidler, B., Russell, S. and Simkins, T., eds, *Choices for Self Managing Schools*, London, Paul Chapman.

Jirasinghe, D. and Lyons, G. (1996) *The Competent Head*, London, Falmer Press.

King, R. (1968) The headteacher and his authority, in Allen, B., ed., *Headship in the 1970s*, Oxford, Blackwell.

Kolb, D.A. (1984) *Experiential Learning: Experience as a Source of Learning and Development*, Englewood Cliffs, NJ, Prentice-Hall.

Maguire, M. and Ball, S.J. (1994) Researching politics and the politics of research: recent qualitative studies in the UK, *Qualitative Studies in Education*, Vol. 7, no. 3, pp. 269–85.

Møller, J. (1997) Some moral dilemmas in educational management, in Kydd, L., Crawford, M. and Riches, C., eds, *Professional Development for Educational Management*, Buckingham, Open University Press.

Musgrave, P.W. ed. (1970) *Sociology, History and Education*, London, Methuen.

Ogawa, R.T. and Bossert, S.T. (1997) Leadership as an organizational quality, in Crawford, M., Kydd, L. and Riches, C., eds, *Leadership and Teams in Educational Management*, Buckingham, Open University Press.

Ouston, J. (1998) Introduction, *School Leadership and Management*, Vol. 18, no. 3, pp. 317–20.

Ozga, J. (1990) Policy research and policy theory: a comment on Fitz and Halpin, *Journal of Education Policy*, Vol. 5, no. 4, pp. 359–62.

Ozga, J. ed. (1993) *Women in Educational Management*, Buckingham, Open University Press.

Preedy, M. ed. (1989) *Teachers' Case Studies in Educational Management*, London, Paul Chapman.

Smith, P. (1997) Values and ethical issues in the effective management of CPD, in Tomlinson, H., ed., *Managing Continuous Professional Development in Schools*, London, Paul Chapman.

Smith, P. (1998) Managing CPD – issues of continuity, collaboration and coherence, *Professional Development Today*, Vol. 1, no. 4.

Smyth, J. ed. (1993) *A Socially Critical View of the Self-Managing School*, London, Falmer Press.

Taylor, W. (1968) Training the head, in Allen, B., ed., *Headship in the 1970s*, Oxford, Blackwell.

Teacher Training Agency (1997) *National Standards for Headteachers*, London, Teacher Training Agency.

Wallace, M. (1991) *School Centred Management Training*, London, Paul Chapman.

Watkins, R. ed. (1973) 'In-service training: Structure and Content, London, Ward Lock.

Primary

1

Strategic Management in an Infant School

ANGELA BIRD and LES BELL

INTRODUCTION

This chapter reports efforts made by the staff of an infant school to identify and implement a vision for their school in an attempt to cope with the major changes that have confronted everyone in education during the 1990s. It is written largely from the head's perspective and traces the development of her own understanding of the head's role over a 14-year period. The school itself was opened in 1967, serves a range of private and council housing and has 188 pupils on roll plus 40 part-time pupils in its nursery unit which was opened in 1986.

THE FOCUS OF HEADSHIP

In the decade following the Education Reform Act 1988 a considerable burden has rested on the shoulders of heads. They have received much of the credit for the success of schools and have had to take personal responsibility for failure. This remains the case: 'The leadership qualities and management skills of the headteacher are a major factor contributing to a school's performance. When a school is put into special measures, one of the factors leading to this decision is often poor leadership . . . In many cases the headteacher leaves the school' (OfSTED, 1998a, p. 4). Furthermore, the role of headteachers will become even more demanding in the future:

> The vision for learning set out in this White Paper will demand the highest qualities of leadership and management from headteachers. The quality of the heads can often make a difference between the success or failure of schools. Good heads can transform a school; poor heads can block progress and achievement.
>
> (DfEE, 1997, p. 46)

1

No concept of shared or distributed leadership can be found here. Such has been the emphasis on the centrality of the role of the head in recent times that Grace (1995, pp. 156–7) could argue:

> Many contemporary texts on educational management . . . use a discourse of 'leadership', 'vision' and 'mission'. Bottery . . . lists the characteristics of the educational leader as 'critical, transformative, visionary, educative, empowering, liberating, personally ethical, organisationally ethical, responsible' . . . The rhetoric of the qualities which headteachers . . . should display . . . is becoming part of the check-list culture of educational management studies. Bottery's listing of these qualities constitutes a description not only of the ideal school leader but also of a person who must be seriously considered for canonisation as an educational saint.

The almost inevitable outcome of this focus on the head as the centre of management expertise and the locus of leadership within schools is that perceptions of headship are located within an hierarchical view of school management in which the head is the solitary, heroic leader who exemplifies the totality of leadership skills and managerial competencies (Bolman and Deal, 1991). This is the myth of the hero-innovator reborn.

Leadership and management in all schools are inextricably linked and the head is the focal point. This is especially true in small schools with a cohesive staff group. At its most strategic, management involves formulating a vision for the school based on strongly held shared values about the aims and purposes of education and translating it into action. Leadership involves the articulation of this vision and its communication to others. The fundamental flaw in the conceptualisation of educational management that leads to the overemphasis on the role of the head is that the analysis stops at this point and fails to recognise that, just as the vision and the mission are derived from overarching values and beliefs, so their realisation requires action at the organisational and operational levels. If management at the strategic level involves translating the vision into broad aims and long-term plans, then it is at the organisational level that the strategic view is converted into medium-term objectives supported by the allocation of appropriate resources and the delegation of responsibility for decision-making, implementation, review and evaluation. In turn, the implementation of these medium-term plans requires them to be further subdivided into the totality of the delegated tasks that have to be carried out. At the operational level, therefore, resources are utilised, tasks completed, activities co-ordinated and monitored. The three levels of management must work in harmony towards a common purpose. This will not happen if the vision is not shared by all members of the school community and if values are not largely communal. Each level of management depends on the other two. To emphasise one and ignore the others is fundamentally to misunderstand the nature of educational management. Headteachers cannot manage schools alone nor can they carry the burden of motivating others to achieve objectives and complete tasks without significant support from colleagues. Nevertheless, ensuring that the school has its vision is the responsibility of the head in her capacity as strategic leader.

A vision is essential to sound leadership in schools. It is the starting point for all heads who wish to provide leadership for their school community. In today's turbulent times, with such an ambitious and all-pervading emphasis on school improvement, vision is essential: 'It articulates values, supplies direction, initiates activities and provides standards for trouble shooting problems that emerge in the hurly-burly work of implementing projects' (Blase and Blase, 1997, p. 92). The vision for this particular school developed as the head's perception of headship changed and developed. It was established through informal and formal processes which involved all staff and governors. Its production was not a one-off event but a strategic process over time. It is not static but constantly evolving both in response to change and as an outcome of change. The vision is: 'A mental image of a possible and desirable future state of the organisation . . . a view of a realistic, credible and attractive future for the organisation, a condition that is better in some important ways than what now exists' (Bennis and Nanus, in Preedy *et al.*, 1997, p. 48). Such a simple statement belies a complex challenge in a climate of extensive change. The formulation of such a vision became the central focus of this entire school community. As a result the head reconsidered her role.

The head of this school has been in post since 1984. Her view of her headship is that it has had three distinctive phases clearly linked to very specific stages of educational change and development. The initial four-year phase had a distinctive management emphasis, one where she concentrated on establishing administrative systems, on the building, furniture, resources, the presentation of children's work and the expansion of the school to include a nursery. At the same time she was concerned with operational aspects and spent a considerable time working with teachers and children, leading by pedagogical example. She inherited a stable and experienced staff, some of whom found it difficult to come to terms with the demands being placed upon them by the new young head. Strategic leadership was, at best, only implicit in her work.

The second phase began with the advent of the Education Act 1988 and the introduction of the National Curriculum, local management, grant-funded professional development and increasing choices for parents. This period of her headship demanded of her the development of new skills and talents, particularly those of writing policies, reports, curriculum plans, responses to consultations and, for the first time, financial documentation. By this time staff changes were taking place through promotions and retirements. Her staff needed considerable support to come to terms with the new demands which faced them. Her focus shifted towards the curriculum, but this was still largely an operational and organisational focus since her main concerns were to improve classroom practice, to establish common procedures and to develop further the broader understandings of her staff with the context of the struggle to implement the National Curriculum and its assessment.

As the confidence of the staff team grew and as the struggle to come to terms with the implementation of new educational policies continued, the head consciously and deliberately changed her role to incorporate a more strategic style of leadership. Strategic would not have been the term she used or would have recognised then but the changes were an attempt to take control of an increasingly challenging situation. There was a growing feeling within the staff that too many decisions being taken and too many plans made on behalf of the school community that did not sit easily with what they believed to be the purpose of the school. Genuine and effective consultation seemed to be missing. Through the many agonies that surrounded the planning and introduction of the National Curriculum and financial delegation the staff team developed the beginnings of their own organisational strength and felt the power of their own planning and decision-making. This feeling was reinforced, initially at a senior management level, by early attempts at development planning, the first steps in creating a real sense of direction which marked a new approach to managing change in the school and the third distinctive phase in its management.

MANAGING CHANGE

In the early 1990s the context within which this school was operating changed. Staff came under pressure from parents, competition from nearby schools with new, purpose-built nursery facilities, and from their own high expectations and intentions. In order to cope with this new environment a way was needed to manage the necessary changes. It became clear that the head needed to adopt a different leadership style, one which could encourage and enable the school to change and develop. This process started by adaptation and adjustment as attempts were made to incorporate the changes within the school's current structures and processes. This was a minimalist response based on limiting the extent of change: change was accommodated but this did not lead staff to review their capacity to manage change. This approach did not work and the whole staff team felt uncomfortable with it. It was beginning to become clear that, as Hargreaves and Fullan (1992) have noted, an inner driving force is necessary to lead a school through a period of intense change such that schools are not allowed to become negative by default but are made positive by design. This driving force emanated from the formal evaluation of the first school development plan.

At the start of the new cycle of planning which followed this evaluation, the staff team recognised the need to underpin the next phase of development with their own vision, values and beliefs. Through extensive debate initiated through an in-service day, staff exchanged views and shared personal philosophies about the kind of school to which they wanted to belong and the kind of classrooms that would enable teaching and learning to be effective. A collective view emerged. This was formulated into a vision for the school against which to measure the growing external emphasis on continuous development improvement. The vision had three elements. The statement itself committed the school to providing a caring, stimulating environment in which each child has the opportunity to develop emotionally and intellectually. This was followed by five action points which shaped all that was done within the school and against which each new initiative and aspect of the development plan was tested. Those action points were the provision of:

- an environment which stimulates learning;
- a broad and balanced curriculum which provides maximum opportunities for achievement;
- caring and supportive relationships;
- an ethos which fosters positive qualities, values and attitudes; and
- a dedicated, professional and well trained staff.

The action points were further divided into ten aims which pointed clearly to the pedagogical focus to be adopted in implementing these actions and realising the vision. The statement, its action points and aims are not, in themselves, especially novel or significant. Their significance comes from the ways in which they have been employed throughout the school to inform decisions, allocate resources and shape actions. Through this process of formulating and implementing the vision the staff developed into a creative and talented group who had an immense confidence in themselves and in the capacity of the head to offer leadership.

In 1992, the long-term benefits of a whole-school in-service day devoted to the formulation of a vision of a good school could not have been foreseen. The development, for the first time, of a vision for the school shared by all staff and governors set in motion many internal processes that resulted in more effective and more widely distributed leadership. The staff experienced collective and personal growth, high standards of achievement by pupils and the external recognition by OFSTED. The head shifted her management style from one based on positional authority to personal leadership and the development of a sharper focus on people with a deliberate emphasis on teaching and learning. She relocated herself from the apex of a management pyramid to the centre of the school and a focal point in a network of human relationships. She began to function as a change agent. She helped her staff to develop a strategic view, to establish the necessary processes to move the school in an agreed direction and, through facilitating, empowering and supporting at the operational level of the school, to implement the vision for the whole school which now informed internal policy-making and shaped responses to external demands. This approach to change management based on an agreed vision for the school has enhanced the capacity of all the staff in the school to benefit from a more strategically based leadership, from strategic planning and from a significant cultural change within the school.

STRATEGIC LEADERSHIP

In 1992 the school moved from a one to a three-year cycle of development planning in order to review all policies and practices against the newly stated vision and the aims and objectives derived from it. The emphasis of the plan was to provide a policy framework within which the staff could be more proactive and less reactive, especially about the content and timing of what was changed within the school. All decisions about planned changes within the school could now be tested against a clear view of the strategic direction in which it was planned to move the school. The changes themselves could be mapped, not only at a strategic level but also at organisational and operational levels. This helped to ensure that appropriate decisions were taken, responsibilities were clearly allocated and resources adequately mobilised. This was not an attempt to ignore the forces of change. Rather, it was an approach that allowed the staff team to take control of what was happening in their school through the planned choice of what and when to change and, more importantly, how and why to change? Such decisions are the essence of strategic planning.

Over the past decade the use of the term strategy has become increasingly used to identify the planning of the long-term development of organisations. It can be defined as 'a disciplined effort to produce fundamental decisions and actions that shape and guide what an organisation . . . is, what it does and why it does it' (Bryson, 1988, p. 5, cited in Fidler, 1996, p. 1). For schools, strategic planning must involve long-term decisions informed by known opportunities and constraints – future trends in the wider environment in the context of information about present and future resource levels. Thus, it can be argued that strategic planning underpins 'a key management process, drawing together institutional values and goals, and providing a framework for the quality of provision and the deployment of resources' (Preedy et al., 1997, p. 5).

Strategic planning was not a familiar term when the school's three-year development plan was formulated in 1992, yet it could be argued that this was the beginning of a strategic view of the way the school needed to develop. The purpose of that process was to plan a specific rolling programme of policy review and revision in order to improve teaching and learning in the school. It generated, for the first time, the feeling that the staff were able to take control of the direction of their own development. At the same time, the head took the stance of leader manager. She made the choice to use the educational reforms as an opportunity to transform the school. The outcome of this decision had a significant strategic importance for the school. It provided for the school community the opportunity to move ahead, to place its school in a strong position, with an enhanced capacity to manage strategic change. The staff soon recognised that the development plan was just a framework, a map within which actions and choices about emphasis are necessary to transform that map into a journey. The nature and quality of the journey are dependent on the contributions of the travellers and their collective ability to solve the problems met along the route. Arriving at the destination is only the quantitative measure of success and this may not be achieved because the destination may change while the journey is in progress. What matters, and is remembered, are the values, the attitudes and the behaviour of those involved. Strategic planning at its most effective, therefore, is a journey to cultural transformation.

CULTURAL TRANSFORMATION

A cultural transformation was necessary in the school to ensure that the whole staff had the ability and the confidence to make choices, to solve problems and to be fully involved in implementing, monitoring and evaluating the strategic plan. To the extent that a school's culture can be related to its internal conditions, its vision, its values and the attitudes and relationships that influence behaviour, its quality is closely related to the capacity to change and improve. An approach to managing change such as the one reported here, with its focus on the cultural development of the school, is based on the pursuit by all members of the school community of common goals and a common vision.

During the years 1992–95 the school began to approximate to Rosenholtz's (1989) description of schools that are 'moving' or 'learning enriched'. She identifies 'moving schools' as those that have the power to grow and change, that is to succeed. Transforming the school into a strong learning-enriched organisation, one capable of achieving its vision, was the head's goal. Beare *et al.* (1989) identify this as a leader's main task since in the final analysis the headteacher is the custodian of a school's culture. Fullan (1994) also identified the creation of a culture, one characterised by its ability continuously to improve, as part of a leader's 'big agenda'. This is not a task that any head can achieve alone. It requires the unlocking of the leadership forces of all the staff, identified by Sergiovanni (1995) as technological, human, educational and cultural forces. To achieve this the head focused her role on the operational and organisational levels of the school's activities which she ensured were based on a well developed strategic intent. She was able, therefore, to support, facilitate and enable staff to transfer the vision for the school from paper to practice and to encourage the staff to support each other within a wider strategic context. The quality and strength of the culture of any school depend on the individual contribution of all members of staff and their need to become stewards of the school vision. The choice made by this head to place such a strong emphasis on cultural development derived from her growing understanding that the achievement of vision succeeds or fails with individuals. The empowerment of the individual leads to the transformation of the culture which, in turn, enhances the capacity of the school to develop, grow and respond to the challenges of imposed external change.

Though the staff had helped to formulate the vision, were committed to it and had identified the processes that would support its realisation, it seemed important to her that the head's leadership recognised and tried to meet the layers of need that exist beneath those connected to processes, systems and action plans. She recognised the need for the focus of her leadership to be concerned with the spirit, the energy, the motivation, the values of staff, and most importantly with the relationships within the school. Though she attended to the processes surrounding implementation and monitoring she placed her emphasis and gave her time to supporting staff as they developed the skills and attitudes they needed to manage change. Time was spent on personal and professional development and on building the kind of culture that facilitated and enabled both personal and organisational growth.

This process was based on ensuring that everyone, not just teaching staff, played a full part in planning internal changes. This was a new departure for the school and initially was met with scepticism by some teachers. Nevertheless, it proved to be a significant decision and has had enormous impact within the school. It gave all members of staff an enhanced understanding of their own roles, a clearer view of the roles of others and of the contributions that they made and might be able to make to the entire enterprise. It resulted in the active involvement of every member of staff in the achievement of the vision. An example of this was a whole-school development day in 1996. Every member of staff, together with the governors, was asked to identify the contribution he or she had each made towards the achievement of the school's vision. Every one had the confidence to respond to this challenge and was able to do so with pride and enthusiasm. It was evident that they felt recognised and valued for their specific and individual roles as well as members of one whole-school team. As a result of this day 'role books' were produced which are used within staff working groups and for the induction of new staff. These are descriptions of responsibilities but go beyond job descriptions because they are dynamic and developmental rather than static and limiting. Two whole-school team in-service days were established. One in the autumn focuses on increasing the shared understanding and the implementation of aspects of whole-school policy and the one in the spring involves all staff in annual school development planning.

Underpinning all this was the head's genuine belief that a school is greater than the sum of its parts. She saw it as essential that leadership roles were devolved to all staff and supported this process by acting as a supporter, facilitator, critical friend and guide. All senior staff were given the role of supporting individual groups within the school. Time was given to regular group meetings designed to support staff in the realisation of the vision, to respond to problems and to identify training need. With the support of the Professional Development Co-ordinator all staff were provided with high-quality professional development both from internal and external sources. Through the revision of annual staff development interviews professional development was closely linked to identified needs and training was related more closely to personal competencies, specific roles and whole-school development. Termly professional development newsletters were introduced to inform staff of the outcomes of training and, more importantly, to celebrate and praise staff and governors.

This emphasis on celebration and praise was a small step but it had a positive and powerful impact. The school had always celebrated genuine efforts of pupils but not necessarily those of the adults who were contributing so much. This realisation led the head to note that a leader's behaviour is as important as skills and knowledge. Sensitivity and empathy are essential components in both personal management styles and in the management of change. As West-Burnham (1992) puts it: 'Sensitivity is about caring, respecting . . . It only has meaning when it is expressed in action and this means; listening first, understanding, collaborative problem solving, emphasising process issues and awareness of others (p. 112).' This, then, exemplifies the learning culture to which the school community aspired.

The head wanted the culture of the school to be one that related to the art of the possible, to the potential of development Her focus on people as a leadership strategy began through an instinctive 'feel' that this was a key element in the realisation of the vision. Only by penetrating more deeply into the operational and organisational layers of the school could she support staff to gain a clearer understanding of the relevance of their day-to-day activities to the realisation of their strategic vision. Handy (1989) identifies this aspect of leadership as the 'nourishment' of a school's most effective resource, its people. Fullan and Steigelbauer (1991) provide a useful and timely reminder about where the ultimate power to change is and always has been. It is in the heads, hands and hearts of those who work in the school. Through an instinctive focus on people the head found the most effective operational tool for matching her strategic thinking to the organisational and operational management of change and, in so doing, identified the most effective approach to translating the vision into reality. Through a process of strategic development which informed the organisational and operational arrangements within the school significant changes have been made.

STRATEGIC DEVELOPMENT, STRATEGIC IMPROVEMENT

During the years 1995–98 the staff team in this school had been able to capitalise on the benefits of the outcome of their first three-year development plan. Those benefits paved the way for the successful future of the school, the positioning described earlier, but the journey is not over. The journey of school leadership is never over. The next stage of the planning process had already started as the school entered its second three-year planning phase. As they set about formulating the next phase the staff team sought to locate the development of the school in a wider context, one that took greater account of the external environment. The plan itself was restructured to incorporate a new section, 'Rationale and trends'. This section, placed immediately after the vision, aims and objectives, set out the results of a scanning of the local and national environments, including proposed legislation. It identified the trends that were important and that would, therefore, be incorporated into the next stage of development. It provided a rationale for these decisions based on the vision for the school. These decisions were taken by all the staff and governors working in partnership. From this strategic scanning of the raft of legislation facing everyone in education it was clear that the specific and measurable outcomes of teaching and learning were going to be the main external measure of the success of all schools and were becoming increasingly important to external stakeholders. In their strategic discussions staff also incorporated a review of current literature about development planning which had begun to focus on the lack of direct impact of school development planning on teaching and learning which later informed the implementation of their plans. The staff team agreed that the vision statement was still relevant but that it needed adjusting to acknowledge their shift to a more explicit vision in relation to pupils' achievement. This helped staff and reflected the head's desire to make teaching and learning the central theme of the plan rather than just a strand within it. The whole-school approach to developmental decision-making had now become a strong feature of a flatter, more collaborative style of management and ensured the involvement of everyone in a continued alignment towards the school vision. The incorporation of other stakeholders' views into strategic planning was an attempt to ensure that the direction for the school reflected those of external stakeholders, the people who were the receivers of its tangible outcomes related to learning and its intangible ethos and values.

In 1996 the revised vision was shared with parents for the first time. Instead of just being displayed on the walls it was published at the front of every document, particularly those prepared for new parents. It was used by governors as the benchmark against which to measure success in the annual report to parents. A questionnaire relating to the vision was sent to parents prior to the 1997 development day to find out the relevance of the vision for them. Parent governors used the information to prepare a report concerning parents' perception about both the content of the vision statement and its relevance for them, the key stakeholders. The outcomes of this survey were discussed and taken into consideration in the preparation of the current improvement plan. At the same time the LEA pastoral inspector was asked to adopt the role of critical friend and provide an external commentary on the internal strategic decisions. Such a view was necessary since all the school's strategic decisions about the focus of its planned development were taken in an internal context. In order further to establish an effective external context against which to match the school's existing strategic, organisational and operational arrangements and future plans and to celebrate the achievements of the staff in the creation of such a strong and positive learning culture the staff team began to work towards the Investors in People (IIP) standard. They were awarded the standard in 1997. The IIP report recognised the quality of the culture and the commitment to learning of all staff.

In outlining the development of strategic planning it could be thought that the focus of the head's role had shifted once again to the organisational level and was not taking into account strategic considerations. This was not the case. What she sought to do was to move between the levels as and when it was appropriate to her strategic vision for managing change. Thus she moved from boundary spanner to central change agent to meet the needs of the school and the increasing demands of government legislation. The application of such a flexible leadership role was possible because of the effective administration systems previously established and to the significant role played by the management team in the day-to-day management of the school. The division of the role of the deputy head between two competent and skilled practitioners added a deep layer of leadership that gave her the freedom to place the emphasis on strategic leadership related to key aspects of development and improvement. At the organisational level she was able to articulate responses to the challenges facing the school relating to target-setting and the introduction of the literacy hour. Her focus at the operation level provided significant knowledge that she could use to inform strategic thinking and strategic action plans. Extensive knowledge of the skills and abilities of staff meant she could offer appropriate support. In other words, she could walk the talk of her strategic leadership and continue to make the shifts necessary at the organisational and operational levels to keep the implementation of the change aligned to the vision.

Such a flexible role was helpful in the preparation for the school's impending OFSTED inspection. The head needed to maintain a strategic view of the school, but her emphasis was placed within the operational aspects of teaching and learning which would be most important in the OFSTED judgements. Everyone in the school was delighted with the outcome of that inspection. The extensive review conducted by the inspection team challenged all aspects of the school but their findings confirmed that progress was being made. Achievements in Standard Attainment Tests were well above the national average in core subjects:

> The school's results in National Curriculum Key Stage I assessment (1997) indicate that the number of pupils achieving level 2 and above was well above the national expectations in reading, writing, mathematics and science. The number of pupils attaining level 3 was well above national expectations . . . These high standards have been exceeded in the 1998 end of key stage assessments, where 100% of pupils have achieved level 2 or higher.
>
> (OFSTED, 1998b, p. 1)

The public recognition of the quality of the learning environment provided by the school, together with an understanding of the significant contribution of every member of staff to the work, quality, achievements and vision of the school indicated that the strategic, organisational and operational levels of leadership combined effectively to ensure that the school was achieving its vision and could move forward with confidence.

THE NEXT VISION

In the next stage of its development, which began through the preparation of OFSTED action plan, the staff and governors identified jointly the need for a new vision for the school. The OFSTED inspectors identified no key areas for action so the staff team decided to use the action plan as a link to the formulation of a new three-year improvement plan. This action plan would reflect the staff team's own internal vision for the future of the school and would be directly related to teaching and learning as this was clearly where the government's externally driven changes were designed to impact. In the next cycle of strategic development planning there would again be a review of the environmental context with its extensive public focus. The key question now to be asked and, more importantly, to answer was 'Whose vision?' The school effectiveness and improvement research which has been incorporated into government policy, especially for language and literacy, offers recipes for improvement that could enable schools to become more effective and key indicators of success. Both the recipes and the performance indicators are derived from a view of an effective school which is rooted in the notion of targeted performance and is measured by the achievement of limited objectives: 'From September 1998, each school will be required to have challenging targets for improvement. The use in school of reliable and consistent performance analysis enables . . . headteachers to monitor the performance of classroom teachers' (DfEE, 1997, p. 26). These targets, however, only relate to aspects of literacy and numeracy. This is far too narrow a view of both schools and the educative process. Slee and Weiner (1998, p. 6) note that 'Students' achievements in pencil and paper limited and culturally specific tests are then used as the data for comparison and the compilation of published league tables'. Such reductionism resonates with the discourse of performance, efficiency and restrictive notions of academic standards and their assessment. It makes simplistic assumptions about the nature and purposes of education and suffers from an impoverished, mechanistic and narrow view of what counts as achievement.

Performance objectives are a necessary part of what is required to achieve high standards in education but they are not, in themselves, sufficient. Every school should be tested against its capacity to offer a broad curriculum not a narrow and basic educational menu. The effective management of a school requires that the entire school community has a concern for standards but this concern must be closely linked to a strategically based approach to leadership that is based on a wider view of education than narrow performance indicators and must enable all the members of that community to contribute to its further development. The new vision for this school will be based on these considerations because, as in all schools, it is the community of teachers that makes the difference.

REFERENCES

Beare, H., Caldwell, B. and Millikan, R. (1989) *Creating an Excellent School*, London, Routlege.

Blase, J. and Blase, J. (1997) *The Fire is Back*, San Francisco, Corwin Press.

Bolman, L.G. and Deal, T.E. (1991) *Reforming Organisations: Artistry, Choice and Leadership*, San Francisco, Jossey-Bass.

Bottery, M. (1992) *The Ethics of Educational Management: Personal, Social and Political Perspectives on School Organisation*, London, Cassell.

Bryson, J.M. (1980) *Strategic Planning for Public and Non-profit Organisations: A Guide to Strengthening and Sustaining Organisational Achievement*, San Francisco, Jossey-Bass.

Department for Education and Employment (1997) *Excellence in Schools*, London, HMSO.

Department for Education and Science (1988) *The Education Reform Act*, London, HMSO.

Fidler, B. (1996) *Strategic Planning for School Improvement*, London, Pitman Publishing.

Fullan, M. (1994) *Changing Forces*, London, Falmer Press.

Fullan, M. and Steigelbauer, S. (1991) *The New Meaning of Educational Change*, London, Cassell.

Grace, G. (1995) *School Leadership: Beyond Educational Management: An essay in Policy Scholarship*, London, Falmer Press.

Handy, C. (1989) *The Age of Unreason*, London, Business Books.

Hargreaves, A. and Fullan, M. (1992) *What's Worth Fighting for in Headship*, Buckingham, Open University Press.

OFSTED (1998a) *Making Headway*, London, HMSO.

OFSTED (1998b) *Inspection Report Number 104053*, London, OFSTED.

Preedy M., Glatter R. and Levacic R. (eds) (1997) *Educational Management; Strategy, Quality and Resources*, Buckingham, Open University Press.

Rosenholtz, S. (1998) *Teachers' Workplace: The Social Organisation of Schools*, New York, Longman.

Sergiovanni, T. (1995) *The Principalship: A Reflective Perspective*, London, Allyn & Bacon.

Slee, R. and Weiner, G. (1998) Introduction: school effectiveness for whom? In Slee, R., Weiner, G. with Tomlinson, S., eds, *School Effectiveness for Whom: Challenges to the School Effectiveness and School Improvement Movements*, London, Falmer Press.

West-Burnham, J. (1992) *Managing Quality in Schools*, London, Longman.

2

Building the Vision: a TQM Approach

GWENN BROCKLEY and RAY MOORCROFT

The aim of this chapter is to illustrate how implementation and sustainability of long-term strategic development strategies are enhanced by the use of total quality management (TQM). It will demonstrate the effectiveness of such an approach in securing wider stakeholder/community involvement and an enduring partnership for school improvement.

The chapter explains the philosophy behind the TQM approach, and explores the benefits and deficiencies of this management concept. The case study illustrates its strengths and weaknesses, and the opportunities and threats which arose from implementation. It offers a critical analysis of the process, and relates this to educational imperatives in government plans before concluding with a summary judgement as to its effectiveness at Ysgol Gwaenynog. We do not suggest that this approach is a readily transferable instrument which will provide school management with instant solutions: it is recognised that each school exists in a unique context. The aim is to advance understanding of successful management practice: it is for the reader to judge how far this is transferable.

INTRODUCTION

Although TQM principles are now widely accepted in industrial/commercial organisations, it is still much as Stephen Murgatroyd and Colin Morgan pointed out in 1993, 'very early days for TQM in schools'. Unfortunately, many schools have experienced difficulties when implementing TQM, mostly from poor change management, lack of training and most significant of all, a lack of commitment to the process. These difficulties are exacerbated by the fact that it is not a single philosophy, with a clear thrust of reasoned argument and exemplars which 'prove' the model. Thus each 'guru' appears to offer a different model, with Deming, Juran, Shingo, Ishikawa, Crosby, etc., each making convincing cases for their philosophies, principles, techniques and methods to be regarded as superior.

There is, however, general agreement on the first step in implementing TQM; that is, ensuring that there exists in the organisation what Deming (1986) calls 'a constancy of purpose for continual improvement'. Others talk of 'determining goals' (Juran), or 'Setting quality standards' (Feigenbaum), while Philip Crosby goes one step further, and actually sets the 'purpose' in a short phrase – 'Zero defects'. In implementation, both industry and education have translated this as 'setting the vision', and in this guise it is familiar to most schools. Indeed it is a central tenet of the TTA's national standards for both headteachers and subject leaders: 'Headteachers, working with the governing body, develop a strategic view for the school in its community . . .' (Key Area of Headship A, National Standards for Headteachers, 1998). However, if the original TQM texts are revisited, behind the different phrases lies an underlying imperative: long-term, deep involvement of management in partnership with the stakeholders of the organisation, which is based on identified needs. There are two key issues here:

1) That the improvement inherent in any vision is long term, and therefore the involvement of stakeholders must be based on true commitment.
2) This commitment can only be secured if needs and wants are accurately identified.

Most school managers accept the long-term nature of the vision, reasoning that 'if you don't know where you are going, you will probably end up somewhere else' (Peter, Lawrence, 1929, Manchester Metropolitan University (MMU) teaching notes). It is commonly agreed that the vision helps the organisation to use and decipher what Juran, J. (1979) calls the 'quality planning road map' by providing a destination. As a result, most schools now have mission statements which reflect the vision. These are usually well thought-out and inspire messages of hope, reflecting long hours of deliberation by the head and/or the senior management team. Unfortunately, they often fail to inspire and secure long-term improvement, and are themselves either changed (through organisational change) or ignored (becoming irrelevant as a guiding influence). They can even become counterproductive, as Fullan (1991, p. iv) wryly observes: 'Visions can blind if they remain the prerogative of one person.'

We believe that this arises because the vision is not grounded in accurate identification of the needs of all the stakeholders, and therefore any commitment gained is relatively short term. The commitment is based on the goodwill evident in most schools from those already committed to the school, and from those who are willing to see how it works out. It fails to bring on board the disaffected, and soon loses those who are initially neutral: 'Having vision alone is not of course, sufficient . . . Recent studies have highlighted the importance of the leader gaining the commitment of others to that vision, and then ensuring that it shapes the policies, plans and day-to-day activities in the organisation' (Caldwell and Spinks, 1988, p. 174). To secure long-term commitment demands knowledge of what will drive stakeholders to support and participate, of what it is that *they* see as a desirable institution. Unfortunately, as Morgan and Murgatroyd (1993, p. xii) succinctly put it: 'Customers will have different perceptions of what constitutes quality. It may well be that many customers of schooling have a similar common core definition of quality, but the totalities of their definitions of "quality" will differ.'

It is therefore advisable for heads at least to *ask* the stakeholders what their vision is, before embarking on a programme of school improvement. It is this process of discovering the needs of the 'market-place' of the community and incorporating them into the vision which is the focus of the case study: a 'customer-led' process. This is the first part of the TQM paradigm, and here it is worth noting the views of Malcolm Greenwood and Helen Gaunt (1994, pp. xiii and xiv): 'This new management paradigm is not just a new "fad" which will go away. The quality revolution is here to stay, since our customers insist that it should.' The case study is valuable in that there are so few educational exemplars focused on the *process* involved in this important first step: indeed, only 'a handful of schools in the USA and the UK . . . have gone down this route' (*ibid.*). It is a deliberate attempt to encompass management science in a fundamental school process, and its success is based on the firm and unwavering convictions held by the headteacher, Gwenn Brockley, that the TQM philosophy offered a chance to break some ideological chains which restricted school improvement performance. The first 'chain' is the belief that the headteacher knows best, and her or his vision can be devised and implemented in isolation. Gwenn believed that implementing and sustaining the school vision is best served by rooting it in the community it serves. After all, helping all parts of the organisation to acquire a sense of purpose (a 'vision') is one of the most important components of effective leadership (Ribbins *et al.*, 1991).

THE CONTEXT: BACKGROUND OF THE CASE-STUDY SCHOOL

Gwenn Brockley has been headteacher of Gwaenynog School since September 1995. The school is an infant school with 107 full-time pupils and 40 part-time nursery children. The staff comprises the headteacher, deputy head, three class teachers, a part-time teacher designated for special educational needs, two nursery nurses and an auxiliary support worker assisting a child with physical special needs. The school is built on the outskirts of the town of Denbigh and is one of two English medium infant schools serving the town and surrounding rural area. The natural catchment area of the school is Upper Denbigh. The housing profile of the area, as taken from the 1991 census data, comprises 42% owner-occupied housing and 58% rented accommodation. Some 58% of children who stay for school dinners have an entitlement for free school meals, an indication of the socioeconomic profile of the catchment area.

MSc EXPERIENCE FOR THE HEADTEACHER

In 1997 the writer was studying for a master of science in educational management with Manchester Metropolitan University. The focus for these studies was implementing and sustaining a vision for the school considering the process of stakeholder involvement. Stakeholders in this study refer to parents, governors and the school staff. It was intended that the vision would impact on the production of the management planning strategy for the forthcoming years in the form of the school development plan.

From her studies, Gwenn was aware of the 'place' of the vision within school improvement and TQM theory: by late 1996, this awareness had crystallised into clear ideas regarding what was needed, and initial thoughts about how to do it. Gwenn recalls:

> I knew that a vision statement needed to be brief and memorable. The vision should ideally consist of no more that three words and is something staff, governors, parents and pupils can remember. A vision should take you from the past and commit you to the future. I made a strategic management decision to develop and implement a Vision for the school which would be sustained by ensuring it impacted on the School Development Plan. I considered that the contribution of the stakeholders to the development of this strategy was vital to ensure long-term development and my aim was:
>
> * to consider and explore the involvement of the stakeholders in creating a Vision for the school and
> * strategically manage the planning – the School Development Plan – to implement and sustain that Vision.
>
> However, whilst the management theory was clear about the need for involvement of all, there was little to assist me in terms of specific exemplars of the processes involved – of how to do it.

DESIGNING THE STRATEGY

It was at this stage that a series of meetings were held with the university tutor (Ray Moorcroft) acting also as a management consultant. A number of options were considered and discarded for various reasons – generally those of time and resources. It is worth noting that some of these (e.g. focus groups) are considered an essential part of relationship marketing, which was a technique the authors considered offered much to the process, given appropriate circumstances.

However, given the restrictions of the time and space, it was decided that the involvement of the stakeholders in the process of the development of the school vision should be through the mechanism of a questionnaire, in the style of the Likert attitude scale. The decision to assess the attitudes of the stakeholders using a questionnaire designed on the Likert format was because:

* the format is clear, uniform and standardised; and
* many of the parents were familiar with the format, as it is similar to the questionnaire used by the OHMCI/OFSTED inspection team: the case-study school had been inspected 18 months prior to the questionnaire.

The questionnaire statements which demanded an opinion reflect issues which had a long-term impact on the development of the school, and more importantly were issues which the management team in the school have a control over.

IMPLEMENTATION OF THE PROCESS

A working group was formed in November 1996 as a direct result of the TQM literature relating to the development of a vision statement. This was a direct derivative of the wider 'focus group' concept. The working group for the case-study school comprised

- three teachers (including Gwenn);
- three governors (including the chair of governors); and
- three parents from the Parent Teacher Association.

The members of the working party were volunteers who indicated an interest after an initial explanation given by Gwenn about the vision development process of involving all the stakeholders in the school. This explanation was given verbally to the teaching staff and governing body in the regular staff and governor meetings and via the regular newsletter to the parents. Discussions with the working party developed the issues which formed the statements in the questionnaire. Table 2.1 contains the statements which made up the final questionnaire: respondents were asked to indicate, on a scale, whether they agreed or disagreed with the statements, and how strongly they felt.

Table 2.1   Statements used in the final questionnaire

---

1. Creating a happy atmosphere in the school should be a high priority.
2. Newsletters are the most efficient form of communication between home and school.
3. Good 'home/school' relations are important to the children's learning.
4. Being able to approach teaching staff informally is important.
5. Parents/governors coming into school should be encouraged.
6. The school building should be secure during school hours.
7. Continued staff training and updating is important.
8. What is acceptable/unacceptable behaviour should be clearly known by all pupils, parents, staff and governors.
9. Parents should listen to their children read for homework.
10. Parents and governors need detailed knowledge of the curriculum.
11. Children have different teachers for different subjects.
12. Children should become familiar with computers and modern technology.
13. At times, teaching pupils with special needs in small groups 'outside' the class is the best way to help.
14. Opportunities for parents, teachers and governors to meet informally helps strengthen relationships, e.g. fund-raising events.
15. Parents learn most about their child's progress at formal meetings with the teachers.
16. The best way to communicate a child's progress is through the annual school report.
17. Helping children to be aware of their own responsibilities and the needs of others is important.
18. Links with the community should be fostered.

The questionnaire was piloted on parents from a neighbouring primary school in the authors' residential locality: it is a smaller school than the case-study school but considered suitable for a pilot study. The pilot questionnaire went out to the 40 stakeholders in the pilot school. The stakeholders included 3 teachers, 9 governors and 28 parents. The headteacher explained by letter that this was a pilot exercise and that written comments on the questionnaire or verbal remarks would be welcome. The return of 23 pilot questionnaires by the recommended date was felt enough of a response to assess the correctness of the questionnaire. As a direct result of the pilot questionnaire, the instructions for the final questionnaire were revised from 'Please tick the choice after each statement that indicates your opinion' to 'Please carefully read the statements below then tick the box, after each statement, which most closely matches your views in relation to the education in the school'. The written and verbal feedback from the pilot respondents indicated that the design of the format and the wording of the statements appeared to offer no difficulty to the pilot respondents and, therefore, the format and statements remained in the initial form.

The questionnaire was then distributed to 90 parents who represented the 90 families in Ysgol Gwaenynog, all 12 governors and the 5 teaching staff. Gwenn and Ray decided that as the total number of stakeholders was 107 this was not an unreasonable amount to analyse and that it was not necessary to reduce this total number by taking a sample. In larger schools greater care regarding a statistical model may be needed, but the authors believe it is important that all stakeholders should be involved.

ANALYSIS OF THE RESULTS – THE STRATEGIC ANALYSIS

The questionnaire was collected at the end of the week and 77 stakeholders had responded. The 72% return rate was an acceptable and worthwhile response validating the results of the questionnaire. Gwenn considered this to be a good response and one which would provide an adequate reflection of the attitudes of the parents, the governors and the teaching staff. There was some discussion about making efforts to increase the response, but this was negated by the timescale of study deadlines.

The structure of the analysis is such that the results for each issue are represented initially in a numerical percentage form; directly following those is a bar graph which is a visual representation of the respondents' attitudes. The suggested strategies have been considered by the senior management team in the school and are detailed for development in the school development plan.

DEVELOPING THE VISION

This vision is a reflection of the attitudes of the stakeholders as to the future development and ethos of the school. This section describes the next stage of the process and illustrates how the data were used to inform the vision. A letter detailing these next stages was sent to parents.

The analysis of the responses to the questionnaire was initially done by Gwenn and discussed with the working group. The results of the questionnaire in the form of percentage results were given to all the stakeholders, thus fulfilling the commitment from the authors to report the findings and the results of the questionnaire. The analysis of the results in percentage form, bar-chart form and the 'strategies for action' was discussed with the working group with invited responses from all the parents. From this discussion the main issues were extracted from the questionnaire responses and it was agreed that Gwenn should devise the first draft of the vision. The author was mindful of the literature suggesting the vision should be short and concise, and the first draft of the vision was 'happy as we learn'.

However, issues which are important to the stakeholders should be contained in the vision for the school, issues which will impact on the school planning over the forthcoming years, and therefore the first draft of the vision was revised after consultation with the teaching staff and the governors. The respondents to the questionnaire ranked highly:

- the security of the pupils – question 6;
- a happy atmosphere in the school – question 1;
- an effective learning environment – questions 3, 9, 12 and 13; and
- knowing the needs of others: acceptable behaviour between pupils – questions 8 and 17.

Mindful that the vision statement is brief and memorable and is something that the staff, governors, parents and pupils can remember, the following statement was compiled selecting the issues of perceived importance in the questionnaire. The 'vision' for the case-study school is: 'Happy and secure as we learn together.' This has become the vision for the school and the school development plan reflects the stakeholders' desire to implement and sustain that vision.

IMPLEMENTATION

The process so far can be regarded as strategic environmental analysis, which involved gathering information about the attitudes of the stakeholders in order to secure long-term commitment. It was recognised that the greater commitment engendered by the process would not be sustained, unless it was *seen* to be used and become embedded in the school's development priority plan. The next step, implementation, involved the formulation of 'strategies for improvement' which meant analysing the respondents' attitudes, and deciding which strategies would achieve the desired outcomes; that is, those which reflected the attitudes of the community/stakeholders, as encapsulated in the vision statement. This process was also widely publicised and a commitment made to ensure that the vision would be reflected in the published 'strategies for action' – i.e. in the school development plan (SDP), which becomes a tool to ensure the planned future development moves towards the vision.

Therefore the school is now guided by four clear and memorable principles:

- *Happy* – a happy school where there is an effective pastoral care system and children can effectively concentrate on school life, parents feel comfortable approaching staff and feel able to participate in the life of the school, e.g. helping in class, working with the PTA, attending open evenings.
- *Secure* – high standards of security to endeavour to ensure the safety of the pupils, staff and the recognised visitors to the school.
- *Learn* – an effective learning environment where the quality of education is reflected in high standards of learning for the pupils. An environment where the importance of development needs of the staff is dictated by those which will impact on the quality of teaching and learning.
- *Together* – a social structure which respects the needs of others and where the standards of what is acceptable behaviour and what is unacceptable behaviour are clearly known by all staff, governors, parents and children. The school aims to promote good working relationships between all the stakeholders and the officers in the local education authority.

These principles can be seen embedded in the 'strategies for action' contained in the third section of the SDP.

To ensure the process is remembered and (thus further embed the principles of the vision), the school development plan document has been divided into sections and these sections relate to:

- *the context* – the uniqueness of the school, the principles of teaching and learning in the school and the experience of the process;
- *the management plan* – a description of the information collected in the questionnaire, a step-by-step analysis of the questionnaire; and
- *the management matrix* – includes an 'at a glance' three-year 'time line' of the key strategies for action. This section fulfils the commitment made by the management to translate the vision into actions, and publicly details which element (security, partnership, etc.) is guiding which development.

An example of this can be seen in Table 2.2. Thus the development planning process has been directly informed by the responses of the stakeholders of the school. The vision developed for the school is a direct reflection of the views of the stakeholders and acts as a constant benchmark indicating the direction and planned development of the school, and will sustain commitment.

ANALYSIS

The initial aims and purpose of the project were to

- consider and explore the process of maximising the involvement of the stakeholders in creating a vision for the school;
- manage the implementation of the vision by using the process to inform the school development plan; and
- ensure sustained commitment.

Table 2.2 Strategies for action: vision – 'Happy and secure as we learn together'

Vision principles	Area of activity	Strategy	Key events (Sept. launch)	Dates
Learn	Assertive discipline	*Ensure:* 1) All stakeholders familiar with the concept (through training) 2) Status/position of initiative by use of external organisation/ consultancy	1) Secure 　a educational psychologist 　b education social welfare speakers 2) Arrange open evenings (2) which are training focused (all stakeholders)	April May June for Sept.
Together		3) Commitment through invitations to extend training to all 4) Set up MER system	3) Explore accreditation for training 4) Involve children 5) Arrange review audit (NB: Ongoing audit compilation)	July Sept. Nov. Dec.

All three of these have been fulfilled at a pragmatic level: the school has a vision and a school development plan to bring the vision to fruition.

The vision compiled for the case-study school of 'Happy and secure as we learn together' is rooted in the needs of the stakeholders and the process provided the element of ownership which the literature indicated was an important element of a vision for an organisation. The vision of the case-study school is a reflection of the elements which the stakeholders considered important issues, i.e. a happy atmosphere, the security of the school, the learning process for pupils and staff, and a school which encourages involvement from the stakeholders in a social structure which respects the needs of others – where the standards of what is acceptable behaviour, and what is unacceptable behaviour are clearly known by all involved. The fact that the vision then affects the policies, plans and activities of the organisation has been an indicator of school management's (head, governors, staff) commitment to the expressed needs of the stakeholders.

The process was based on the premise that an organisation cannot simply adopt another's vision statement: the process of evaluation and development should respond to the unique conditions of the individual institution. There are approximately five generally agreed steps to producing a vision statement:

- *Solicit commitment from the stakeholders.* The author explained to the governing body in the regular governors meeting, the teaching staff in a staff meeting and the parents in a regular newsletter about the nature of the initiative being undertaken and that their views and opinions about a future vision for the school would be obtained and collated as part of the process.

- *Development of a vision statement working group*. The working group was formed and comprised volunteers from the teaching staff, governors and parents. The discussion process was fairly time-consuming but it was this discussion process with the working group that formulated the issues which made up the questionnaire which was ultimately distributed to the stakeholders. The group continues to meet informally in a monitoring role.
- *Gathering the data*. Information was gathered by the questionnaire.
- *Analyse the responses to the interviews or questionnaires*. This was initially done by the author and discussed with the working group. The results of the questionnaire in the form of percentage results were given to all the stakeholders as there had been a commitment from the author to report the findings of the questionnaire. The analysis of the results in percentage form and bar-chart form was discussed with the working group. From this discussion the main issues were extracted from the questionnaire responses and the first draft of the vision was compiled.
- *Seek consensus*. The teaching staff and governors had an opportunity to discuss the responses and the first draft of the vision in the respective meetings. Consensus of staff and governor opinions was that security, the issue of the working partnership and living together in a sociably acceptable way, should be included in the vision for the school. The final draft of the vision statement 'Happy and secure as we learn together' was compiled by the working group and sent to all parents as part of the process. Informal monitoring continued at this stage through discussions with parents on an *ad hoc* basis.

One issue which arose that was not part of the original focus was that of 'relationships'. As a direct link to involving the stakeholders in the vision-making process the relationship between the various stakeholder groups has grown stronger. The stakeholders are proud of the vision of the school and the authors feel this is a reflection of the corporate nature of its development: being committed to the vision they also act as ongoing motivators to each other. The importance of this cannot be underestimated as it helps *sustain* the vision.

In retrospect, the rewards of collaboration and partnership with the parents, pupils, governors and staff were worth the risk of potentially providing a forum for negative debate. What came from the partnership was a mandate of support for involvement, not just in the social aspects of the school but via the curriculum. Parents and governors have their ideas for effective education at Gwaenynog School and they have ideas about the role they can play in this, which can be capitalised in the future. The vision in the school forms the foundation for future planning, the established vision belongs to everyone in the school and the role of the senior management team is to ensure the vision is implemented and sustained.

CRITICAL REFLECTION

It is perhaps difficult, at first glance, to see how the time and resources dedicated to this process can directly aid schools in meeting the range of initiatives which constantly crop up. This is not made any easier by the authors' agreement with Hardie (1995, p. 16): 'In order to get the vital element of "ownership" it is necessary to spend some time, and it will take time, probably a long time, developing a statement to which everybody has some commitment.'

The temptation for heads just to 'do it' seems overwhelming, as staff react to initiative overload and other pressing concerns by pleading for paternal autocracy. However, the simple answer to these concerns is that the outcome, the vision, is too important not to spend the necessary time on the process. Indeed, research shows that most success recipes have vision as a key ingredient (Timm and Petersen, 1993).

The link to school improvement is commonly accepted, and also makes a strong imperative: 'Vision-building . . . permeates the organisation with values, purpose and integrity for both the what and how of improvement' (Fullan, 1995, p. 81).

Underlying all this is a fundamental element of TQM: 'do it right first time.' The principle rests on the tenet that if the time is spent on analysis, and 'preaction thought', then the implementation of the process, and quality of the 'product', are much enhanced. This is a study about the involvement of stakeholders in this 'front-end' school development planning process – i.e. in developing the vision and the planning strategies to implement and sustain that vision. How should it be judged?

The initial performance indicators set at the beginning of the project revolved around how many people would know of the initiative, how many would respond and so on, and these are valid indicators of the success of the methodology.

In addition, the concept of 'revisiting' the vision was built in to the review process, although as Gwenn points out, the effect is long term, and many indicators were not evident until at least two terms later. Indeed, judging whether or not the vision *does* reflect the needs of the community could not be undertaken until the vision was put in place, and even then presents difficulties in quantitative measurement. There is, however, no doubt that the process has developed co-operation and empowered the community to find a voice, and say something about matters which affect them. Gwenn is in no doubt as to the success of the process, summing it up thus:

> The vision for Ysgol Gwaenynog has become a fundamental part of school life and can be seen in many ways. For example, in driving out fear of change: we have found that initiatives (e.g. Family Learning) are much more readily accepted, parents' involvement with all events has improved, governor assistance increased, visitors have commented upon the friendly culture, and so on. However, perhaps the most significant feature has been the 'adoption' of the vision by the children; this is understood by them as 'our special words', and each is constantly used throughout the day.

It is this ongoing self-motivation which helps provide continuity and sustainability of the approach, working in exactly the same way as it did for their parents.

The evidence from industrial/commercial exemplars affirms these benefits with specific reference to greater motivation, creativity, partnership, improvement and perhaps most importantly, 'a lack of fear' (Deming, 1982). While all these are evident in Ysgol Gwaenynog, it is interesting to note that the sense of 'driving out fear' is mentioned by Gwenn: change is not something to fear, but to deal with. This in itself is a remarkable achievement, given the truism, 'The human spirit does not adapt easily to change' (Mikhail Gorbachev, 1995, MMU teaching notes).

RECOMMENDATIONS AND CONCLUSIONS

There are many things which Gwenn says she would 'do differently next time', but when pressed, these reduce to four:

1) Involve the children. It is argued that this was done through parents, but Gwenn believes direct, initial involvement may yield benefits which would speed things up.
2) Explain the process at the beginning, giving an overview to all stakeholders. This, of course, requires knowledge of the process, and appropriate experience of the facilitator.
3) Use social/informal mechanisms much more, including 'an official launch', with a higher profile throughout. This is, of course, very much dependent on the headteacher's confidence in the process. There is also a need to ensure as many people as possible are involved: the authors feel that there is much to gain from 'chasing responses'.
4) Build on the use of focus groups in a wider capacity – for example, as 'culture-marketing agents'.

However, it must be remembered with TQM, there is no 'one best way'. Add to this assertion the fact that improvement and development are not rational, as any study of change will reveal, the fact that each school is the sum of its different parts, that industrial models do not always transfer well to education, and the result is a complex equation. It is not the intention of the authors to reduce this equation to the simplistic (i.e. 'imitation = success'), but to offer a framework for action requiring professional reflection from educational leaders.

REFERENCES

Caldwell, B. and Spinks, J. (1988) *The Self-Managing School*, Lewes, UK, Falmer Press.
Deming, W.E. (1982) *Out of the Crisis*, Mass MIT, USA, Cambridge University Press.
Fullan, M. (1991) *Visions that Blind; Leadership for Institutional Development*, London, Educational Leadership.

Fullan, M. (1995) *The New Meaning of Educational Change*, London, Cassell.
Greenwood, M. and Gaunt, J. (1994) *Total Quality Management for Schools*, London, Cassell.
Hardie, B. (1995) *Evaluating the Primary School*, London, Northcote House.
Murgatroyd, S. and Morgan, C. (1993) *Total Quality Management and the School*, London, Open University Press.
Ribbins, P., Glatter, R., Simkins, T. and Watson, L. (1991) *Developing Educational Leaders*, Harlow, Longman.
Teacher Training Agency (1998) *National Standards for Headteachers*, London, TTA.
Timm, P. and Peterson, B. (1993) *People at Work*, USA, West Publishing.

3

The Culture of Counselling as an Engine for Change

CAROLYN CLARKE and TERRY MARTIN

INTRODUCTION

The appointment of a new leader provides a window of opportunity for changing the culture and dynamics of any organisation but there are still big challenges to face and surmount. Carolyn was appointed headteacher of the junior school in 1992 with a mandate from the governors to bring about change. The school is located in a semi-rural area of southwest Hampshire and has a wide catchment area containing small hamlets and villages to the fringes of mass urban sprawl. The pupils come from varied backgrounds with children from affluent middle-class homes to children from families on very low incomes. Within the school population of just over 300, approximately 10% of the pupils come from families with single or remarried parents, and these pupils are from across all social backgrounds. The school has a relatively high level of special needs, currently indicated at 14% on the Hampshire Special Needs Audit, with a further 10% of children being monitored.

The school Carolyn inherited was organised around a traditional culture where the micropolitical structure was fissile (Hargreaves, 1995), inherently liable to break into groups quarrelling over status, power and resource. Staff would meet in groups and plot against each other, whilst others would court favour with people they believed had influence. The routines of the school were organised on a tight positional basis, linked to the historical routines of the institution, preventing innovation and making change difficult as the previous hierarchy had had a strangle hold on development. Many of the staff were demoralised and discontented; no matter how hard they worked there seemed to be few rewards. The eager were disenchanted and those who were tired had become disillusioned. Children who were identified as having learning or behavioural difficulties remained with those problems until they left, despite the best efforts of the school.

Another key feature of the school culture was an emphasis on 'control', ensuring that teachers were 'winners' and the risk of 'losing' was minimised at the expense of pupil independence. Relationships between many staff and parents were strained as there was a definite divide that did not encourage parental involvement in the educational process. As the political structure began to change towards a more 'collegial' one, a number of staff wanted to introduce self-action management techniques for pupils. Whilst recognising that the style of a collegial school structure was not one where staff had been able to appoint her as headteacher, the opportunity for involvement in decision-making was nevertheless greatly increased. Governors with staff representatives had been involved at some stages of the selection process and as relationships have improved all teachers have now been given equal rights to participate in school issues. Prior to these changes thinking staff were thwarted by others who were defensive and railed against the drive towards the notion of a participating culture where the assignment of duties was related to trustful delegation.

Co-operation at this time had been limited and there was general malaise that any development or problem belonged to someone else. This belief was evident in the teaching and non-teaching staff and was reflected in the general state and disrepair of the building. As staff began to audit and identify the needs of the children within the school a realisation began to dawn that those remaining could no longer rely on defensive behaviour, identified by Ashforth and Lee (1990) as overconforming, passing the buck, playing dumb, depersonalising, stretching, smoothing and stalling.

THE PROCESS OF CHANGE

The first moves within the school came slowly as staff began to recognise that their voices were being listened to and that they could participate in the decision-making process. They recognised, for example, that they could not change the behaviours of pupils by bullying or aggressive behaviour, or influence the environment or mental health of the institution without working together and taking responsibility. To move forward the climate of trust had to be improved so that staff could accept one another, encouraging information to flow between different groups. This would then allow goals and targets to be set, some of which would be linked to social control and responsibility. For this situation to arise it was important that the staff had a shared vision and that all could participate in formulating it. This was achieved very simply by all staff and governors listing those aspects of school life that were important, throwing them away and then only retrieving those that they could not live without. Although the final wording took some time to produce it was surprising how quickly all agreed on what was important and this formed the basis of the mission statement. The formation of the mission statement was the beginning of change as it opened the door to discussion; for some it introduced feelings of defensiveness and aggression as control moved from the hierarchy to the staff as a whole in which all contributions were welcomed. By collectively producing this mission statement we had identified the group's ideals. Where staff found that their beliefs did not match those of the majority it simulated them as individuals to review their thinking: 'The value of organisation can be measured by the expertise of its staff and their ability to work together. The bottom line will reflect the skills of staff and the quality of their relationships' (McConnon and McConnon, 1996, prelims).

Developing trust within the school is dependent upon members of the group trusting and understanding themselves. Handy (1993, p. 116) describes trust in the management situation as 'consistency and integrity, the feeling that a person and an organisation can be relied upon to do what they say'. The open management systems for children and staff was encouraging this to happen, for individuals to make decisions and to carry out their plans. Those who felt uncomfortable or threatened were given support to recognise the importance of their contributions. When working with children it has been important to examine the ethical procedures in operation, to ensure that we still perform our duty of care, including our statutory obligation to disclose information when child safety and protection are threatened. Therefore children and staff needed to know the limits of confidentiality and the framework in which they were and continue to operate. This includes a code of practice, guidelines on confidentiality and methods of storing, passing and giving information as mentioned by McLaughlin (1995). This information is given at the end of the chapter.

SUPPORT AND CHALLENGE

In 1995, about half-way through her current headship Carolyn embarked on a two-year part-time MA(Ed) at the University of Southampton where Terry Martin was her course tutor for much of her studies. The course has a distinctive philosophy and declared set of values which are shared with the group as the basis of their work together. As laid out in the course handbook these are

- both the detailed content and the topics for assessment are negotiated between participants and the course tutor;
- participants value and respect each other and their contributions;
- learning is enhanced through group commitment; and
- close links between theory and practice by analysis and reflection.

Many key interpersonal issues have to be resolved within such a group; the manner in which this is done will exemplify the principles taught and the group will therefore be a key resource within which to learn together. Although we did not use the precise expression at the time, we were seeking to establish a culture of counselling within the group, in the deep conviction that in such a culture effective learning and personal development can occur.

This culture can be encouraged by getting the group members to establish a set of ground rules early in their life together. In formulating ground rules it is helpful to express them in positive rather than negative ways if possible. The purpose of ground rules is not only to prohibit certain behaviours but to define the ways in which group members wish to relate and the sort of climate they wish to encourage; the intention is to improve the quality of their learning. The physical and social contexts in which learning occurs are very important. The leader's role is to lead by example and to encourage those features that will be most conducive to establishing and maintaining a good climate. A good climate will be one in which conflict is handled constructively, and each member is valued and respected.

For example, the group to which Carolyn belonged agreed and affirmed the following ground rules which would inform the way they would work together and relate to each other:

- Listen to others.
- Show consideration especially when criticising ideas.
- Support and help each other.
- Attention to time boundaries.
- Confidentiality.
- Be sensitive.
- Value the views of each other.
- Allow equal opportunity to contribute.
- Keep an open mind.
- Respect choice – join in or not as you wish.
- Socialising.
- Humour.

There is nothing particularly surprising or controversial about this particular set of ground rules; they are typical of the kind of understandings most people, given the choice and opportunity to do so, will suggest and readily commit themselves to. They create a safe and nurturing climate, and the group leader may have to point out that if the climate is too safe people will not challenge each other sufficiently. Growth and development occur in response to such challenges. However as in a counselling relationship a safe climate of trust has first to be established and experienced before we can embark on challenge and confrontation. Within such a safe climate ultimately greater risks will eventually be taken and deep and permanent learning can occur. A culture of counselling is not, as is often believed, a soft option, but a highly disciplined method of regulating our behaviour with each other.

Headship, as with any leadership position, can be a lonely and isolating experience, and some form of external support network can be crucial. This particular group and the course provided Carolyn with ongoing support and challenge for two years during which time she was consolidating many of the changes initiated earlier and introducing new ideas to her staff which she had experienced and learned first hand on the course. The course also provided an opportunity for group members to report back, in confidence, on events within their own schools. These case studies of management problems, issues and predicaments became an important strand of the course woven into the structure through the creation and reviewing of a shared agenda. A course and group are not the only means through which heads and others can get the support they need. Providing those in leadership with appropriate personal and professional support (of a developmental rather than remedial focus) remains a significant issue.

We illustrate how support and stimulation can work in practical terms by describing three examples of issues which were considered and modelled on the MA course and then adapted and used in school with staff:

- teams and team-building
- self-esteem
- problem-solving techniques.

Working with each issue involved practical activities which helped confront important and difficult issues in as non-threatening way as possible. Given the right climate most people will welcome an opportunity to share concerns about their effectiveness in working together and achieving the shared task which has drawn them together in the first place.

TEAMS AND TEAM-BUILDING

To gain an understanding of how the school staff felt about themselves as a team, we examined self-perception when measured against the characteristics of what makes a good team. We undertook this exercise in January 1996 having worked together for some time using the 'Building blocks to effective teamwork' identified in Woodcock and Francis (1994), scoring each section out of 10:

- balanced roles
- clear objectives
- openness and confrontation
- support and trust
- co-operation and conflict
- sound procedures
- appropriate leadership
- regular review
- individual development
- sound intergroup relationships
- good communications.

The staff were strongest in the area of support and trust, which was a significant improvement from the situation I had found in 1992. Appropriate leadership and sound intergroup relations also scored highly. The team were pleased that we had scored highly in most aspects but believed we could continue to work on the areas of balanced roles, co-operation and conflict and regular review. Open management team meetings have started to move us towards more 'balanced roles' as all members of staff are encouraged to contribute towards management issues should they wish. Peer group support between colleagues and the inclusion of transactional analysis problem-solving techniques as discussed below have helped us to become more efficient at coping with conflict which was the area staff identified as needing most support. Finally, we have identified and included in the management cycle a regular pattern of review with a specific timetable and identified personnel.

What had occurred to bring about these changes was less easy for staff to identify. However, a cross-section of personnel identified physical changes in the building and grounds, improved resources and facilities which have made the school appear a calmer and more gentle place in which to learn. From a personal view point all staff identified the notion of active teams which co-operate with one another, and a spirit of openness which encouraged discussion of success and failures with supportive colleagues as vital components for making progress. Several identified the team-building exercises that have been undertaken including the two day residential visits. In-service training undertaken by staff and encouraging team co-operation was another underlying factor supporting the recognition of the change in ethos. On the subject of trust the discussions, although similar, had differing bias. All staff agreed that a high level of trust was evident at times when the establishment was not under stress. The majority also felt that during periods of stress, such as the period at the time of writing in the lead-up to an OFSTED inspection, colleagues were generally more supportive. There were one or two individual exceptions who found the stress difficult to handle and who used displacement techniques to cope with their own problems. Already we have begun to see the calmness and support of staff helping colleagues complete preparation for next term ahead of schedule without anxiety or tension despite obvious fatigue of all staff. As we moved into the six-week period before the OFSTED inspection it was important to recognise the role that support and trust play in supporting the culture within the school and the role that good communication plays in lessening the stress in institutions.

SELF-ESTEEM

Knowing more about how we felt about ourselves as a team led me to wanting to discover how the staff felt and whether they saw themselves as 'winners or losers'. Staff completed a questionnaire developed by James and Jongeward (1971) as did Year 6 pupils (however, this questionnaire was adapted to a child's perspective).

Staff appeared extremely confident and responded positively as winners. All staff believed

- people could trust them
- they enjoyed life
- they enjoyed work.

The staff generally believed themselves to be 'Winners'. Teachers and other adults, who work in education, are often seen as insecure, and it was therefore interesting to see that amongst peers they were extremely confident. Relating these results to Stevens (1983) most adults working within the school environment would be at the seventh stage of generativity. At this stage the adult's 'concern in establishing and guiding the next generation' is evident. Stevens (*ibid.*) in discussing Erikson states that although this does not necessarily mean one's own offspring it is the prototypal form. With a young staff, care needs to be taken to ensure that they do not become too close to their pupils, reacting to them as though they are parents. In addition they need to be encouraged to teach in a non-didactic manner allowing pupils to grow towards the next stage of 'competence'.

Analysis of the pupil questionnaire identified that the children were less confident, corresponding to 'School Age' (industry versus inferiority) as discussed in Stevens (*ibid.*). At this point pupils may become aware that they are being judged on their performance in comparison with peers, and 'play is transformed into work, games into competition and co-operation and freedom of imagination into the duty to perform with full attention to the techniques which make imagination communicable, accountable and applicable to the defined tasks' (Stevens, 1983, p. 48).

I was concerned by the lack of confidence within the group relating to relationships and work. However, as these questionnaires were completed on the Monday following national Standard Assessment Tests (SATs), a particularly stressful time for pupils, the results would reflect the tension that children had felt the previous week. The nature of the tests would leave many feeling inadequate to the task, and cause a sense of inferiority amongst the group. This is of some concern, for as SATs results within the school show an above-national average and improving score rate, the anxiety reflected in the questionnaires appears disproportionate to the performance of the school. The expectation for pupils to perform and produce ever-improving results appears to invoke a fear that could constrict the horizons of pupils even amongst this normally quite exuberant group.

On reflection I hope that our Personal Social and Health Education (PSHE) programme including the use of circle time has increased pupil confidence. I also believe that pupils are working within an active yet considerate learning environment in which they can contribute to the development of the school organisation and reflect upon management issues. Their involvement is evident through the elected school's council and over the last three years there has been involvement in the following projects:

- Developing the anti-bullying policy and 'Children's Charter'.
- Planning development of the school grounds.

- Introducing and reviewing the rewards system.
- Problem-solving the control of movement around the school.
- Raising funds for charitable appeals at their own instigation.

Individual pupils in need of support have trained learning support assistants to talk to, as well as all teaching professional staff and time is always prioritised to this need. Children are also able to use a circle of friends with the support of special needs staff if this is appropriate.

PROBLEM-SOLVING TECHNIQUES

Creating a climate of trust is dependent upon members of the group trusting and understanding themselves. To discover more about themselves as individuals all staff completed a transactional analysis questionnaire and were able to identify which of their ego states were more prominent. Although this work was carried out confidentially, concluding discussions revealed that the predominant aspects of staff ego states were 'nurturing parent and adult'. Staff involved in the sciences and mathematics erred more towards the 'adult state'. There were some exceptions. One teacher's 'free child' was high, as was 'adapted child' of another. As a staff we recognised there were no right answers but still believed this was a useful tool in understanding how we and others react to different situations.

We have taken this idea a further step forward and it is now used to help us confront and understand difficulties that arise in our organisation that rely on human reaction for smooth running. I use a problem-solving technique (Hay, 1992) to help find solutions to some of these problems. For example, an area that we identified as a problem earlier this year was that of controlled movement around the school. The school is situated on a large site with vast grounds that discourage those working and learning within it to take responsibility, as it was thought to be too large to monitor with a limited number of staff. Adults and children could operate in 'free child' mode expecting others to take responsibility for health, safety and security issues. I involved pupils (school's council) and staff in the following problem-solving activity which valued people's opinions, allowed them to take responsibility and moved them collectively into 'adult' mode:

1) One person (the problem holder) in each group outlined the problem.
2) All brainstormed solutions.
3) The problem holder identified one or more solution to take forward, paraphrasing the practical ideas, giving three reasons why they liked the suggestion and one reason where they found difficulty with the idea.
4) Finally when the problem holder felt he or she had workable solution/s, he or she then shared this with the group.
5) The solutions were acted upon.

Working in this way we changed the emotional state of the stakeholders, allowing them the freedom to take responsibility from a reasoned, rational information base. All members of the school community, who had made an input, recognised that their input was valued and listened to and that they had the ability to contribute and make decisions within the 'collegiate' school structure. They were able to move into 'adult' mode to problem solve, which is a useful tool for life and I hope to give all pupils through the PSHE programme and all staff through the school/staff development programme the opportunity to work in this way, thus valuing their contributions and developing their belief in self-worth.

This problem-solving approach was taken one step further with a small group of children who were not able to learn and function effectively in the school environment. To help these children we used aspects of 'Solution-focused brief therapy' (Rhodes and Ajmal, 1995), which allowed children to solve their own problems without an emphasis on the past. Children are encouraged to identify where problems occur less frequently and use their own resources to set goals related to the conditions and actions when problems were reduced. The children engaged in problem-free talk and developed hypothetical solutions to miracle questions: 'Suppose that one night, while you were asleep, there was a miracle and this problem was solved. The miracle occurs while you are sleeping . . . When you wake up what is the first thing that lets you know there has been a miracle?' They were then given the support to move towards their goals with time to discuss solutions and, by using a rating scale of 0–10, put themselves on the scale working towards their identified goal.

By 1996 the institution had changed to an extent that the staff recognised they had moved to a situation where they were offering, as part of the pastoral care and behaviour management, a 'culture of counselling' without having considered its implications. At this point we needed to give this development further consideration to be clear that this was the direction the school should move in. Following whole-staff discussion, the group belief was that this was the way in which the school wished to develop to improve the learning environment and that further staff training was required. 'In-house' and professional training from Terry Martin identified that the work we were doing incorporated the different models of counselling and needed to be aimed at helping the institution and the individual learn more about themselves to facilitate learning and acceptance. Although all staff now had first-hand experience of basic counselling skills training they were not aiming to act as 'counsellors'. Staff spent time looking at their own perceptions of events and reflected upon their attitude and feelings towards pupils and others. All these processes aimed to develop understanding, control from within, increased self-esteem and a furtherance of the climate of trust.

GROUND RULES AND GOOD PRACTICE

As stated earlier in this chapter, it was important for staff to be clear about the ground rules under which they operate and the passing and storing of information. The passing and storing of information is carried out in the following way:

- note for file
- incident forms
- solution-focused record sheets.

All records must be completed within 24 hours and passed to the relevant personnel or authorities. Children and adults are always made aware that if the information given breaches child protection issues then social services will be informed. In one particular case the work was developed at the instigation of social services and a parent. Informal passing of information also occurs, however, and these reporting forms are designed to ensure that communication is always maintained. Included in these forms will be referrals to peer group support both of adult and child groups.

Staff have recognised the importance of individuals' perceptions and identified that if they wished to promote the counselling culture further then they needed to work to the agreed ground rules which would be confirmed at the start of each session and be able to engage in active listening. Initially I believed we did this quite well but on further exploration the staff identified the characteristics and core conditions of good listening for ourselves and recognised that this skill takes practice. The characteristics of good listening identified by the staff are listed below:

- eye contact;
- affirmation (nodding);
- focused on person;
- empathetic body language;
- empathy;
- summarising what has been said;
- no suggestions given;
- do not take over with own experiences;
- ensure the listening remains active;
- allow time;
- encourage;
- ensure room and space non-threatening, friendly and warm;
- learn to be comfortable with silence;
- read situations;
- build trust;
- where possible, remembering duty of care, respect confidentiality.

These characteristics are in line with those advocated in numerous books and courses on counselling; nevertheless there is value in staff creating such a list for themselves as the process demonstrates the shared understanding they already have.

The core conditions or qualities of good listening, as formulated by Carl Rogers and confirmed by countless others since, are

- *empathy* (perception, understanding, communication);
- *acceptance* (warmth, respect, non-judgmental); and
- *genuineness* (honest, transparent).

Having identified the characteristics and core conditions it was important to rehearse and use them. We have practised listening triangles with one person recounting an area of difficulty he or she has had in his or her working life, another engaged in active listening and the third person observing. This session was enlightening yet exhausting having to stay on task, reflect, respond ensuring our responses were open ended and not letting internal thoughts distract us. Active listening is now a fully integrated part of the PSHE curriculum with children and staff making using it for problem-solving and decision-making procedures.

After building an atmosphere of trust and acceptance the listening process encompasses the four skills described below:

- *Observing*   The listener should engage in non-evaluative attention, including eye contact, providing a warm accepting atmosphere. The observation tunes the listener into the speaker's words.
- *Reflecting*   Reflecting back improves clarity and lets the speaker know that you are hearing correctly. Staff felt that it was important that during this process they did not make interpretations of the message.
- *Paraphrasing/summarising*   Paraphrasing and summarising helps both parties to review and check the clarity and understanding of the message.
- *Reflecting feelings*   Reflecting these back will test perceptions and will give information and feedback to the person about the speaker and his or her feelings. This helps both parties if words and emotions appear incongruous. Reflection continually tests and expresses understanding.

This process allows the speaker to 'off load' negative feelings and helps them to clear their emotional vision to help them find solutions to their problems. It also allows those working with them to hear clearly the message and begin to use their knowledge more flexibly to recognise their own and the problem holder's use of filters. The culture developing in the school is for an integrated approach to the use of counselling skills but as in all institutions some problems require support to individuals and we have found this most successful when working with some individual pupils who have emotional and behavioural difficulties.

SCHOOL ORGANISATION

A belief in positive management, raising self-esteem and a positive approach to problem-solving has also been essential in developing the climate for a culture of counselling. Care is needed to ensure that within this culture of counselling academic rigour and educational excellence are pursued so that all children reach their potential and that staff have the opportunity to develop the necessary skills and competencies. Monitoring of classrooms, maintaining teaching standards, increasing results and target-setting are an important part of this programme. Targets must be realistic and achievable and children and staff must be clear in their aims.

This project began as a development programme for the school and not as an original research project. To provide objective data for the assessment of progress I have detailed reading age scores and SAT results (Tables 3.1 and 3.2). Whilst recognising that these results are 'crude' it is interesting to compare the gains by year group with the percentage of pupils with special needs. Special needs are not only those related to specific learning difficulties, such as dyslexia, but also include social, emotional and physical difficulties that delay children's learning communication skills and mobility when compared to an average child. In Year 6 there are a considerable number of pupils who were monitored on behavioural aspects which were not recorded on the Hampshire Special Needs Audit and therefore did not receive extra funding. This lack of inclusion distorts the figures. The school is making gains with pupils in Years 3, 4 and 5. Year 4, with the poorest gains, have already been identified for specific target-setting related to the school's literacy improvement project which will seek to promote a continuation of a compassionate learning

Table 3.1 Average reading ages by year group

Time	Year 6	Year 5	Year 4	Year 3
Beginning of Year 3	6.9	7.6	6.9	7.6
End of Year 3	8.6	8.6	8.9	8.9
End of Year 4	9.6	10.6	9.9	–
End of Year 5	10.0	11.3	–	–
End of Year 6	11.6	–	–	–
% of special needs	11	14	23	17

Table 3.2 SAT by subject and year as percentage of pupils for English, mathematics and science

	1995			1996			1997		
Subject	E	M	S	E	M	S	E	M	S
Absent	0	0	0	0	0	1	0	1	3
1	1-5	3	0	1	0	0	0	0	0
2	6	1-5	0	4	4	0	6	6	0
3	32.5	32	9	21	32	8	22	16	10
4	52	54	71	58	48	77	45	56	57
5	8	6	20	16	16	14	27	21	30

environment. The year group has at present the highest percentage of special needs. Standard Assessment Tests have shown year-on gains.

These figures, when taking into account the percentage of special needs pupils, have shown significant gains in mathematics and in the percentage of pupils achieving Level 5. The key question is: Can these improvements be attributed solely to the improved curriculum planning, delivery and preparation? I believe that the improvements in these areas would not have been possible unless the climate had been prepared for teachers to examine their practice and to develop new skills and curricula or for children to take responsibility for their learning. I also recognised that there were pupils within Year 6 who were not achieving satisfactory levels to enable them to cope with secondary education. If these children had identified specific learning difficulties and we have helped them reach their potential then staff have been successful. For the future we need to use this culture to raise emotional intelligence and enhance levels of achievement for pupils who find learning difficult.

THE WAY FORWARD

To maintain the culture of counselling regular reviews and assessment by all involved in the school are necessary. Future work to enhance the culture will include the development of a solution-focused therapy for both problem-solving and raising educational standards. By using this approach teachers can analyse and find solutions for raising standards in the classroom. However, whilst seeking to raise standards for our pupils and assisting them in achieving their potential there is merit in Anita Roddick's (founder of the Body Shop, and former teacher) statement that she made when commenting on the recent government white paper *Excellence in Schools* (1997); she made the fundamental point that schools should be developed '. . . as wisdom schools. The word "education" comes from the Latin *educere* meaning to "lead out". In this context we have to work on leading out the wisdom within us. It's a process of reconnecting with ourselves. Without this, education is trivial, dogmatic and doomed to failure' (Roddick, 1997, p. 12).

If we as educators are to help our pupils become the citizens of tomorrow then all involved in education should move away from the 'poverty of praise' that society perpetuates and remember that self-esteem is the root of all learning. Education needs to be valued by children as well as politicians; they are the stakeholders in the process and thus their needs, aspirations and problems require consideration so that they can become not only well educated but emotionally mature and responsible adults.

REFERENCES

Ashforth, B.E. and Lee, R.T. (1990) Defensive behaviour in organisations: a preliminary model, *Human Relations*, Vol. 43, no. 7, pp. 621–48.

Handy, C. (1993) *Understanding Organisations* (4th edn), London, Penguin.

Hargreaves, D. (1995) School culture, school effectiveness and school improvement, *School Effectiveness and School Improvement*, Vol. 6, no. 1, pp. 23–46.

Hay, J. (1992) *Transactional Analysis for Trainers*, Maidenhead, McGraw-Hill.

James, M. and Jongeward, D. (1971) *Born to Win*, Massachusetts, USA, Addison-Wesley.

McConnon, S. and McConnon, M. (1996) *Rewarding Relationships*, Barton on Sea, People First.

McLaughlin, C. (1995) Counselling in schools: its place and purpose. In Best, R., Lang, P., Lodge, C. and Watkins, C., eds, *Pastoral Care and Personal–Social Education: Entitlement and Provision*, London, Cassell.

Rhodes, J. and Ajmal, J. (1995) *Solution Focused Thinking in Schools*, London, BT Press.

Roddick, A. (8 August 1997) Lead out, Mr Blunkett, *The Times Educational Supplement* 12, Times Newspaper Group.

Stevens, R. (1983) *Erik Erikson – An Introduction*, Milton Keynes, Open University Press.

Woodcock, M. and Francis, D. (1994) *Teambuilding Strategy*, Aldershot, Gower.

4

Leading a Primary School to Enhance its Distinctively Catholic Identity

FRANCES HARDY

Gallagher (1988, p. 33), a Catholic writer, believes that 'our Catholic schools are, or should be, distinctive because their entire educational policy and approach are inspired by and flow from the vision of life which is enshrined in our faith tradition'. Yet, this distinctively Catholic ethos has rarely been investigated. In 1988 the Sacred Congregation for Catholic Education (p. 60) recognised the need for 'further study, research and experimentation . . . in all areas that affect the religious dimension of education in Catholic schools'. In the same year the Bishops published a document to encourage Catholic schools to study their own practices (Bishop's Conference for England and Wales, 1988).

I began my research in 1993, intending to identify what makes a Catholic school distinctive from others schools and, through an examination of my practice, to clarify the role of the headteacher in developing and leading the school towards that distinctive nature. My school is a Catholic primary school of 250 pupils, 13 full-time and 2 part-time teaching staff, and some 20 auxiliary staff. It has 14 governors and a school chaplain. The school is part of a London borough and a Roman Catholic parish within one area of a diocese. Undertaking *action* research as the headteacher of a *British* Catholic *primary* school is fairly unique. I see my responsibility as ensuring that the school is fulfilling its mission. I engage in action research for very much the same reason, and agree with Eisner (1993, p. 10) that 'we do research to understand. We try to understand in order to make our schools better places for both the children and the adults who share their lives there'. Anthea Millett (1996), Chief Executive of the TTA, stressed the importance of the role of the headteacher in this when she said: 'the best headteachers play a central role in creating a climate in which pupils are able and willing to learn and teachers have the best opportunities to do the best possible job'.

Bryk *et al.* (1993) in their investigation of the American Catholic school also identified the principal (headteacher) as the critical agent for the translation of the formal commitments of the school into practical lived experiences. They noted (*ibid.*, p. 156) that all principals valued academic excellence and students' educational attainment, but

> for principals in Catholic schools, however, there is also an important spiritual dimension to leadership that is apt to be absent from the concerns of public school administrators. This spirituality is manifest in the language of the community that principals use to describe their schools and in their actions as they work to achieve the goal of the community.

Using action research, I aimed to investigate my contribution to the provision of the appropriate facets of a Catholic education for the children in my school in order to satisfy the Catholic church and to improve this distinctive Catholic aspect of the school. I was fully aware that the school had to satisfy the requirements of the National Curriculum and the OFSTED inspectors in relation to the development of the children's spiritual and moral understanding. At the time I began the research, the murder of James Bulger was giving particular impetus to a national debate on the spiritual and moral development of children. Conferences and lectures were organised (e.g. Froebel, 1994) and new periodicals published (e.g. *SPES*, 1994). The School Curriculum and Assessment Authority set up the National Forum for Values in Education and the Community (1996) and began consulting on the values that schools should be promoting. In the same year a debate on spirituality and the part that schools should play in developing the spiritual in children was held in the House of Lords. The National Curriculum Council (1990; 1993) drew attention to the fact that the Education Reform Act 1988 set education within the context of the spiritual, moral, social and cultural development of pupils and of society. The OFSTED framework for the inspection of schools (Office for Standards in Education 1993) *Handbook for the Inspection of Schools*, London, OFSTED, which followed the Education Act 1992 meant that schools were to be inspected in these areas. Suddenly schools were to be accountable not just for teaching the subjects of the National Curriculum but also for teaching the values that society expects.

Although I have been a headteacher of a Catholic school for many years, it was not until I began this research that I questioned what was distinctive about a Catholic school. I started by researching into the literature about Catholic education and about the management and leadership of Catholic schools, both in the UK and overseas. Research such as this could provide a background against which schools can begin to assess whether they are fulfilling their Catholic mission. I deepened my understanding of the unique contribution that the teaching staff, and especially the headteacher, make to the school in the area of faith development. These insights have moulded my action research. I began by using the rewriting of the school's mission statement as a focus for exploring the Catholic nature of the school and, in 1996, when the school was involved in OFSTED inspections, I was able to show how the spiritual development of the children was seen by the two teams of inspectors.

ACTION RESEARCH

I decided that action research was the most appropriate research method to use to assist me in my work. I needed the action research process of negotiation to try to explore what different people felt and thought if I was truly to obtain a 'living' mission statement for the school. My intention to work within a representative working party and to involve a critical friend (Lomax *et al.*, 1996) to help me reflect on my own process of learning were important to this. I believe that the rigour of the action research spiral, which necessitates constantly reappraising decisions, would help to ensure that the decisions made were the right ones. This was appropriate not only for the writing of the mission statement but also for implementing changes in practice within the school. I needed to feel confident that, although I was the headteacher and therefore in a position where I could impose my values and beliefs on others, I wished to lead the rest of the team as collaborators and fellow researchers and not as unwilling and uninvolved participants. I was convinced that 'action research precipitates collaborative involvement in the research process, in which the research process is extended towards including all those involved in, or affected by, the action' (Carr and Kemmis, 1986, p. 199). I wanted to stress the importance of acting from a strong value position when engaged in action research. This element was important to me as imparting strong Catholic values is an important aspect of my work as the head of a Catholic institution. I share the belief that 'the underlying values of the institution – shared by its members – provide the animating force for the entire enterprise' (Bryk *et al.*, 1993, p. 279). I saw action research as being the most effective research method to use. By giving examples from the data I have gathered I can illustrate how my values have been used as standards to judge two separate but interlocking elements of my work: the writing of a mission statement and the analysis of two inspection reports.

THE MISSION STATEMENT

The Sacred Congregation for Catholic Education (1977, p. 24) have pointed out that 'what is perhaps fundamentally lacking among Catholics who work in a school is a clear realisation of the identity of a Catholic school and the courage to follow all the consequences of its uniqueness.'

One appropriate way for a school to identify this 'uniqueness' is to write a mission statement – a document which describes the aims of the school. In some schools and other institutions, the mission statement is written by an individual or a small group of people. It is then handed out to employees who are expected to feel inspired and motivated by this piece of paper. But these people have had no involvement in the discussions, they have no 'ownership' of the statement and therefore no commitment to it. Moreover, they did not learn about their institution as a result. Obviously, then, the document has limited success, employees paying 'lip service' to the mission statement that is meant to generate a sense of commitment and service towards a common goal.

Because I wanted the mission statement for my school to be a document that was not just understood by all and believed in by all, but was also delivered by all, I decided that the collaborative rewriting of the school's mission statement would include contributions from all involved in the life of the school – staff, governors, associated clergy, parents and children. The Bishop's Conference for England and Wales (1988, p. 3) suggest that 'in a Catholic school the mission statement should be developed through a process of consultation'. The exercise would also increase my own knowledge about what other members of the school community believe to be the Catholic nature of the school, and increase their awareness too. We would be learning together. I wanted to generate a team spirit and a sense of belonging to the school. The writing of the document was one outcome; a greater awareness of Catholic education in general and our school in particular was the second and far more important one. I would therefore be in a more informed position to carry out my role in the future and also I would be leading a more knowledgeable team. I agree with McLaughlin *et al.* (1996, p. 137): 'Catholic educational leaders and policy makers, and Catholic teachers themselves, need a clear sense of what it is they are striving to achieve. Shared clarity of educational vision is a well known general requirement for educational effectiveness.'

The process of constructing the mission statement

During 1994 I worked with a committee of eight members representing staff, parents, governors and clergy to involve as many people as possible in developing the school's mission statement. I minuted and tape recorded all planning meetings. I had frequent meetings with M, my deputy head and critical friend, to review progress. I kept a diary so that I could record how, as my knowledge increased, my thinking altered.

The committee sent questionnaires to all the parents. We analysed these and used the results as a focus for discussion with colleagues at the staff meetings that we arranged. We also arranged an INSET day for staff, governors and some interested parents, and we were able to use the papers relating to this to inform the mission statement. We wrote a draft mission statement based on data from these sources and asked for critical responses from all – teachers, support staff, governors, parents and clergy.

The questionnaire to parents

We studied literature (Bishop's Conference for England and Wales, 1988; Sacred Congregation for Catholic Education, 1988; Duncan, 1990; Louden and Urwin, 1992) to help us formulate the questionnaire which asked five questions, some closed and some open. When the questionnaires were returned, I analysed the results and fed the information to the working party. Question 1 asked parents why they sent their children to the school. Below is the rank order of responses:

1. I want him/her to be brought up as a Catholic (63).
2. I am a Catholic, my husband/wife is a Catholic (60).
   I feel sure that my child will be taught Catholic morality (60).
4. I wish my child to experience what it means to live in a Christian Community (50).
   The staff are friendly and approachable (50).
6. There is good co-operation between home, school and parish (49).
7. Prayer and worship are important (43).
8. The standards and approaches to discipline (42).
   The school has a high reputation (42).
10. It has high academic standards (38).
    People in the school care about everyone (38).
    It involves the parents/guardians in the education of their children (38).
    The pupil is valued as an individual person (38).
14. The atmosphere is welcoming and encouraging (37).
15. The school is involved in Christian Action locally and overseas (26).
16. It was recommended by others (19).
17. It is on a convenient bus route or conveniently located (11).

I have included the above because it raises a number of interesting issues. The first two statements are simply to do with the fact of being a Catholic. The third and fourth statements, however, flag up the importance of the moral and spiritual elements of Catholic education. The one item to do with Liturgy is ranked seventh. When we discussed the questionnaire results in the working party, one member said: 'I think that people feel that as their children are at a Catholic school they should be putting those things higher. But is that reality?' (Tape 14/4/94). Other members of the group were less suspicious, believing that, as the returns were anonymous, the parents genuinely believed that the school was providing a firm Catholic education for their children.

The INSET day: a collaborative exercise

We arranged an INSET day for staff, to which we invited governors and parents, for the purpose of getting their contributions for the mission statement. INSET days are usually arranged by the headteacher or the staff member responsible for staff development, so involving the working party was unusual but I wanted to benefit from the diverse and differing knowledge of the group. I was becoming aware of how I listened carefully to advice and comments and I was beginning to realise how important collaboration and consultation were to my management style. I agree with Loftus (1996, p. 95) who says:

> I recognise how crucial it was to collaborate closely with my teaching staff, ancillary staff, governors, the inspectorate, parents and the wider community. All too often head-teachers make decisions without consultation so as to save time. I have learnt that time saved in this way could be costly in the long run. Beside which, there is an immeasurable advantage to be gained from positively seeking participation with others so that they 'partner' you in bringing about the changes that are required in schools today.

It thus came as a shock to be confronted by a value conflict with a parent member of the working party at one of the INSET day planning meetings: 'I think that if parents were invited [to the INSET day] they would get in the way, there would have to be a lot of explaining. This would waste time for everyone else' (Mary, Tape 8/3/94). I wanted as many parents to be involved in the day as possible. All the school staff and the clergy were to attend, and I felt it was important that there also was a strong parental representation. Yet, here was a parent suggesting that they shouldn't even be invited. I felt uncomfortable. Mary was concerned that parents would get in the way of the discussions on the INSET day. I wanted parents to be as involved as possible. In the end we agreed to compromise. We decided to find out whether any parents wanted to attend and go from there. In the event, 14 wanted further involvement, so we invited all of them to attend the day and 7 of them were able to do so.

The INSET day was attended by all teachers and support staff, nine governors (although four were also staff members), three priests (including the parish priest who is also a governor) and seven parents (other than staff members). During the day we discussed issues concerning the nature of Catholic education and our school in particular, and participants drafted statements which they felt ought to become part of the mission statement. The presence of parents at the INSET day greatly enhanced the collaborative aspect of the writing of the mission statement.

Constructing the mission statement

I believe that 'it is in the living reality of people that thought is turned into action' (McNiff, 1988, p. 8). I value the opinions of others and I wanted the mission statement to be the result of a collaborative exercise. It was important to me that every staff member, governor, priest or parent saw that they had been involved in the process of writing the document, that they had been instrumental in its evolution, that they had ownership of it and that they could see their contributions in the text. It was this process of discussion at working party meetings, stimulated by the questionnaire responses and the ideas from the INSET day, that was to help us develop the mission statement. Care was taken to ensure that all the ideas we had collected in our consultations were considered. Some suggestions were combined, some expanded and some linked together. We tried to use people's own language:

The Mission Statement
The School community, inspired by the spirit of Jesus of Nazareth, aims to provide all its pupils with a broad education to a high standard of excellence. We endeavour to provide a happy, caring and stimulating environment, which enables each child to achieve his or her greatest potential and where each member of the community will experience the call to faith in Jesus and explore that faith in the light of the Catholic Christian tradition. Through this process of education and formation we aim to equip pupils to be valuable members of society and work to fulfil God's plan for his people.

We acknowledge the fact that our pupils come from a wide diversity of backgrounds and some are strangers to the faith.

We value the good they bring from their families and cultural traditions. We aim to be aware of and respond to the particular gifts, pressures and needs of each child.

The school was founded by a Religious Society and, following their educational tradition, we work in close partnership with all who are concerned with the total well-being of the children and their families.

We aim to offer a secure and welcoming environment for all.

Respect for each individual is a priority regardless of race, sex or creed.

We will encourage an attitude of respectful listening at every level, value the contribution of each individual and foster open and honest communication.

Worship and prayer from the Catholic tradition will form an integral part of the daily life of our school appropriate to the needs and faith development of the children and adults.

Each member of the school community, inspired by gospel values, will seek to witness in action what they celebrate in worship. In particular the adults will be sensitive to their position as role models and their commitment to pastoral care within the school.

The school seeks to realise the full potential of each child in every aspect of their development, academically, physically and aesthetically. We have the highest of expectations for all the children.

Staff will take account of the spiritual, religious, moral, social and cultural aspects of education throughout school life.

Staff, and especially teachers, will monitor the progress of each child's development and endeavour to cater for the needs that have been identified.

We seek to assist and support one another in our personal growth and continue to develop the necessary professional competence so that we are able to give the highest possible level of service to the children in our care.

An analysis of the mission statement

The completed mission statement is in two parts; the first section is one paragraph which sets out over-riding principles which are expanded in the second part of the document in twelve shorter statements encompassing most aspects of school life (Bishop's Conference for England and Wales, 1988).

In his work on school leadership, Grace (1995, p. 162) noted: 'the special mission of Catholic schools was expressed in three interrelated features, i.e. Gospel values, the teachings of Christ and the nurture of community.' I can find all these within the mission statement of my school. Although it is not *solely* Catholic it incorporates the Catholic aspects of school life into the other secular reasons for the existence of the school.

In the first sentence of the mission statement we wrote: 'The School community, inspired by the spirit of Jesus of Nazareth, aims to provide all its pupils with a broad education to a high standard of excellence.' Not all the expanded statement is therefore concerned with particularly Catholic aspects of the school as some parts obviously relate to the academic, physical or aesthetic development of the children and some to assessment, monitoring and equal opportunities. But the first sentence explains the rationale – the fact that, as a Catholic school, we take our inspiration from Jesus. This explains *why* we act as we do. Again later in the statement we describe our actions as being 'inspired by Gospel values'.

The importance of community, both within and from the school, is also seen as an important element, being mentioned several times. We state that we 'work in close partnership with all who are concerned with the total well-being of the children and their families', and that we have 'a commitment to pastoral care within the school'. We also describe ourselves as a 'school community'. Our inclusion of this aspect of school life is acknowledged by the Sacred Congregation for Catholic Education (1988, p. 26) when the Bishops stated: 'primary schools should try to create a community school climate.'

The seventh and eighth statements highlight our emphasis on Catholic liturgies being integral to the life of the school and in the latter we are also stating that everyone will try not just to listen and worship, but also to *live* a Christian life, to practise what we preach! But this last statement also contains an important phrase that has particular significance to me as the headteacher, that 'the adults will be sensitive to their position as role models'. As I led the working party in the year-long consultation on writing this mission statement, I was, and still am, very aware of my position as headteacher and the example that I give to others, staff, children and parents – especially in an area so sensitive as the development of the faith of others.

The writing of the mission statement was important in getting all concerned to focus on the nature of schooling in a Catholic school. It confirmed my view that parents, staff and priests place a great value on Catholic education and that this places a tremendous responsibility on the headteacher who must lead a school to achieve its mission. The statement is displayed as widely as possible, both within the school and beyond, thus becoming a benchmark for good practice. I have placed framed copies in every classroom, both halls, the entrance foyer and my office. It also has a central place in the school prospectus and is quoted in all policy documents as they are rewritten.

But it must not remain a piece of paper. As headteacher, I must lead the staff constantly to review school practices and procedures so that we are making sure the mission statement is a living document 'which actually guide[s] and shape[s] the educational processes of the school and the relationships within it' (Bishop's Conference for England and Wales, 1997, p. 36).

THE OFSTED INSPECTION

When writing the mission statement I was aware that there was an impending OFSTED inspection and I thought that this would provide an opportunity for the mission statement to be assessed by an independent body who would provide data about whether they believed I was facilitating the development of a distinctively Catholic education. In fact, being a Catholic school, we had to have two inspections, one being a section 9 (OFSTED) and the other section 13 (Diocesan), forming part of the implementation of the Education (Schools) Act 1992. (These numbers have now been altered – section 9 is now called section 10 and section 13 is called section 23.) Although it is the OFSTED report that the general public study, for a church school the Diocesan report should provide a rationale for its existence. If this report is unfavourable and if the inspectors cannot find examples of good religious education, an awareness of the spiritual and moral needs of the children and appropriate and meaningful acts of worship, then there is no reason for the school to exist. The children would be educated just as well in a county school, possibly better. This was one of the main reasons why I wanted to get a good report from the Diocesan team.

Analysis of the inspection reports

My analysis of the mission statement had led me to the idea that the spiritual development of the children was an area in which the distinctiveness of a Catholic school will partially be manifest. In looking at the two inspection reports, I was struck by the differences in them concerning their perspectives on spirituality. In writing the inspection reports, the two teams of inspectors worked from different briefs. The task of the OFSTED inspectors was to study all aspects of school life except *the school as a Catholic community* and *classroom religious education*, while the task of the Diocesan inspectors was to study only *the school as a Catholic community, spiritual and moral development*, and *classroom religious education.*

Spiritual and moral development was therefore the only area that both teams of inspectors examined. I set out to analyse the inspection reports to see if there were similarities and differences in how *spiritual development* was inspected from a Catholic perspective (by the Diocesan team) and from a generalist perspective (by the OFSTED inspectors).

Spiritual development

The OFSTED discussion paper, *Spiritual, Moral, Social and Cultural Development* (1994, p. 8) describes spiritual development as relating 'to that aspect of inner life through which pupils acquire insights into their personal existence which are of enduring worth'. This is, therefore, the starting point for both teams of inspectors.

The OFSTED inspectors are advised to look for evidence to show that the school 'provides its pupils with knowledge and insight into values and beliefs and enables them to reflect on their experiences in a way which develops their spiritual awareness and self-knowledge' (OFSTED, 1995, p. 82). The Diocesan inspectors, on the other hand, take their direction from the document written by the Bishop's Conference for England and Wales. Although they agree with this definition, they feel that it does not go far enough. Spiritual development is considered to be 'inseparable from growth in faith', it relates to the ability of the human individual to 'surpass the material universe'. It is 'the quest and love of what is true and good' (*ibid.*, p. 11). Evidence will be found by looking at opportunities for the pupils to 'recognise, reflect on, be moved by the existence and experience of others'. The school should also provide opportunities for worship and liturgy: 'opportunities provided by a Catholic school for pupils to deepen their personal relationship with Christ in personal prayer, public liturgy and the celebration of the sacraments bring the spiritual life of the school to its most explicit expression' (*ibid.*, p. 16).

The broad-based definition was therefore to be used by the OFSTED team but the Diocesan inspectors were also to look for ways in which the school helps children to explore 'beneath and beyond mere factual knowledge' so that they come to an understanding of the way in which God works in the world – a more 'religious' interpretation of spirituality.

The inspection findings

Both teams of inspectors looked for evidence to show that the school provides for spiritual development in different areas of the curriculum and both found examples in many areas. The OFSTED inspectors made references to spiritual development being fostered in 'art, history, science and mathematics' whereas the Diocesan team stated that several curriculum areas contributed to broad-based spiritual development, 'including art and music'. But as the Diocesan inspectors only watched religious lessons they must have gained their evidence from displays around the school and music at assemblies. If this is so it could be a significant finding in terms of exploring the distinctive identity of the school.

The Diocesan inspectors placed emphasis on opportunities for worship, listing the types of assemblies that took place as well as noting that morning, evening and lunchtime prayers were said in the classroom. This highlighted a distinctive aspect of *religious spirituality* that is promoted in denominational schools rather than other schools. They also acknowledged that other liturgies took place on different occasions.

The Diocesan report also stated: 'The Catholic nature of the school is also reflected in the provision of carefully maintained religious focal points throughout the school and in the class displays.' The report also acknowledged strong home/school/parish links: 'Over a long period of time, the governors and senior management of the school have sought to develop and foster a good and active partnership between home, school and parish. This partnership underpins much of the life of the school.'

These extracts highlight for me some of the ways in which we have been striving to carry out the aims of the school as written in our mission statement. Both inspection reports have also helped me clarify what are some of the significant aspects of a Catholic education and thus to try to understand how the headteacher can and should lead the school to enhance this distinctive area.

CONCLUSION

My research so far has concentrated on identifying those features of my school which suggest its distinctively Catholic identity. By looking at the collaborative development of a mission statement and the official reports from two inspections, I have identified three features that seem to be of particular importance. These are

- spiritual and moral development within a Catholic framework;
- Catholic worship and liturgy; and
- Catholic community and commune.

I am continuing to research into my practice as a headteacher as I try to understand more about the Catholic nature of my school. I am aware that I want the children in school to be given a firm foundation on which they can build the rest of their lives. By this I do not just mean in academic, aesthetic or physical terms; I want the children to have an awareness of their own spiritual and religious lives – to have begun to know and love the God who made them. If I am to give these children the best possible start in life, then I need to continue to discover what provision is needed to achieve that aim. But I know that I cannot do this alone; I need the support of a dedicated governing body, a diligent parish team, a hard-working and inspired staff and a committed parent body. Together we could provide the optimum conditions for the children so that 'From the first moment that a student sets foot in a Catholic school, he or she ought to have the impression of entering a new environment, one illuminated by the light of faith and having its own unique characteristics' (Sacred Congregation for Catholic Education, 1988, p. 16).

REFERENCES

Bishop's Conference of England and Wales (1988) *Evaluating the Distinctive Nature of a Catholic School*, London, Catholic Education Service.

Bishop's Conference for England and Wales (1997) *A Struggle for Excellence*, London, Catholic Education Service.

Bryk, A.S., Lee, V.E. and Holland, P.B. (1993) *The Catholic School and the Common Good*, Cambridge, Mass, Harvard University Press.

Carr, W. and Kemmis, S. (1986) *Becoming Critical*, Lewes, Falmer Press.

Duncan, G. (1990) *The Church School*, London, National Society.

Eisner, E. (1993) Forms of understanding and the future of educational research, *Educational Researcher*, Vol. 22, no. 7, pp. 5–11.

Gallagher, J. (1988) *Our Schools and Our Faith*, London, Collins.

Grace, G. (1995) *School Leadership: Beyond Educational Management*, London, Falmer Press.

Loftus, J. (1996) Enhancing the image of a first school in the immediate and wider community. In Lomax, P., ed., *Quality Management in Education*, London, Routledge.

Lomax, P., Woodward, C. and Parker, Z. (1996) How can we help educational managers establish and implement effective 'critical' friendships? In Lomax, P., ed., *Quality Management in Education*, London, Routledge.

Louden, L. and Urwin, D. (1992) *Mission, Management and Appraisal*, London, National Society.

McLaughlin, T., O'Keefe, J. and O'Keefe, B. (1996) *The Contemporary Catholic School*, Lewes, Falmer Press.

McNiff, J. (1988) *Action Research: Principles and Practice*, Basingstoke, Macmillan.

Millett, A. (1996) A head in more than a manager, *The Times Educational Supplement*, 21 June.

National Curriculum Council (1990) *Curriculum Guidance 3. The Whole Curriculum*, York, National Curriculum Council.

National Curriculum Council (1993) *Spiritual and Moral Development – a Discussion Paper*, York, National Curriculum Council.

Office for Standards in Education (1994) *Spiritual, Moral, Social and Cultural Development – an OFSTED Discussion Paper*, London, Ofsted.

Office for Standards in Education (1995) *Guidance on the Inspection of Nursery and Primary Schools*, London, HMSO.

Sacred Congregation for Catholic Education (1977) *The Catholic School*, London, Catholic Truth Society.

Sacred Congregation for Catholic Education (1988) *The Religious Dimension of Education in a Catholic School*, London, Catholic Truth Society.

SPES (1994) (ed.) Halstead, J., RIMSCUE Centre, University of Plymouth, Devon.

5

Coming to Grips with the Realities of Marketing

JOHN LOFTUS and NICK SELLEY

THE REASON FOR MY PROJECT

In September 1992 I was appointed headteacher of a first school built in 1973 for children aged 3–8 years in an outer London borough. In 1993, under my borough's reorganisation plans, my school gained primary school status. This meant that my school would now have to cater for the needs of children aged 3–11 years. This meant a massive change of character for my school in the following areas: a whole new key stage National Curriculum requirement, two sets of SATS instead of one, increased resourcing to support the above, to name but a few.

SCHOOLS IN THE MARKET-PLACE

This, however, was not the only challenge I was to be faced with as a new headteacher. The government's policies in the form of the Education Acts 1980 and 1988 have 'put schools in competition for pupils' (Barber, 1994, p. 356). The Education Act 1980 promoted competition between schools by reducing the circumstances in which admission to a school may be refused, by allowing parents to send children across LEA boundaries, and by schemes such as the Assisted Places Scheme. It also provided that parents, as the 'customers', 'clients' and 'consumers' (e.g. Bowe *et al.*, 1994, p. 33) should be given information on which to base their choice of school. The Reform Act 1988 supported these trends. The resulting situation is that if there are sufficient applicants schools must admit up to the number of pupils that the school building actually holds, so the abolition of catchment areas makes schools depend on popularity for their existence (Sullivan, 1991, p. v); popular schools unwillingly put their neighbours out of business (Deem *et al.*, 1994, p. 537). The National Curriculum has become a 'product' on offer (Grace, 1993, p. 353) and SATS test results provide the publicity material which is demanded by the 'free market'. Formula funding with age-weighted pupil numbers focuses primary school managers on their relationship with the local community, because under LMS each child with per capita funding brings an income into the school and schools need money to exist (Furse, 1989, p. 56; Deem *et al.*, 1994, p. 26; DFE, 1994, p. 22; Vincent *et al.*, 1994, p. 261). In addition to this there are now simply fewer children due to a falling birth rate. Between the mid-1970s and mid-1980s there has been a drop of over 25% of children in the main-tained primary sector. Some schools have closed and some are well below their standard number. In short, the government wishes to see schools as 'competing individual firms subject to the incentives and disciplines of the markets' (Flew, 1991, p. 43).

I am most certainly aware that 'the market philosophy' has been responsible for 'the pushing of the nation's schools out of local educational authorities where most want to stay and into the market-place' (Whitehead, 1994, p. 9). I feel like the parents tied in the education market-place described by Ranson (1993, p. 337), whose plight causes him to ask the question 'why is it that individuals are trapped into acting within the rules of a game which they did not produce?'

THE EXISTING SITUATION

In addition to this, I had the added predicament that the schools nearest to my school are well established primary schools which are well resourced from pre-vious years, with good staff expertise, their own science labs, music rooms, playing fields on site, good libraries and offering a good Key Stage 2 National Curriculum. I have none of the above. There is also a shortage of space. Because each primary-aged child has to have 9 sq m playing space by law, my yearly intake has been reduced from 2 to 1.5 form entry, i.e. 60 to 45 pupils. This has implication for teaching and learning, such as automatic vertical grouping, which parents do *not* like. In the last two years, the education budget for my borough has been reduced by £4 million (1992–93) and £5–6 million (1993–94) with more cuts pending. The shrinking budget is being devolved to schools which will control 90% by 1995. It is incredibly difficult to resource a growing school in this financial climate. The intention to enable my school to survive in this climate of change is at the centre of my research. My concern is that to survive I need to compete with other schools and convince my parents and community that my school is a quality school. Much of the literature on LMS argues a case for marketing the school which is seen as 'a means of identifying and satisfying your customers' (CSCS, 1991, p. 2). As parents are now critical consumers in the educational market-place seeking out services required and rejecting those which do not conform to their specifications (Riddell *et al.*, 1994, p. 241), in short, 'if schools do not respond to their views, parents may vote with their feet and send their children elsewhere' (Bush, 1981, p. 467).

Marketing involves 'attempting to put yourself in the consumer's shoes so as to identify with their hopes and expectations and finding ways of meeting these' (Sullivan, 1991, p. 1). To market the school I needed a quality product which means that marketing must be a collaborative effort with staff and pupils involved. I believe that 'schools . . . are institutions at the heart of a local community. They can and should command the loyalties of staff and parents, of pupils' (Vincent *et al.*, 1994, p. 366). Building on this belief it is my aim for our school to become

> as much part of the community as the church, the bank or the supermarket. Our neighbours have as much right to know what is going on in the classroom as they do to be informed of the times of the church services, the financial opportunities provided by the bank, and the range of goods available in the store.
>
> (Kent, 1989, p. 142)

MY PERSONAL CONFLICT

I was most certainly aware that I had been forced into a situation that I did not wish to be part of. Yet in spite of this, I was most definitely an active participator in carrying out the government's philosophy. In short, I was a 'living contradiction' (Whitehead, 1993, p. 70).

I realised that as I was in this situation I would have to look very closely at my values and intentions 'up front' because as my project progressed I, along with my collaborators, would be closing the gap between 'the way I would like to see the world with my set of values, aims and ideals and the world of my practice' (Whitehead, 1985, p. 701). Before reaching this stage, however, I was aware that I would, as a researcher, be engaging in a continuing critique of my own educational and professional values as part of the research process, as I sought answers to the questions that my practice as an educator posed.

I was aware that marketing is not a concept that had received much exposure in educational circles prior to the 1980s. In short, it was considered unprofessional and the idea that schools were in competition with each other 'selling' their curriculum was considered unethical. Furthermore, my reading of Jackson's (1994, p. 23) statement that 'In Great Britain it is only very gradually that the concept of marketing schools has gained respectability' worried me immensely. I did not warm to this statement in the least as I am of the opinion that 'there are few wrongs more disturbing to those who are involved in education than schools competing for pupils like a market trader' (Pardey, 1991, p. 7); taking this further 'making a living is one thing, building lives is quite another, and I remain unconvinced that schools have much to gain from mimicking the language or techniques of the marketing men' (Finch, 1990, p. xix).

MY VALUES

The above views were influential in causing me to think long and hard about my values, which were as follows. That

1) all children should have access to quality education;
2) when a school is proud of the education it offers, then the community – both immediate and wider – should be made aware of this;

3) all staff (teaching and ancillary) should share the commitment to any major change imposed on an educational institution;

4) a wider curriculum outside the National Curriculum should be followed and that staff and parents should work as a partnership in bringing this about;

5) the growth and survival of a school should not be pursued in a manner compromising the education of the children in that school;

6) one headteacher should not criticise another headteacher's school as a means of promoting his or her own;

7) the 'quality situation' which we portray should be a true reflection of the curriculum on offer in the school, and not just a publicity front; and

8) in spite of the present system of formula funding under age-weighted pupil numbers, pupils are *not* to be seen as merely 'little pledges of income' (Stenner, 1990, p. xxiv). Pupils should be valued for their personal qualities, and not for the income they bring.

STRIVING TO LIVE MY VALUES IN MY PRACTICE

As an action researcher I have striven to live my values in my practice. This has not been easy. No sooner do I feel that I am accomplishing the above when suddenly my reflection brings forth more uncertainties, and further questions.

In this chapter I wish to share where I am at present in relation to my values. This is as follows.

Value no. 1 (Quality education for all)

The fact that we were a primary school operating on first-school facilities meant that this value was not being lived fully in my practice. It was only when new resources were bought and new curriculum such as swimming, outdoor education, field games were introduced that this value began to reach fruition.

Value no. 2 (Publicising achievement)

Marketing in the form of constant press releases, a school video being lent out, children's work being put in the public library, prospectus being sent out, curriculum evenings for parents, Christmas and summer concerts, school assemblies with parents present – these are are all ways in which we have shown the quality of work achieved in our school, to our immediate and wider communities. So I do not feel that this value has been compromised in my practice. In fact the feedback received and suggestions offe `ed have led to better marketing of the school's achievements.

Value no. 3 (Whole-staff commitment to any change)

I believe strongly in utilising staff's views, collaborating with them (Winter, 1989, p. 45; Lomax, 1991, pp. 103–4). Staff in my school feel that the above has taken place effectively (Loftus, 1996, p. 17). I, however, am not in total agreement with this. I am aware that for my project I have been the 'main change agent' (Lomax, 1989, p. 188) and because of the urgent need to market, I have spent much time pondering over the possibility that my value of collaboration has not been 'lived in my practice' (Whitehead, 1985; Loftus, 1997, p. 12).

Sometimes the pace of change has been so fast, with opportunities to market arising suddenly, that I have grasped these opportunities and although I have collaborated strongly with colleagues implementing these opportunities, on reflection what has happened is that collaboration has taken place *after* the initiative has been set in motion. This reduces the staff's role to one of being my followers or assistants.

This has proved to be one of my values which it was hardest to keep to. I cannot really claim to have involved the staff fully in planning changes: their workload was so heavy that they often had little opportunity to think about marketing. There were not enough occasions when the staff contributed to putting forward suggestions and initiatives, as opposed to merely carrying them out.

Value no. 4 (Broad curriculum; staff–parents partnership)

A wider curriculum has most definitely evolved which has been of great benefit to the children. The need for marketing has actually been a force towards this. Staff have been fundamental to initiating this range of activities, but parents have never actually been involved to the extent I would have liked them to be. They have been involved in large numbers but not as collaborators. The reason for this appears to be that the activities introduced have been teacher directed, being linked in most cases to certain constraints, e.g. health and safety. The real breakthrough has come in terms of extracurricular activities, e.g. football, where parents actually run the team. So, within limits this value has been fulfilled.

Value no. 5 (No compromise on the children's education)

I feel on reflection that 'growth' and 'survival' are completely different processes and should not necessarily be put together. However, the situation my school found itself in was unique and therefore 'growth' had to go hand in hand with 'survival' although I would not have liked this to be the starting point. I was in fact marketing 'growth' as a means of ensuring 'survival'. I pondered on whether children's education had, on occasions, been compromised for the sake of marketing mainly because of the extra things we did to gain recognition for our school.

The staff, however, saw things differently. In semi-structured interviews (Loftus, 1997, pp. 8–10) I asked 'Has the pupils' education been compromised', with my mind on their academic achievement. To my surprise a number of staff answered the question in terms of the children's whole development and well-being. For example:

It gives them the opportunity to show that they're proud of their school.

The pupils, you know, they've been doing all this wonderful work and they see it all presented nicely.

I think they love it. They all love having their photo in the paper and it makes them proud of their school. It shows they take a keen interest in their school. I think it's great!

Some saw it as offering an opportunity to break free from the confines of the National Curriculum: 'I think it's nice for the pupils to do things other than sit in the classroom and do things from just one angle or perspective.' A minority warned that there was a danger of giving the show priority over the learning: that the teachers had to avoid slipping into the view that the school needed the pupils to spend their time on work for display purposes alone.

A similar question could be asked about the educational value of getting the children to make posters advertising the school music festival or the carol concert. Even though the events themselves were judged to be beneficial to the children (see discussion of Value 4 above), the designing and making of the posters might have been tasks which did not really advance the children's learning.

However, the general consensus was that the projects we undertook outside the normal curriculum were in fact a reflection of Value 4, and not in conflict with it.

Value no. 6 (Not to criticise other schools)

I have used an industrial marketing concept USP ('unique selling position') as a means of living this value in my practice. Comments such as we have 'a leafy countrified environment', 'are well away from busy main roads', 'have little pollution', 'don't have concrete and tarmac as main school fabric' are comments which I have been using consistently in marketing the school. These 'selling' points have been strongly stated in our school video, school prospectus, in the 'strengths' section of the SWOT (strengths, weaknesses, opportunities, threats) proforma in our school development plans, in a full-page profile of our school in the local paper and by myself whenever I show prospective parents around our school.

I had always felt good about USP as I felt it had helped me become aware of the uniqueness of my school. It was not until the BERA conference 1997 when, as I was giving my paper, it was pointed out that by emphasising the unique advantages (e.g. 'lack of concrete and tarmac') I was drawing attention to the deficiencies of other schools. Can marketing ever really be non-competitive?

Value no. 7 (Claimed success must be genuine)

I feel that this value has been lived in my practice as the 'quality situation' has grown throughout my project. New initiatives brought in to analyse and meet children's needs have evolved and are now responsible for a higher standard of education. Our prospectus plus analysis of parent questionnaires relating to the work and initiatives operating in our school show that the education we say we offer is actually being delivered in our school.

Value no. 8 (Pupils not to be regarded as income)

This has been incredibly difficult for me to come to terms with because under the present system the money brought in is necessary for a school to survive. Not only that, but the quality of education can be enhanced. The more money you bring in the more resources you can buy, the more support staff you can employ and the smaller you can make your classes. All the above give children more learning opportunities. As a committed educationalist striving to give your pupils the best learning opportunities, it is very hard not to see money as an attractive option.

Because of the above, I feel there is a dichotomy of which I am as yet unsure. I feel very strongly that my priority should be to do the best by my pupils (i.e. the ones already enrolled), but this is compromised by the realisation that 'getting pupils in' is a prerequisite for it.

CONCLUSION

I strive to come to terms with my personal conflict and to live by what I believe to be just in a continuous cycle of relentless change. It has been a solitary struggle, especially since LMS puts heads into a position of competition and not co-operation. Other heads whom I meet, who might formerly have been supportive of a colleague in difficulties, are now preoccupied with worrying about what is happening in their own schools, and especially how to balance the budget. This atmosphere of suspicion and even hostility cannot bode well for the educational futures of our pupils. I continue to implement my values as a guiding light in providing quality education for our pupils and in bringing a school community together.

ACKNOWLEDGEMENTS

This chapter was written by JL, based on interim research reports prepared in the course of studies for a higher degree at Kingston University, and in consultation with NS who was his Director of Studies. We are grateful to the school staff and parents for their helpful participation.

REFERENCES

Barber, M. (1994) Power and control in education 1944–2044, *British Journal of Educational Studies*, Vol. 42, no. 4, pp. 348–62.

Bowe, R., Ball, S. and Gewirtz, S. (1994) Parental choice consumption and social theory: the operation of micro markets in education, *British Journal of Educational Studies*, Vol. 42, no. 1, pp. 38–52.

Bush, A. (1987) The management of contraction. In Bush, A. *et al.*, eds, *Approaches to School Management*, London, Harper & Row.

CSCS (1991) *Broadsheet 17: Schools in the Market Place*, Centre for the Study of Comprehensive Schools.

DFE (1994) *Education Means Business*, London, DFE.

Deem, R., Brehony, K. and Heath, S. (1994) Governors, schools and the miasma of the market, *British Educational Research Journal*, Vol. 20, no. 5, pp. 535–49.

Finch, R. (1990) Brochures and Brouhaha, *The Times Educational Supplement*, London.

Flew, A. (1991) Educational services, independent competition or maintained monopoly. In Grant, D., ed., *Empowering the Parents: How to Break the Monopoly*, London, London Institute of Economic Affairs.

Furse, J. (1989) Marketing in a primary school. In Fidler, B. and Bowles, G., eds, *Effective Local Management of Schools*, London, BEMAS.

Grace, G. (1993) On the study of school leadership beyond education management, *British Journal of Educational Studies*, Vol. 41, no. 4, pp. 353–65.

Harrison, M. and Gill, S. (1992) *Primary School Management*, Oxford, Heinemann Educational.

Holt, K. (1990) Monitoring and evaluation: some thoughts. In Gilbert, C., ed., *Local Management of Schools*, London, Kogan Page.

Jackson, T. (1994) Changing attitudes to marketing in British schools, *Education Today*, Vol. 44, no. 2.

Kent, G. (1989) *The Modern Primary School Headteacher*, London, Kogan Page.

Loftus, J. (1996). How can I elicit information from teaching and support staff so as to gain an insight into the culture which exists in a newly formed primary school? Paper presented at BERA conference.

Loftus, J. (1997) How can I elicit the views held by staff in the marketing of a newly formed primary school? Paper presented at BERA conference.

Lomax, P. (1989) *The Management of Change*, Clevedon, Multilingual Matters.

Lomax, P. (1991) Per review and action research. In Lomax, P. (ed.) *Managing Better Schools and Colleges: An Action Research Way*, Clevedon, Multilingual Matters.

Pardey, D. (1991) *Marketing for Schools*, London, Kogan Page.

Ranson, S. (1993) Markets or democracy for education, *British Journal of Educational Studies*, Vol. 41, no. 4, pp. 333–54.

Riddell, S., Brown, S. and Duffield, J. (1994) Parental power and special educational needs: the case of specific learning difficulties, *British Educational Research Journal*, Vol. 20, no. 3, pp. 327–44.

Stenner, A. (1990) Do be optimistic, London, *The Times Educational Supplement*, 23 March.

Sullivan, M. (1991) *Marketing your Primary School*, Longman.

Vincent, C., Evans, J., Lunt, I. and Young, P. (1994) The market forces? The effect of local management of schools on special educational needs provision, *British Educational Research Journal*, Vol. 20, no. 3, pp. 261–77.

Whitehead, J. (1985) An analysis of an individual's educational development. In Shipman, M., ed., *Educational Research: Principles, Policies and Practices*, Basingstoke, Falmer Press.

Whitehead, J. (1993) *The Grant of Educational Knowledge: Creating your own Living Educational Theories*, Bournemouth, Hyde Publications.

Whitehead, J. (1994) Action research as a form of life. *Action Researches*, Vol. I, Bournemouth, Hyde Publications.

Winter, R. (1989) *Learning from Experience*, London, Falmer Press.

6

Developing and Sustaining School Effectiveness

MO WILLIAMS

INTRODUCTION

This chapter explores my philosophy and vision and the educational developments and research that have had a major influence on my management style. Being a headteacher has been the most challenging and rewarding experience of my life – but at times has also been daunting, exhausting and frustrating. Many people in senior educational management positions have offered me advice but I have learnt that it can only be advice – the final decision in any situation is mine. As headteacher I am the end of the line! This has been the most daunting part of the job and I soon realised that no matter how clear I am about my vision it is vital that 1) it can also be understood and owned by all the stakeholders and 2) it is based on strong philosophical and practical educational foundations.

The aim of my chapter is to tell the story of one school's development in both implementing a vision and then sustaining this through teamwork. Our commitment is to TEAMS – Trust, Education, Achievement, Motivation, Security, which makes us a learning school where achievement is recognised, encouraged and celebrated.

MY PHILOSOPHY

As a headteacher, being in a leadership situation and having the opportunity to help every individual to achieve their full potential, is an exciting and stimulating goal. I believe my prime responsibility is to create a vision and ethos that will enable pupils, staff, parents and governors to work together, for the benefit of all, in an atmosphere of mutual trust and respect. It is my role to ensure that staff and pupils are motivated to take on challenges with confidence and be able to manage change, in an atmosphere that is caring, calm and secure. I endeavour to ensure the highest quality of teaching and learning to enable every child to achieve high standards academically, morally, socially, physically and spiritually. A framework for managing developments within the school to move it forward towards that vision is vital.

61

I have worked in four schools in particular where a team approach was at the centre of their philosophy. Team teaching, management teams, working parties, team initiatives and developments were in operation and working effectively.

A letter sent to staff and governors of schools states that successful management (and implicit in this – a successful school) depends on the whole staff working as a team with the governing body. The principles underpinning the taskforce approach are summarised below:

> . . . the prime purpose of management is to help the school promote and support better teaching and learning in the classroom, all staff will need help to improve their management skills . . .
>
> Given the right conditions, all professionals are capable of learning from their experience of the job. If the everyday experience of school management is challenging but supportive, frequently resulting in successful recognisable achievement, then the climate will be positive and much personal and team development will occur spontaneously, with training playing a supporting and enhancing role. If the regular experience includes high levels of uncertainty and work overload, leading to inconclusive achievements and a sense of personal inadequacy, there will be a negative climate and little or no development, with or without training.
>
> A management development policy must create conditions in which managers find it easier to succeed and harder to fail. We cannot be satisfied with the situation where only the very best can succeed, where the average are constantly unfulfilled and demotivated, and where anyone with a weakness goes to the wall taking other staff and students with them. It is a prime responsibility of the head inside the school and of the LEA's external support services to ensure that positive conditions are established.
>
> (*Management Development in the School*, 1992)

I believe firmly in these principles. As a headteacher I see each member of staff as 'a manager' – a manager of his or her classroom and a manager of his or her particular curriculum area. It is important, therefore, to 'create conditions in which managers find it easier to succeed and harder to fail'. It is important to ensure 'positive conditions are established'. My primary aim, when appointed, was to involve the collective effort of the whole staff working with the governing body to satisfy the principles laid down by the school management taskforce – for everyone to feel a valued and valuable member of 'The Team'.

When I became a headteacher encouraging 'teamwork', whilst empowering each individual, was a priority. Developing each teacher according to his or her individual needs (but with the concept of them contributing positively to the whole team) led to a staff who were ready and able to participate actively in whole-school planning for improvement.

The school had no detailed school development plan. My first task was to involve all the stakeholders in deciding 'Where are we now?' 'Where do we want to be?' 'How are we going to get there?' 'How will we evaluate if we are being successful?' with the emphasis on *we* and *success*.

School improvement is an approach to educational change that has the twin purpose of enhancing pupil achievement and strengthening the school's capacity to manage change. School improvement seeks to enhance pupil achievement by specific changes in teaching strategies, the curriculum and/or assessment procedures and by strengthening the school's internal conditions for supporting the work of teachers.

At the centre of my philosophy and vision is 'the child' and the importance of providing the best possible education for every child. As a headteacher I know that often what is best for the child results in an enormous amount of work for the teacher in planning, preparation, teaching, assessing, recording and reporting. Research has and is continuing to indicate that quality of learning and standards of achievement are dependent on quality teaching.

As educationalists we are answerable and accountable. Results of Standard Assessment Tests, local and national inspections, league tables are all open to public scrutiny. There is considerable debate about the pressure involved in this. However, I believe that the education of our children is of paramount importance and that the quality of education they receive in their 11/12 years of compulsory schooling should be the best possible. Enormous sums of public money are spent on education and, as educationalists, we must be accountable for this.

However, in order to be effective, we must be clear about what constitutes effectiveness and what factors or indicators characterise this. As schools, we are expected to set ourselves goals or targets, implement an action plan to achieve these targets and set clear criteria by which success can be judged.

EFFECTIVE SCHOOLS

A review of school effectiveness research by Sammons, P., Hillman, J. and Mortimore, P. (1995) summarises current knowledge about factors identified in this research as important in gaining a better understanding of effectiveness. It draws together all the threads of the other research I have explored. The aim of this study was to provide 'an analysis of the key determinants of school effectiveness in secondary and primary schools'. The primary focus of the research was on school effectiveness, but the research also examined the related field of teacher effectiveness. (Sammons *et al.*, 1995). The key results of this research are summerised below:

11 Factors for effective schools

1. Professional leadership: Firm and purposeful; a participative approach; the leading professional
2. Shared vision and goals: Unity of purpose; consistency of practice; collegiality and collaboration
3. A learning environment: An orderly atmosphere; an attractive working environment
4. Concentration on teaching and learning: Maximisation of learning time; academic emphasis; focus on achievement

5. Purposeful teaching: Effective organisation; clarity of purpose; structured lessons; adaptive practice
6. High expectations: High expectations all round; communicating expectations; providing intellectual challenge
7. Positive reinforcement: Clear and fair discipline; feedback
8. Monitoring progress: Monitoring pupil performance; evaluating school performance
9. Pupils' rights and responsibilities: Raising pupil esteem; positions of responsibility; control of work
10. Home–school partnership: Parental involvement in their children's learning
11. A learning organisation: School based staff development

(Ibid.)

This research uses the work of Mortimore (1991) in defining an effective school as one in which students progress further than might be expected from consideration of its intake. An effective school thus adds 'extra value' to its students in comparison to other schools serving similar intakes. The central focus of school effectiveness research concerns the idea that 'schools matter, that schools do have major effects upon children's developments and that . . . school's make a difference' (Reynolds and Creemers, 1990, p.1).

Although they accept that there is no recipe for success or 'quick fixes' because every school is unique, they use the work of Firestone (1991, p. 9) to observe:

> There is a core of consistency to be found across a variety of studies conducted here and abroad with a wide range of different methodological strengths and weaknesses. Moreover, there is considerable support for the key findings in related research on organisational behaviour in a variety of work settings and countries.

This research lists key characteristics of effective schools. It is important to note that these factors should not be regarded as independent of each other. However, the 11 factors for effective schools highlighted in the research of Sammons *et al.* (1995) pull together the strands of other research. The list is not intended to be exhaustive or a 'magic formula' but it provides a summary of relevant research. The authors 'hope it will provide a useful background for those concerned with promoting school effectiveness and improvement, and the processes of school self-evaluation and review' (*ibid.*, p. 8).

Each of the factors of school effectiveness is important and many are interconnected and interdependent. I have used these key characteristics of effective schools to analyse Lee-on-the-Solent Junior School in terms of school effectiveness. My aim is to show how, from my starting point as headteacher, I have endeavoured, through a continuous and systematic school development process, to implement and sustain my vision to make this an effective school.

Professional leadership

Research has shown that the key role of leadership is in initiating and maintaining the school improvement process, in the headteacher as the leading professional and in the headteacher sharing leadership responsibilities, i.e. a participative approach. Even in my first staff meeting I attempted to begin to address these issues: 'Headship is a job which requires vision, it requires strong professionals who have consistent value systems that are relevant to the school, its pupils and its community. You cannot afford to find yourself in your new staff room on day one without a strong sense of the "vision-value" thing!' (Whittle, 1996, p. 23).

I asked the staff in this first staff meeting to decide on the important issues that needed to be addressed: 1) in the first term; and 2) during the first year.

I gave out two questionnaires and gave them time to fill these in. I also shared my letter of application with them. I felt that it was important that the teachers should share the details of my vision, my experience, my view of primary school education and my priorities for development at Lee-on-the-Solent Junior School. In my letter of application I stressed my commitment to teamwork and to staff development. I agree with Murphy's (1989) views that the headteacher's impact on pupil achievement levels is likely to operate indirectly rather than directly by influencing staff and school culture, behaviour and attitude which in turn affects the quality of teaching and learning in the classroom.

By the end of the first term all staff, governors, pupils and parents had been consulted as part of a whole-school audit to prioritise developments in order to improve our school. Everyone's views had been read, discussed, considered and valued. A plan was taking shape that would enable us to become a successful, effective school. However, it was very much my role, i.e. the headteacher's role to be the 'leading professional', the central person who communicated with all the stakeholders, who encouraged a participative approach, but who was firm and purposeful.

By the end of my first year as headteacher all the staff were committed to teamwork, and each year group were team-teaching.

Shared vision and goals

The research on school effectiveness has shown that schools that are more effective are those where practice is a result of a consistent and collaborative way of working and decision-making. Consensus on values of the school is associated with improved educational outcomes.

At the first INSET day all the teaching and support staff were involved. We all participated in a visioning activity where everyone drew his or her vision of the school he or she wanted. We then discussed each other's in groups and common key words emerged from each group. Rigorous discussion on the meaning of words focused everyone's attention on a common vision. Everyone's views were represented, seriously considered and valued. Everyone felt a real sense of achievement with the final result and everyone is able to relate positively to it:

Lee-on-the-Solent Junior School = *Our Vision*
Trust
Education
Achievement
Motivation
Security

We all felt the 'softer' words of trust and security were the protective ones on the outside. We moved towards our central work 'Achievement' through education and motivation with 'TEAMS' being the key word – teams involving teachers, support staff, pupils, governors, parents and the wider community. At the centre is 'Achievement' for all, and a pride in our common goal.

When activities or developments are initiated and implemented it is important to build review into the process – monitoring, evaluating, reviewing and amending need to become part of the culture of continuous improvement and increased effectiveness.

A learning environment

I was very fortunate to inherit a deputy head who very closely shared my vision and educational philosophy. She made it clear to me that she would like to set up a pilot team-teaching year group in Year 3 with her colleague. This pilot worked so effectively that other teachers were keen to work in a team-teaching situation. This was discussed in detail, but needed to be built into the school development plan in order to manage the building and financial implications, and for discussion to take place in order for staff to decide on the optimum teams. Time in particular was an important factor in order for a whole-school approach to be developed.

The governors were very supportive of planned developments in the building. Huge, impractical storage cupboards were removed from upper school classrooms, plasterboard walls removed and sound-proofed, carpeted conference screens installed between each pair of classrooms. Doors were removed and high-quality printed curtains hung in their place. The shared practical area was cleared of 'junk' and furnished with tables, chairs and resources to teach science, art, craft, design technology and IT. The staff and children were really appreciative of the change and the whole atmosphere and ethos of the upper school have improved.

Whilst this has happened internally we have developed the grounds externally. This is built into the development plan. We have planted a copse of 1,000 trees in conjunction with our infant school and have developed the playground at the front of the school as a quiet sitting area with trees, shrubs and planters for both parents' and children's use. Our school environment is not only a learning environment but an inviting and welcoming environment too. Morale has been raised considerably. Staff, children, parents and governors are very positive about the building developments. Visitors to our school always comment on how warm, bright and welcoming it is. Through careful, planned developments we have been able to manage this process in order to create a 'learning' environment in which quality teaching and learning can take place.

Concentration on teaching and learning

Quality of teaching and learning has been the focus of our school development plan since I became headteacher and will continue to have a high profile. Our learning policy is central to teaching and learning across the school. Teachers use this when they are planning, and it is central to the formulation of curriculum policies. Having agreed our learning policy, with all staff and governors involved, it became a focus of our planning. However, as a school, we believe that monitoring is important in order to evaluate success and review developments to assess their effectiveness. Feedback to staff individually and collectively has been an important feature of building the team. Trust, honesty, mutual respect and valuing have become part of the culture of our school. Staff are now much more prepared to say to each other 'I can do . . . well but I need help and support with . . .' We have reviewed our organisation, evaluated our strengths and weaknesses and subject managers have been empowered to manage their subjects.

Through careful planning of time, budget and curriculum, each subject manager has had time to become clear about the National Curriculum requirements in his or her subject and to work on policies, scheme of work and guidelines to ensure quality teaching in his or her subject. Each subject manager and subject has equal value, although extra resources are allocated to the subject managers of core subjects. Each subject manager has also been allowed funds which he or she manages to 1) develop resources in his or her subject and 2) to 'buy in' subject expertise from LEA inspectors. Adaptability, co-operation, collaboration are words that sum up the teamwork concept at our school. However, careful planning with the involvement of all stakeholders is crucial in a participative approach.

We have certainly taken the words of Alexander *et al.* (1992, p. 54) to the heart of our school when they say 'Schools will need to ensure that they have a range of specialist expertise to sustain the national curriculum and to deploy such expertise in more flexible ways than hitherto, considering a variety of teaching roles from generalist to specialist'.

Purposeful teaching and high expectations

(I would like to add high but appropriate expectations.) A major focus for our development planning is 'what is quality teaching and how do we ensure this?' The overview of the development plan focuses on planning for long, medium and short term, on assessment to inform planning and on the use of subject manager's strengths to develop quality teaching using the criteria in the OFSTED *Handbook* (1995). These criteria for quality teaching also reflect the criteria for effective schools.

At the heart of quality teaching is quality planning. The role of the deputy head over the past two years has been curriculum planning and organisation.

Our school planning policy has been developed in practice, drafted, discussed, reviewed and finalised. Each level of planning has a different emphasis. The long term has a clear 'learning aim', the medium term a 'learning focus' and the short term 'learning objectives'. Our planning is linked to clear organisation and clarity of purpose, it ensures breadth and balance, continuity and progression.

Team teaching allows for adaptive practice. Teachers are clear about 1) what they want the children to learn and 2) what is the best teaching method to promote this learning in order to ensure high standards of achievement. They work as whole-year groups or classes, in groups, in pairs and, when appropriate, individually. Sometimes children need to collaborate in groups and at other times need to work in silence on an individual task.

We are adaptable, non-dogmatic and prepared to use the teaching method that best facilitates quality learning – the outcomes being measured in standards of achievement. We aim to make all our lessons intellectually challenging. Our vision is concerned with education and motivation in order to raise achievement.

The various research findings on effective schools use factors like 'positive climate, discipline, pupil care and welfare, clear and fair discipline, positive reinforcement, rewards and disciplinary rules rather than punishment and criticism'. The key elements are clear and fair discipline and feedback.

During the first staff meetings when I became headteacher the whole staff unanimously requested that we address the issue of discipline. They felt it was a priority and was a key factor in implementing a plan of effective school improvement. The implementation of the policy was carefully planned. It took a whole term to draft the policy and a term to share the draft with pupils, support staff, governors and parents. The policy was finally agreed, and an annual review cycle built in. It has taken careful planning, implementing, monitoring and reviewing of the policy in order to ensure it is effective.

The children were very much involved in the process. Each year group decided six 'golden' rules that were needed to ensure our school was a safe and happy environment for everyone. We recognise that it is also necessary to have a system of fair and clear sanctions, and for this we base our approach on assertive discipline. Both rewards and sanctions are clearly understood by all staff and pupils. The reasons for the introduction of this policy are as follows:

- It gives children a feeling of stability within the school through a fair and consistent application of the rules.
- It emphasises learning and teaching as the prime purpose of our school.
- It gives more opportunities for rewarding positive behaviour and attitudes.
- It allows greater involvement of parents and encourages home/school partnership in both rewards and sanctions.

This area is very much linked to the section on positive reinforcement. Reid *et al.* (1988) use pupil care and welfare as important in an effective school. It is concerned with encouraging pupils to take responsibility for their actions. Where pupils are given responsibility and a voice within the school structure and organisation the pupils respond in a mature way. At our school everyone is valued and given a voice.

Our strengths statement, at the front of our school development plan, says 'All the staff and pupils are valued and involved in decision making. Their development is a high priority.' We aim to help our pupils 'have high self esteem, feel valued, confident and have a positive and enthusiastic attitude to life'. In our learning policy we say 'the environment and organisation encourages independent learning; they [pupils] are helped to develop self discipline and co-operative skills; there is a positive approach with praise and encouragement'. We value 'positive, supportive, caring relationships where every member of our school community is respected and appreciated'.

Children are consulted during the school development plan audit and review. They are encouraged to fund raise and choose areas where they wish to spend money raised. We encourage them to take a pride in *their* school.

Children in Year 6 are pupil librarians and are co-ordinated by our school librarian. They were involved in agreeing their own job descriptions. Representatives of the pupils are part of the School Grounds Development Steering committee and help plan and prioritise developments as well as supporting fund raising.

Pupils are consulted in deciding our 'Golden Rules' and in agreeing both rewards and sanctions in our policy for managing pupil behaviour. Children are the heart of our school.

There are many opportunities for the children to be given responsibility. They contribute ideas that are built in to the development plan and contribute to our school prospectus. I feel that our whole-school approach is summed up by one of the Year 6 pupils whose contribution to our *School Prospectus* says 'Lee Junior School is a school where they ask the pupils what they want before they make any big decisions. There is not much that I don't like at this school'. There is much evidence across our whole school that pupils are positive, motivated and enthusiastic about their learning and teachers are positive, motivated and enthusiastic about their teaching.

HOME–SCHOOL PARTNERSHIP

Harris and Russ (1994) write that treating education as a partnership between home and school proved to be an important element in raising pupil achievement. In schools where raised pupil achievement was evident every opportunity was taken to involve parents in the life of the school.

We encourage parents into our school in a variety of both formal and informal ways. As part of our policy for assessing, recording and reporting achievement we ensure that parents have the opportunity to visit the school each term to discuss their child's work. At the end of September parents are invited in for an informal group meeting to 'meet the teacher'. Each team of teachers working with a particular year group talks to parents over a cup of coffee about plans for the year – how they will teach, how the children will be grouped and what they will teach in order to ensure high-quality achievements. The ground rules for the year are set at these meetings.

In November each parent is offered an individual parent/teacher consultation. In March written annual reports are sent to parents giving clear indications of areas where their child is succeeding and areas of focus for improvement. Teacher, child and parents add comments to these reports – the positive triangle:

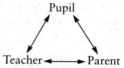

In May/June parents are invited into school again to discuss progress since the written report, i.e. if targets are being met. We have found that the format of consultations has led to considerable progress in home/school relations and in pupil progress.

We encourage parents (and grandparents) to help in the classroom, and to help with visits. I send out a monthly newsletter informing parents about our achievements and developments. They are consulted as part of the development plan audit and review and I keep them updated and informed about planned developments for each term.

We have an active Parent Teacher Association, which we share with the infant school, called Lee Schools' Association. This does much to promote and develop positive home/school relationships and strong community links as well as fund raise. They are an invaluable support to the school, motivated and enthusiastic and always willing to help.

A LEARNING ORGANISATION

This final section, I feel, is one of the most important in ensuring an effective school. Every piece of research on school effectiveness refers to 'the learning school' or 'learning for all' – it comes within ethos and within a work-centred environment. OFSTED (1995) highlights in-service training and use of GEST in developing subject managers' expertise in sharing pedagogic expertise. The whole culture and ethos of an effective school need to view learning as an ongoing process. Our teamwork statement shows how all staff value each other and work together to strive for excellence.

Our staff development policy rationale illustrates this commitment to quality: 'We believe that development/training opportunities should be available to all staff so that they are clearer about expectations of them, feel valued as individuals, are better motivated and are more effective.'

The aim of the policy is to recognise and support the professional needs of individual staff at different stages of their career. It also considers the needs of the school and the related training that both individuals and teams of teachers require in order to carry out their responsibilities effectively. Staff development aims to produce more effective teachers which, in turn, will produce better learning for our pupils.

Development/training opportunities should be available to all staff at Lee-on-the-Solent Junior School. All staff have an entitlement to these development opportunities, within budgetary constraints. Initially our development plan focused on empowering and enabling subject managers to gain expertise in their specialist subject. Then time and resources were allocated to give staff the opportunities to share that expertise, to plan, implement, monitor and review developments in their curriculum area. However to ensure this is effective the planning must be systematic, detailed, cost-effective – value for money is an important consideration.

A FINAL THOUGHT

Since I became headteacher, the school has undergone a number of monitoring visits/inspections by the LEA and OFSTED. The resulting reports have given us objective judgements as to where we are on our pathway to being an effective school. The school's OFSTED Report in April 1997 stated that

> The school's leadership and management are of excellent quality. The team spirit in this school is of an exceptionally high order. The effectiveness of the headteacher and of other teachers with management responsibilities is outstanding. The support and monitoring of teaching and curriculum development are very good. The high quality school development plan was produced following a process which involved contributions from all of those with an interest in the school, including the pupils.

The importance of this report was that it acknowledged not only the effectiveness of the headteacher but also the effectiveness of other teachers with management responsibilities as outstanding. All teachers have job descriptions which focus on their role and responsibilities as both a classroom manager and subject manager. OFSTED recognised and highlighted that a strength of the school was the fact that the whole team managed effectively and that the 'high quality school development plan' was instrumental in managing and achieving school improvement. Our aim is to continue to work together to manage the constant external pressure for change, to hold firmly on to our vision and through it to sustain and further improve our good practice.

OFSTED (1997) reported we were 'a good school, with a number of very good features, some of which are outstanding'. We are proud of this but know that through continued work as 'TEAMS' we can sustain our development and further improve achievements for all. We are a learning school where achievement is recognised, encouraged and celebrated.

REFERENCES

Alexander, R., Rose, J. and Woodhead, C. (1992) *Curriculum Organisation and Classroom Practice in Primary Schools*, DES.

Firestone, W.A. (1991) *Rethinking Effective Schools: Research and Practice*, Englewood Cliffs, NJ, Prentice-Hall.

Management Development in the School, taken from *Programme Linking Learning to Action for Continuous Improvement – Module 3*, the Senior Team. Open College Publications (1992).

Murphy (1989) – Principal Instructional Leadership, in P. Thuston, and L. Lotto, (eds.) *Advances in Educational Leadership*, Greenwich: JAI Press.

OFSTED (1995) *Teaching Quality – The Primary Debate*, London, OFSTED.

Reid, K., Hopkins, D. and Holly, P. (1988) *Towards the Effective School*, Oxford, Blackwell.

Russ, J. and Harris, A. (1994) *Pathways to School Improvement*.

Sammons *et al.* The nature and findings of school effectiveness research in the primary school, in S. Riddell, and S. Brown, (eds.) *School Effectiveness Research: Its Message for School Improvement*, London: HMSO.

Sammons, P., Hillman, J. and Mortimore, P. (1995) *Key Characteristics of Effective Schools: A Review of School Effectiveness Research*, London, OFSTED/Institute of Education, University of London.

Sharron, H. (1996) Vision: the deputies' Achilles Heel, *Managing Schools Today*, Vol. 5, no. 9.

Whittle, J. (1996) Vision, the deputies' Achilles Heel, *Managing Schools Today*, Vol. 5, no. 9, p. 34, Birmingham, Questions Publishing.

Woodhead, C. (1995) *Teaching Quality: The Primary Debate*, report on OFSTED conference.

Secondary

7

Double Vision: 40 Years On

BERNARD BARKER

My 40-year campaign for comprehensive education has never resolved the double vision with which it began. My London comprehensive in the 1950s was: '. . . a shining glass palace filled with excitement . . . school offered the means through which an effective mass democracy, free of ignorance and subservience, might emerge' (Barker, 1986a, p. xiv). But it was also the place where I endured dreary, socially segregated lessons designed to thwart the democratic, egalitarian aspirations of parents, like mine, who chose all-ability schools for their children. Inspired by the potential, troubled by the reality, I decided to become a teacher, eager to help invent a democratic, community education for all our people.

SCHOOL DAYS

In her *Risinghill: Death of a Comprehensive School*, Leila Berg (1968, p. 17) reports an interview with a pupil who reflects on her time at primary school:

> Once we had the headmaster for writing, you know. And we had to start italic. And you must have an italic nib. If you didn't you'd get told off. I had my own pen – it was an Osmiroid, you know. It had an italic nib. And it didn't seem anything wrong with it. And then the headmaster he come up behind me, and he says 'Your writing's slanting.' You know, I didn't say anything, I just kept on writing. He says 'You'll have to do that again.' And he kept shouting at me and that, you know. I was nearly crying, you know . . . the way he shouts at you and that.

The story captures the bullying ignorance which shapes so much that happens at school. Teachers like this are concerned with submission and obedience, not education. 'Do this because I say so . . .' has always seemed to me an anti-learning strategy, an abuse of authority which induces teachers to expend more

73

time on children's manners and appearance than their understanding of the world. Primary school taught me the unintended lesson that didactic methods disregard the learner's need to connect ideas with experience and to reconstruct unfamiliar thought in home-made language and symbols.

During my schooldays at Eltham Green, a purpose-built, south London comprehensive, opened in 1956, four years before Risinghill, I learned to ask questions about my double vision. Why were the children organised into 'A', 'B' and 'C' bands which so neatly mirrored the divided society around us? Why were we so regimented and drilled? Why was everything we learned so abstract, foreign and hard to understand? When would quadratic equations and the fourth declension prove useful? Why were top sets excluded from art and craft? If Latin was so valuable, why was it offered to so few? Why so many exams, year in, year out? Comprehensives promised opportunity for everyone but success seemed to me rationed and remote, sometimes available for A1 and A2 but never for those in the dozen forms below.

TEACHING CONTROVERSY

When I began teaching, I argued that we should educate communities for their enrichment and improvement, not a small number of 'A' band children for their success and departure. The prevalent, self-help gospel of individual achievement seemed to me a blind alley. The academically adept forge ahead but most young people are taught to see themselves as failures. Half-way up the ladder myself, I could see that 'Education based on merit and differences encourages pupils to view life as a game of careers, an escalator from the classroom to the professions and beyond. Learning and knowledge come to have value only as an applied art of self-advancement' (Barker, 1986a, p. 4). Instead, I believed learning should be defined as 'the fruit of relations between children and their experiences, not as the application of the intrinsic ability of individuals to abstract problems. All children not severely handicapped have sufficient ability to justify schools basing their work on the prospect of co-operative citizenship for everyone' (ibid., p. 9). Education, I believe, should aim to improve our social and political life, not to provide prizes and escape routes for disadvantaged talent.

Early in my career, I discovered that many schools and teachers choose methods which reinforce the authority of established élites and discourage dissent and change. Later, as the National Curriculum loomed, I argued that we should cultivate rather than suppress the critical, reflective instinct:

> Teaching is, quite properly, a controversial, experimental activity, to do with examining values and beliefs rather than with preaching or propaganda. Its aim is to encourage pupils to develop self-awareness and form their own judgements. This ambition cannot be fulfilled if debate is circumscribed by the sensibilities of politicians and whole areas of study are hidden from view.
>
> (Barker, 1987, p. 109)

I believed (and still believe) that teachers should select activities to provoke disagreement. We should seek the maximum possible scope for experiment and exploration. Authoritarian management styles, with their ritualised displays of power and control, should be swept aside. New leaders should be appointed to design an open-minded, collaborative culture where children ask pointed questions and are expected to speak as much as their adult guides. Schools should be reinvented so that teachers imagine their lessons from a student's point of view. Impressed by Aneurin Bevan's remark (cited in Foot, 1962, p. 140), 'These boys and girls are to be asked to wield the royal sceptre; we must therefore give them the souls of kings and queens', I aimed to open children's minds, not to school young people in the disciplines of office and factory.

My developing vision came under pressure almost at once. Prompted by Bernard Donoghue, head of his policy unit, Prime Minister Callaghan (his daughters attended a private school in Blackheath) criticised the education system in the context of the global economy. 'I am concerned,' he said, 'to find complaints from industry that new recruits from the schools sometimes do not have the basic tools to do the job' (Callaghan, J. 1976, pp 332-3). Callaghan began a long process in which educational goals were increasingly defined in terms of skills and training for the workplace. 'There is no virtue,' claimed the Prime Minister, 'in producing socially well adjusted members of society who are unemployed because they do not have the skills' (ibid.). He proposed a 'basic' school curriculum which would fit young people for 'a job of work'. The 'Great Debate' which followed (eight regional invitation conferences were held in January and February 1977) included attempts to explain Britain's economic plight in terms of perceived inefficiencies in the school system. Shirley Williams' subsequent green paper (DES, 1977) included proposals strongly influenced by businessmen's complaints about spelling, handwriting and arithmetic. Royal sceptres were off the agenda.

RESCUING THE COMPREHENSIVE EXPERIENCE

Undaunted, I became head of a large, coeducational, 11–18 comprehensive, Stanground School (renamed Stanground College in 1989, in preparation for designation as a Cambridgeshire community establishment, responsible for adult and youth education across south east Peterborough) in Peterborough, in September 1980. I was young (aged 34), the new Prime Minister, Mrs Thatcher, seemed to have nothing to say about education and I believed I could change the world. My innocence and enthusiasm overcame obstacles that should have worried me. At my first staff meeting, without giving the governing body a moment's thought, I announced the end of the upper and lower bands, which had been school policy for the previous 16 years. My new colleagues applauded and the timetable was changed before anyone else noticed. Seething with disaffected students, Stanground had come to depend on corporal punishment. Senior staff caned or slippered boys and girls alike. I took over, not entirely convincing my deputy, who demonstrated how to make the blows more painful. I prowled the grounds with a stick, persuading the surliest elements not to patronise the five vans which pulled up at noon to serve chips and ice-cream. Deprived of custom, the mobile vendors drove off and I became a legend in my own lunch-time. Nobody was ever beaten again.

I encouraged staff debate, introducing an open meeting at which anyone could table a complaint or suggestion. Working groups bustled to design a new curriculum and to improve the school's administration. I was surprised when backbench critics began to find fault with me and was less than reassured when a sympathetic deputy remarked that the school was like 'Spain after Franco!' My desire to reduce Stanground's reliance on authority and tradition was qualified by my need to build support and consensus. I wanted to scrap the house system but postponed action when I sensed resistance. When the academic honours boards came down there was a public outcry, complete with an outraged editorial in the Peterborough *Evening Telegraph*. I compromised. The boards were restored but no new names were added. An honours book was introduced instead, to celebrate more students and many other types of achievement.

My democratic, child-centred instincts were not well attuned to this conservative landscape. Long-serving teachers bellowed down corridors and lamented the new informality. They sent me pupils caught smoking to test whether I would uphold law and order. Provided none of their traditional assumptions were challenged, these colleagues wanted to be told what to do. Junior staff had grown used to opposition and were reluctant to trust the new freedom. Parents responded best to simple, coded messages, mainly about discipline and standards. Determined to change the culture, I worried about the apparent paradox that a liberal, child-orientated approach could be achieved only by astute political management. To promote divergence and imaginative teaching, I should have to manipulate appointments, resources, the curriculum and the agenda of every meeting. Equal value and equal opportunities would have to be engineered because they were unlikely to develop spontaneously.

AUTHORITY AND MANAGEMENT

I began to fear that my vision would be compromised by the exercise of power necessary for its achievement. Stephen Ball (1990, p. 165) has deepened the discomfort of heads who hope to use authority to secure equality and freedom for others: 'The school as an institution is rendered as a system of shared meanings and common goals and values. But theories of management reflect the particular interests and needs of administrators . . . management empowers the manager and objectifies and subjects the managed.' I share Ball's (1987, p. 278) doubt that freedom and authority can be reconciled: '. . . the control of school organisations, focused in particular on the position and role of the head teacher, is significantly concerned with domination (the elimination or pre-emption of conflict)'.

Despite my anxiety, Stanground became a better, happier place. Modern, professional leadership was injected at deputy head and head of department level. Fewer teachers shouted at children. Our days were better organised, public events were more impressive and we were first choice for the local primaries. Mixed ability worked its way through; everyone studied an entitlement curriculum; expectations rose; examination results improved; the sixth form increased from 45 in 1980 to 240 in 1997. The premises were enhanced by a series of major and minor projects. Despite straitened times, millions were spent. In awe of our vision, we forget how much depends on sustained hard work, careful organisation and boring attention to detail.

REACTION AND REFORM

Before the 1987 general election, schools were more or less free to select their own solutions and remedies. Inertia and culture were more serious obstacles to reform than outside influence. Although monetarism produced budget cuts, youth unemployment and pay restraint, Sir Keith Joseph, as Secretary of State for Education, did not depart from a traditional view of his department's role. After the election, Kenneth Baker's Education Reform Act 1988 changed the distribution of power and reduced the scope for independent vision. Nothing would be the same again.

The teacher unions, through their increasingly militant pay campaign in 1985 and 1986, had created Baker's political opportunity and at least part of his justification. No government could tolerate a union veto on what happened at school. Stanground had lapsed into a state of suspended animation, unable to move forward or back. As the unions experimented with ingenious forms of disruption, heads learned the limits of their power. I wrote these words at the time:

> Alone each day for lunch, I have time enough for despair. No meetings, no teams, no music, no chatter, no buzz of life in an empty school. Apart from the children, who seem less affected than you'd expect, Stanground is slipping into chronic depression. Teachers hold their thin red line but there is no answering fire or flag of surrender in the trench beyond. My youth, self-confidence and energy fade as I realise that events have passed beyond my control or influence. My words and dreams are as wasted as driftwood on an ocean. Meanwhile, my colleagues manoeuvre for position as if nothing has changed.

When he replaced Sir Keith in May 1986, Kenneth Baker moved swiftly to impose a settlement. He raised salaries, scrapped national pay bargaining and drafted a new, 1,265-hour teacher contract, designed to frustrate future attempts at disruption. But then he began work on the Education Bill 1987, using the election victory to introduce a complex apparatus of state regulation.

Brian Simon (1988, p. 43) was among the first to recognise the implications:

> What is new are the modes of control that have rapidly been developed over the last three or four years, now culminating in the 147 clauses of the Education Bill. Significantly, the state, instead of working through and with other social organisations (specifically local authorities and teachers' organisations) is now very clearly seeking a more direct and unitary system of control than has ever been thought politic – or even politically possible – in the past.

Simon believed that the government's intention was to create new types of school (LMS, GMS, city technology colleges) subject to market forces; to downgrade and destabilise local authorities and teachers' organisations; and to achieve 'totally centralised control' (*ibid*., p. 44). Individual schools and students were increasingly obliged to compete for resources, status and survival. Test results, league tables, open enrolment and delegated budgets encouraged a business-like approach to school management which was more or less incompatible with my comprehensive vision.

JIGSAW PIECES

The practical impact on schools was startling. My reaction at the time was close to panic:

> The large number of Department of Education and Science initiatives threatens to overwhelm teachers with incomprehensible circulars. Staff search through the orders, regulations, and non-statutory guidelines for jigsaw pieces, only to discover that they have opened an incomplete box . . . Teachers must learn to manage governors, budgets, and maintenance at the same time as transforming their lessons, record-keeping procedures, and assessment arrangements. This war on a dozen fronts (even the Germans limited themselves to two) is corroding the fabric of our schools even as bemused teachers struggle to salvage something from their own frustration.
>
> (Barker, 1989, p. 18)

Children's learning somehow disappeared as officials tabulated 52 statements of attainment in English, 75 in mathematics and 87 in science. Teachers gave up poetry to assess whether pupils were able to 'use pictures, symbols or isolated letters . . . to communicate meaning'. Creativity, independence, understanding, enjoyment, socialisation and motivation were untouched by the civil service leviathan set in motion by the government. Imposed change distressed teachers but also stimulated them in the wrong direction. The government was not interested in equality, community or child-centred learning. The Conservatives wanted efficiency, productivity and output. Self-help individualism was back, big time.

My reaction was to accept defeat. The Conservatives were entrenched in power; the industrial action was over; the unions were beaten. You could cling to old loyalties but there was no king over the water to rescue us. No opposition of ours could alter the course of events. So I decided to lead Stanground into the first wave of Cambridgeshire's Technical and Vocational

Education Initiative (TVEI) and hurried to implement the National Curriculum. I argued with reluctant colleagues that these innovations were ideological shells that could be colonised and converted to child-friendly purposes. We could still put children first and we could use our new, delegated LMS budget to ensure a better balance between teachers, resources and learning support. With Peterborough's growing population, we felt we had little to fear from market forces.

As the government bungled its way through the National Curriculum, this optimism seemed increasingly well justified. Mr Baker, Mrs Thatcher and Mr Graham (Duncan Graham, formerly Chief Education Officer in Suffolk, became the first director of the National Curriculum Council) argued about everything from testing (simple or elaborate?) to history (facts or understanding?) and technology (craft skills or design?). During the next few years (1988–93) teachers were demoralised by constant change as ministers and their advisers improvised solutions to difficulties caused by their own elaborate edifice of state control. Discredited and excluded from debate, teachers at Stanground felt deskilled as they awaited the latest government circular or working party report. A dependency culture developed. 'OK, you're in charge. Tell us what to do.' But the National Curriculum did not answer the questions with which schools had struggled since the invention of the comprehensive school. Should everyone study the same subjects and take the same examinations? Should subjects be academic or practical? How do you find time for history and geography and modern languages? How do you motivate the less able and the less successful?

MANAGING CHANGE

Ten years into my headship, I was seconded to Cambridgeshire LEA as a general inspector, briefed to keep an eye on a 'patch' of schools and to evaluate and develop management strategies. I badly needed the break from direct, daily responsibility for large numbers of teachers and children. Locked into the micropolitics of Stanground, I felt as if I were dragging a heavy cart up a wooded hill where conifers mask the road ahead. During the course of the year, I worked with teachers in over 30 schools, all of them coeducational comprehensives covering the 11–16 or 11–18 age ranges. The experience showed me how schools were adapting themselves to new, complex requirements. I began to develop a revised vision of management that would support and sustain children's learning in the changed circumstances of the 1990s.

I concluded that multiple change required more careful strategic planning than had been usual before the Education Act 1988. I proposed a 'collegial management style' that would cultivate 'ideas and proposals from a variety of sources, seeking to form them into a logical, integrated sequence before they are scheduled for action'. I detected a gap between senior and middle managers. Critical path analysis was required so everyone could operate within an agreed plan. Development should be mapped in detail and in advance. I argued that schools should be more systematic in

Defining their essential educational purpose
Defining the teams needed to achieve the purpose
Defining the interrelationship between teams
Developing an understanding of the complex tasks to be performed by team leaders
Developing detailed action plans and progress checks to ensure objectives are achieved
Training and developing teachers as team leaders.

Loosely coupled, delegated systems, with their reliance on infrequent, over-large consultative meetings, had failed to cope with the new, intense agenda in education.

REINVENTING STANGROUND

I returned to Stanground in September 1991, eager to apply my improved understanding. I found the staff discontented and unhappy, as the school struggled to come to terms with the volume and pace of unwelcome change. Senior managers had fallen out and I found myself caught up in exactly the unhappy tensions I had observed in near insoluble form in other schools. Determined to try a new approach, I set up a review working group, comprising governors, teachers, an inspector and an LEA officer. We shared the work of interviews, questionnaires and developing new structures. This was my last chance to reinvent Stanground.

We established six year-support teams, each with its own tutorial base in the school, each co-led by a head of year and a head of department. The two co-leaders of each team reported to a member of the senior management team. We aimed to close the academic–pastoral divide and to forge a new closeness between senior and middle managers. We created a college development group (CDG) which brought team leaders together to shape and implement policy. Executive sub-committees of the CDG were responsible for major initiatives. A carefully planned schedule of interconnected meetings was timetabled for the year ahead.

We also began to evaluate teaching, applying techniques I had learned with the Cambridgeshire inspectorate. Senior managers observed lessons and afterwards coached team leaders and their colleagues towards improvement. Paired projects were set up to encourage greater variety in lessons.

TURN OF THE SCREW

My concentration was soon diverted from our big project. Anxious not to be left behind by other schools (by 1993, 16 Cambridgeshire secondary schools and colleges were grant maintained. The rush for the exit was stimulated by the unexpected 1992 Conservative election victory and the prospect of serious LEA budget reductions, unwisely overadvertised by John Ferguson, then director of education), the governors voted unanimously for grant-maintained status. I have never wavered from my inconvenient opinion that GMS damages the cause of democratic education:

> Schools are run as isolated units by managers who are encouraged to concentrate on financial management and resource acquisition. Headteachers are expected to preoccupy themselves with parent-winning public relations, bids for specialist school status or schemes to secure lottery funding for pet projects. LMS and GMS establishments relate to the people as individual customers, not as citizens with an interest in the purpose of education for all.
>
> (Barker, 1997, p. 31)

At Stanground, GMS became another turn of the screw, pushing us towards an alien, finance-focused, market-driven, consumerist version of education. Between 1992 and 1996, my job was to recreate the school as an independent business. We had to reconstruct every aspect of our administration, from health and safety to financial regulations and procedures. I took pleasure in power, control and money but struggled to reconcile privileged status and funding with my past rhetoric. I became a hypocrite who rode with the hounds while extending infinite goodwill towards rabbits and foxes.

My self-contempt and near despair became unbearable as OFSTED approached. Just before our inspection in May 1995 I wrote:

> I have soaked up other people's angst for years and the mark is on me. It's like a rugby match where you don't notice the bruises until afterwards. The league tables, the cross parents, the disappointed staff, the long hours, this chasing after the rainbow, this damned impossible job – they're rusting my steel and rotting my soft bendy willow from the inside out . . . My body and the school's merge as our Ofsted inspection looms. Doctor, there's nothing seriously wrong, is there? Inspector, we're OK aren't we? That churning isn't an ulcer, is it? . . . Tell me what I've done wrong, I promise I'll change.
>
> (Barker, 1995, p. 7)

The OFSTED report seemed a poor reward for my life's blood. 'A significant number underachieve in many subjects,' commented the registered inspector. In her opinion the principal 'exudes ideas which are frequently imaginative and innovatory but are not always fully understood or implemented by his colleagues'. Our collective leadership was 'sound'. The statutory framework provides no scope for disagreement. You are obliged to produce an action plan to deal with the 'key issues that the school needs to address'. Stanground had to conform to OFSTED's vision and criteria.

WORN OUT TOOLS

Rudyard Kipling's 'If' echoed in my ears as we started work on the action plan: 'watch the things you gave your life to, broken, /And stoop and build 'em up with worn-out tools.' We had to tackle again the same old problems of disaffected students, low expectations and underachievement, only this time with Thomas Gradgrind astride our shoulders: 'A man of realities. A man of fact and calculations. A man who proceeds upon the principle that two and two are four, and nothing over, and who is not to be talked into allowing for anything over' (Dickens, 1854, p. 48). I struggled with the Gradgrind-like sciences of action planning and target-setting, hindered by my defiant opinion that GCSE and test results trivialise education and prevent us from understanding how learning depends upon need, desire and expression. No target can make a book, film or sculpture more interesting. I have never seen a dull teacher enlivened by fear.

I had become an embarrassment to my colleagues. After 17 years, I was part of the problem at Stanground, no longer part of the solution. Like so many teachers, I felt oppressed by the constant questioning of my faith. As a head, I had become an accomplice in the humiliation of teachers. After reading Foucault (1975, pp. 154–5), I had no illusions about my own part in this sorry business:

> Discipline . . . arranges a positive economy; it poses the principle of a theoretically ever-growing use of time: exhaustion rather than use; it is a question of extracting . . . ever more available moments and, from each moment, ever more useful forces . . . one could tend towards an ideal point at which one maintained maximum speed and maximum efficiency . . . orders imposed on everyone temporal norms that were intended . . . to accelerate the process of learning . . . In becoming the target for new mechanisms of power, the body is offered up to new forms of knowledge.

My complicity in this intensification of work was considerable. Determined not to be found out, I had driven teachers, students and myself to exhaustion. We became creatures of OFSTED's ultra-regulated world, where there is no space for imagination, love or joy. Nothing matters there but results. My vision had become an 'ideological shell', invaded and colonised by aliens.

In the summer of 1996, I read Prospero's (and Shakespeare's) final words at sixth-form assembly:

> Now my charms are all o'erthrown,
> And what strength I have's mine own;
> Which is most faint.
> And my ending is despair,
> Unless I be reliev'd by prayer,
> Which pierces so that it assaults
> Mercy itself and frees all faults.
> As you from crimes would pardon'd be,
> Let your indulgence set me free.

A few months later (March, 1997) they let me go. Traumatised by my 17-year Odyssey, I wondered what to do with the rest of my life. Leicester University asked for help with their PGCE history course. This led me to visit a student placed at Rowley Fields Community College, an 11–16 school on the outskirts of the city. He told the story. They'd failed OFSTED and were in special measures. The school's action plan had been thrown out in February; an acting head had been drafted in but was due to leave at the end of term. Now Rowley was up for closure. Parents were withdrawing their children in droves.

CHESS MATCH WITH THE EVIL EMPIRE

Shortly afterwards, Rowley Fields advertised a two-year contract for an acting principal. I read the OFSTED report which had dynamited the old regime: 'Rowley Fields School has a number of important weaknesses in standards of attainment, the quality of teaching and in its management and efficiency. Many of these weaknesses arise from serious shortcomings in the quality of leadership and management provided to the school by the headteacher and governing body.' Rowley Fields might need me, but what kind of madness could lead back into this? Were my nerves fit for another chess match with the evil empire? My diary records how I felt: 'So many problems reminiscent of the past. Do I really have the energy to tackle resurfacing playgrounds, relocating home economics? Can I be a maniac again, a maniac of the trivial, catching up 25 years in two or three? I've not got sufficient time.' Above all, I thought of the teachers (66% were rated satisfactory or better) and families of Rowley Fields, labelled and shamed, their professional and human worth impugned and damaged by a passing juggernaut. How much better to fight for them than to lick my wounds in bitter retreat! And whatever mistakes were made at Rowley, they were not mine. I should not have to defend the past. By 21 August I was back in office, ready to fight to the death for my new school.

Fortunately, the parents' action group, the governors and acting head Chris Robinson (Chris Robinson, principal of John Ferneley High School, Melton Mowbray, was acting principal at Rowley Fields from March to August 1997) were already at war and won the first skirmish. The closure threat prompted an extraordinary outburst of carefully orchestrated community energy and had to be withdrawn. The LEA decided to review secondary education across the city instead. Major improvements were initiated and the GCSE 5 A–C tally rose from 27% to 41%. A Rowley Fields student reported his impressions of that heroic summer:

> I think his method was too strict and it made the school feel gloomy and not really enthusiastic. When Mr Robinson came in, everything was happening, the teachers seemed to be more enthusiastic when they taught and now you've come, I think it has gone down a little bit from when Mr Robinson was here . . . things were happening everywhere, there was the student council popping up, there was the downstairs reception, there were the computers coming in, the disabled doors.

At Rowley Fields my vision is valid and relevant again. Amazed by the new, permissive climate, teachers have seized every opportunity to make life enjoyable for the children. In October, 400 crowded into the hall to celebrate Diwali. At Christmas we staged an extravaganza which was rather unkind to Scrooge. Sikh and Hindu students have organised festivals of music, food and dancing. Lunchtime clubs, after-school activities and educational visits have appeared like flowers in a desert. When Year 10 proved difficult, we sent them to an outdoor pursuits centre for leadership training. We're planning a team-building weekend in Snowdonia for the staff. Equal value and equal opportunities underpin a new, entitlement curriculum. Banding has been outlawed; setting reduced. Open-plan classrooms have been closed; broken paving has been resurfaced; and the home economics rooms have been converted. The LEA has decided to make us an 'expanding' school, while OFSTED considers our progress to be 'good'.

HARD TASKMASTER

Despite these delights, the teachers remain oppressed. I have introduced an intensive programme of monitoring and evaluation, followed up by individual and team coaching. Our prime objective is to leave special measures, so there is remorseless pressure to revise schemes of work and prepare detailed lesson plans. HMI reported that I am seen as a 'hard taskmaster'. I have no guilt or regret about my role. Although often unfair to city schools, the OFSTED process offers us the best hope of recovering respect and credibility.

Forty years on, my double vision persists. Schools reflect but may transcend their social inheritance. The state may thrive on regulation but teachers help children learn. My experience has made me optimistic: 'No one who has read children's poems and stories or seen their paintings or heard their music can help but be moved by the creative flair of ordinary people' (Barker, 1986b, pp. 174–5). Unseen, unheard by the fat controller, teachers have become 'the unacknowledged legislators' (Shelley, 1840, p. 156) of the future they have made possible.

(Rowley Fields was inspected (Section 10) 9–11 November 1998. More than 90% of the teaching was sound or better, 40% good. Special measures are no longer required.)

REFERENCES

Ball, S.J. (1987) *The Micro-Politics of the School*, London, Methuen.

Ball, S.J. (1990) Management as moral technology: a Luddite analysis. In Ball, S.J., *Foucault and Education: Disciplines and Knowledge*, London, Routledge.

Barker, B. (1986a) *Rescuing the Comprehensive Experience*, Milton Keynes, Open University Press.

Barker, B. (1986b) After Joseph: teaching, equality and culture, *Cambridge Journal of Education*, Vol. 16, no. 3, pp. 174–5.

Barker, B. (1987) Teaching controversy, *Cambridge Journal of Education*, Vol. 17, no. 2, pp. 107–10.

Barker, B. (1989) Under fire with little cover. *The Times Educational Supplement*, 17 November.

Barker, B. (1995) Bruised by leadership, *The Times Educational Supplement*, 12 May.

Barker, B. (1997) Who killed the local education authority – Cambridgeshire 1974–1998? *Cambridge Journal of Education*, Vol. 27, no. 1, pp. 23-34.

Berg, L. (1968) *Risinghill: Death of a Comprehensive School*, Harmondsworth, Penguin Books.

Callaghan, J. (1976) *Education*, 22 October.

Department for Education and Science (1977) *Education in Schools: A Consultative Document*, London, HMSO.

Dickens, C. (1854) *Hard Times*, Harmondsworth, Penguin Books (1969 edition).

Foot, M.(1962) *Aneurin Bevan, Vol. 1. 1897–1945*, London, MacGibbon & Kee.

Foucault, M. (1975) *Discipline and Punish*, Harmondsworth, Penguin Books (1979 edition).

Shelley, P.B. (1840) A defence of poetry. In Hughes, A.D.M., ed. (1952) *Shelley*, Oxford, Oxford University Press.

Simon, B. (1988) *Bending The Rules*, London, Lawrence & Wishart.

8

A Vision for Lilian Baylis

YVONNE BATES

THE CONTEXT

In May 1997 Lilian Baylis School in Lambeth, south London, was 'named and shamed' by the Secretary of State for Education and described as one of the worst schools in the country. At that time the school had been in special measures for nearly four years. In September 1997 I was seconded from a Hertfordshire school to Lilian Baylis School, as headteacher for one year, with a specific brief to remove the school from special measures and to increase the number of pupils on roll.

Lilian Baylis School is one of the most socially deprived schools in the country. Some 84% of the pupils are entitled to a free school meal. Nearly half the pupils speak English as an additional language. The school admits many children who are newly arrived in the country. Many of these pupils have little English; some have no previous educational experience of any kind. A fifth of the pupils had been excluded from another school because of behavioural difficulties. OFSTED described these exceptional circumstances as 'operating in a challenging context'.

Examination results compared very unfavourably with national averages. In 1997 only 17% of pupils achieved five or more GCSEs at grades C or above. The Key Stage 3 SATs results compared even less well with national averages. Only 14% of pupils achieved Level 5 or above in their maths SAT and the results for English were even lower. Behaviour in the school was exceptionally poor. Teaching was often disrupted by misbehaviour and there were frequent incidents of serious ill-discipline. Despite significant improvement attendance still only averaged 83%. There was casual absence and long-term truancy. Post-registration truancy had become the norm for large numbers of pupils.

The poor reputation of the school meant that few pupils lived locally and the roll, which was declining rapidly, was only sustained by excluded pupils and siblings travelling relatively long distances to the school. The school, therefore, faced an uncertain financial future.

Understandably morale amongst both staff and pupils was extremely low. The school had been publicly 'named and shamed'. The local press had not just been negative but at times vitriolic in its coverage of the fortunes of the school. Teachers had been told they were failing and pupils had internalised this message of failure and many pupils had developed poor self-images and low aspirations. The strength of feeling in the community about the school took me by surprise. They wanted it closed. Few believed that anything could be done to improve the school. Local people told gruesome stories of violence, pensioners afraid to walk the streets, gang robbery and intimidation. On my first excursion into the local community shortly after taking up my post I met a number of the local traders in Lambeth Walk. I introduced myself cheerfully as the new headteacher at Lilian Baylis. Several looked horrified, others looked doubtful, one looked sad, took my hand and said pityingly, 'You poor cow'.

I visited the school in July and made a judgement about the school's potential to turn itself around. If a vision is needed to give people a belief in a realistic, credible, attractive future then Lilian Baylis was certainly in desperate need of a powerful vision. I had less than one year to formulate, articulate and ensure collective commitment to a vision for Lilian Baylis and to define the tasks that would begin the achievement of the vision.

THE TASK

Lilian Baylis had to be removed from special measures within the year or face closure. The immediate agenda for the school had been set by OFSTED. To remove the need for special measures the school had to pass a set of tick-list criteria. For some time these criteria had defined the school's agenda. It was therefore always short term, externally imposed, perceived by staff as unobtainable and was therefore counterproductive. The school had been failing against the criteria for four years. Defining the priorities and tasks that would lift the school out of special measures was not difficult. There was, however, a real danger that the process could lead to a 'quick-fix'. If improvement was to be sustained then the task went beyond a cosmetic exercise to paper over the cracks for the benefit of the inspectors. A vision was needed to lift aspirations. My vision for the school was to effect a significant shift towards an achievement culture based on a genuine belief in the capability of teachers and children.

Brief meetings with teaching staff in the summer of 1997 had left me in no doubt that the school could be turned around. Hidden beneath a veneer of stress-induced, negative relationships was a strongly held set of values underpinned by a fundamental belief that the school was making a positive difference to the lives of young people.

The quality of teaching and learning had been judged to be satisfactory or better in less than 75% of lessons at the last monitoring visit and although this represented a considerable improvement from earlier inspections it still fell short of the OFSTED tick-list requirements. Asking teachers to make teaching their first priority seemed a reasonable focus. Placing the emphasis on pedagogy and curriculum at the level of the classroom, the faculty and the whole school re-established a shared understanding of the core purpose of the organisation. The first and most fundamental task was to establish an expectation that teachers would reflect upon their teaching and discuss their work with colleagues. This would lead to an agreed definition of good-quality teaching. Teachers would then observe each other's work which would lead to the dissemination of good practice.

The emphasis on good practice in the classroom was inextricably linked to the requirement to establish a calm and disciplined environment with a clear focus on learning. The behaviour of pupils had been highlighted by OFSTED as a key issue for improvement and had been found to be unsatisfactory on most monitoring visits. My meetings with pupils in the summer before my appointment, however, had indicated that they shared an unswerving loyalty to their school. This was the starting point of the emergence of a vision which took account of, but was well beyond, OFSTED criteria.

Fostering a sense of belief and pride in the school was imperative. The message needed to be internalised and then disseminated strongly and confidently in the community. Although removal of special measures was necessary it was not sufficient to establish the viability of the school. It would be futile to have HMI declare the school to be offering an acceptable standard of education to its children whilst there were not enough children on roll to justify or finance the school's future. Unless the school could win the confidence of the local and wider community and persuade prospective parents that Lilian Baylis no longer deserved its reputation then the school had no future. This was the more difficult task. The internal improvement agenda was clear and achievable. The prospect of successfully reversing a reputation that had become part of the folklore of Lambeth was much less certain. In almost every primary school I visited I was reminded that the task appeared to be insurmountable. I was always welcomed warmly and excitedly by the children who were waiting to recount the gory stories they had heard about severed limbs, gang violence, arson and their understanding that the school had been designated as a police 'no-go' area. This was not encouraging. Even less encouraging was the frosty reception of one or two of the primary headteachers, one of whom told me that she felt morally bound actively to discourage her pupils from applying to Lilian Baylis.

THE VISION

Vision has been described as a 'mental picture of a preferred future for the school' (Caldwell and Spinks, 1990, p. 50). At this level some rudimentary consensus of a vision was already shared by pupils, staff and governors. The preferred image of the school was that it would continue to exist. Although the image was quite explicit it was based on either hope or denial, rather than expectation and belief. The challenge was to build a vision for the school that was ambitious but credible. I had no doubt that staff and pupils would commit to a vision of a successful school and that this commitment would instantly bring about changes in the procedures, processes and practices of the school. Staff and pupils had indicated to me that they expected significant change and were more than ready for it. It was less certain, however, that they would really believe that the outcomes were possible and that the vision could be realised. This was fundamentally important since only a belief in the credibility of the vision would bring about the cultural shift that was needed to establish sustained improvement.

The need for staff and pupils to build explicit images of a future Lilian Baylis is well illustrated by Fullan (1991, p. 81) who states that 'vision-building permeates the organisation with values, purpose, and integrity for both the what and how of improvement'. Without a clear and robust vision of the future staff had understood the need to improve but did not share an understanding of what needed to be done, or how to do it. Many teachers were too demoralised to risk making changes alone and others were sceptical that where improvements had been made in the past they had been acknowledged by HMI who had then replaced them with other requirements. In other words they felt that they were victims of a 'moving goal post' and that there was, therefore, little to be gained from working towards specific goals, or even in setting them in the first place.

A vision must be based on the values of the school and incorporate beliefs of the fundamental nature of the school. It should be informed not only by future aspirations but also by past achievements and strengths. The staff at Lilian Baylis shared a common belief that their task was to close the gap of disadvantage experienced by many of their pupils. This was not a school where social determinism would be tolerated. It was a school where teachers, despite public humiliation and condemnation over a sustained period of time, worked tirelessly and with extraordinary devotion in the interests of their pupils.

The school also had a strong ethos of providing equality of opportunity. There are over 30 languages spoken by pupils. The sense of worth and respect for other cultures, languages and religions is a quite tangible feature of the school, permeating the curriculum. The performance of some ethnic minority groups was also impressive. I was able to demonstrate statistically, for example, the high relative success of African and African-Caribbean children compared with the national averages of all children at GCSE. If it had been possible to compare Lilian Baylis pupils with the national performance of African and African-Caribbean children I am sure the success of the school and its commitment to equal opportunities would have been spectacularly demonstrated.

These strengths gave a starting point for the formulation of a vision for Lilian Baylis that would first take the school out of special measures but then more importantly establish a culture of continuous improvement. The existing ethos and action plan for improvement had proved ineffective in taking the school forward. A major constraint on the process of formulating a powerful vision was time. HMI were expected only 6 weeks after I took up post by which time there needed to be evidence of some tangible improvement. Many commentators have noted that a successful vision cannot be imposed. Jenkins (1991, p. 40), for example, states that a vision must be '. . . created through collaboration and negotiation with stakeholders'. Caldwell and Spinks (1990, p. 52) agree with this stating that 'Commitment is likely to be high where representatives of the community . . . have been involved in formulating that vision', but they do make a qualification to this generalisation where there is a need to transform the school. They note that in some case studies 'the vision of the leader who took the initiative was not initially developed in association with others' (Caldwell and Spinks, 1990, p. 51). This had to be the way forward for Lilian Baylis.

I met with most staff throughout August and established an understanding of their perceptions of the priorities for improvement. I learned what had constrained their performance and was able to identify what colleagues felt were the strengths of the school. Caldwell and Spinks state that 'the initiator must be energised by a personal vision of what is possible' (Caldwell and Spinks, 1990, p. 51). It was certainly clear to me that Lilian Baylis was a school with loyal children and dedicated, hard-working, capable teachers. I recognised that the school had unlimited potential and formulated a personal vision that would begin to realise it.

The vision for Lilian Baylis had to be simple. It had to reflect and build upon the values and strengths that already existed. It also had to state quite explicitly what would be created and accomplished which was not currently in evidence. It needed to paint pictures of a school in which attendance at all lessons is the norm, pupils are ready and willing to learn and feel secure in a well ordered environment. It needed to bind staff together to repair damaged relationships and focus on positives. It needed to create a culture of good behaviour and zero tolerance by students of the failure of others to meet their expectations. It must be based on pride. Pride in the school, in belonging to the school and in personal achievement. Communicating the vision and disseminating the messages of improvement and success had to become a collective responsibility which included governors and support staff. We all had to become determined that in 6 months there would be public recognition that Lilian Baylis was a school to which we were all proud to belong.

REALISING THE VISION

Lilian Baylis was operating within a divisive and counterproductive political culture. 'Management' was a largely derogatory term for those at senior level whose primary purpose was thought by some teachers to be to conspire against the staff to constrain their performance in some way. The concept of all teachers as leaders and managers was generally not understood. Since few people were managing and issues were inevitably part of a teacher-union rather than management-led agenda their solutions tended not to reflect the core purpose of the organisation: teaching and learning. Many governors had failed to take responsibility for the declining fortunes of the school and had fuelled a culture of blame, which was also in evidence amongst different staff factions. This had led to a breakdown in relationships at all levels of the organisation. Repairing these relationships depended on shifting the culture to one in which all who work for and within the school are expected to operate to the highest levels of professionalism.

There had been a significant loss of confidence amongst teaching staff both collectively and individually. My absolute confidence in the success of the school and in their capability to achieve it was crucial in securing their commitment to an unqualified belief in each other and in a professional culture. We decided that the only way forward for Lilian Baylis that would achieve the desired outcomes in the limited time available was to impose our own 'fresh start'. We defined this as a completely clean break in which negative feelings, experiences and relationships could be put to one side. We adopted the phrase 'improving school', which we undertook to stress at every opportunity to replace the much used headline 'failing school'. We agreed to emphasise success, professionalism and the achievement of our children.

From the first day of term we committed to ensuring that as the pupils returned they would recognise a difference. The building had been painted internally and externally and several rooms and corridors had been recarpeted. This made a significant improvement to the appearance of the building from outside. This had been paid for by the local education authority in support of our fresh start initiative. All staff painted pictures for the children of a 'good' school with 'good' defined in terms of improvements which would address the special measures criteria and would support our own shared values. For example, in a good school pupils attend every day and attend all lessons. Our children had internalised the failure of the school and desperately wanted something of which to be proud. They shared the vision, believed in our success and made immediate, significant improvements. Internal truancy virtually ceased, graffiti was minimal and even litter around the site became less of a problem. Pupils understood the need to promote positive images of the school and relished the instruction to take every opportunity to tell visitors, friends, community partners and especially inspectors about the changes, successes and achievements of their school. They committed to wearing full school uniform to add weight to this message of pride and improvement.

Almost from the first few weeks of term visitors to the school noticed the change. They commented on the calm and orderly environment, the quiet of the building during lessons and the positive messages that greeted them from staff and pupils. The school had a direction, a short-term goal and a vision of the future.

One of the key issues to be addressed that initially looked daunting within the timescale was the academic underachievement of pupils. There was a dearth of prior attainment data, or any data on subsequent performance. The little data I had seen, however, had led me to believe that the school was adding significant value to pupils' achievements. I analysed the Key Stage 3 results of the Year 11 who left in 1997. I used this, along with their GCSE results and national information, to produce an analysis showing that Lilian Baylis adds value to pupils' achievement considerably above national expectations. The analysis was thorough. It examined gender and ethnicity factors and found, again, that the school was producing some remarkable results. The work provided indisputable evidence for OFSTED that the school was not, in fact, underachieving, as had been claimed, but was worthy of national attention for its achievements. At the same time I introduced a system of baseline testing which was administered to all pupils in the school so that this work could continue on a more data-rich basis. It is imperative that the extraordinary results that teachers enable pupils to achieve can be measured more accurately and monitored over time. This was a turning point for staff in their belief in the vision. I had been able to demonstrate to them and to a wider public that they were doing an exceptional job. It was an effective counterclaim to years of bad press and inaccurate analysis and critical reporting by OFSTED. The staff also knew that they were so much nearer to realising the vision than they had first thought. The short-term task now became clearly achievable and our goals attainable.

These data also enabled the school to set realistic but challenging targets for the performance of the school, departments and individual pupils. We agreed GCSE and Key Stage 3 targets for the following 3 years which were published in the school development plan. The target for the first academic year was 20% of pupils achieving 5 or more A*–C grades at GCSE. Prior attainment data indicated that around 8% of pupils could reasonably expect to reach this level.

Despite the relative success that had been demonstrated with examination results another key issue to be addressed was the quality of teaching. It had been found to be 'poor' in almost 30% of lessons on previous HMI monitoring inspection visits, particularly at Key Stage 3. Although this represented an improvement over the time the school had been in special measures it was still unacceptable. The extremely poor behaviour of many pupils, especially when taught by new staff, was proving to be a major constraint on improving the quality of teaching. Although there was a clear understanding of the relationship between readiness to learn and the quality of the curriculum, and several examples of very good practice in existence in the school, improvements in behaviour and in teaching had to be developed simultaneously.

In order to disseminate good practice we introduced a formal system of lesson observation and feedback. Training was provided to middle managers to enable them to observe lessons and provide feedback effectively with the emphasis on improving pace and ensuring effective differentiation. We used OFSTED criteria, slightly modified by the specific needs of the school, to define good-quality teaching. The protocols for observation were agreed and we carried out three complete observation phases, the third of which involved peer observation rather than a hierarchical structure. This reinforced the creation of a culture of talking about teaching, which had been lost amid other agendas. A high level of mutual support between teachers became common practice.

Some constraints on the quality of learning were more easily solved. The school had espoused a commitment to mixed-ability teaching but several heads of faculty felt that this policy was counterproductive to our main school development plan priority: to raise examination performance. The timetable was rewritten over the summer to enable setting to take place in those faculties that wished to set. During the year we undertook a complete revision of the curriculum. We introduced a literacy hour for Year 7, a vocational pathway through Key Stage 4 and revised the option arrangements to enable pupils to focus on their strengths and interests. We established strong business links to complement the vocational curriculum and to minimise the risk of social exclusion for some of our young people whose familial experiences had not involved regular employment for two generations.

Improving attendance and behaviour depended largely on the commitment of pupils to the vision but also involved changes to the processes and structures in the school. I presented staff with a behaviour policy and after minor revisions it was implemented at the beginning of term. The essence of its success depended upon consistent practice and application of a very simple structure. It minimised bureaucracy but emphasised responsibility at classroom level with a responsive and effective support system.

Strategies to raise attendance were based on a reward system. Weekly certificates were awarded to the form with the highest attendance which they used to fill a large wall specially cleared for that purpose. Competition became fierce and pupils were known to be collecting truants on their way in to school to prevent them from lowering their form percentages. Individual awards were also made at different levels and a 'pupil of the month' award was introduced which required, amongst other things, 100% attendance and punctuality. We also targeted the times and days of the year which we knew to be problematic and developed incentives to improve attendance at these times.

It is probably true that the most successful initiatives that result in raised attendance are not always those that set out to address the issue directly. The vision of a 'good school' painted for the children certainly made as much impact as the specific attendance strategies we adopted. The peer-tutoring programme also had a positive effect on attendance and behaviour. Year 11 pupils were given some basic lessons and some teaching strategies to help Year 7 pupils learn about fractions. The methodology followed the work of Professor Carol Fitzgibbon who had inspired staff at a training session when she outlined the work she had done on peer tutoring. An important aspect of the project at Lilian Baylis is that it gave us an opportunity to demonstrate a high level of trust in our pupils and gave them an opportunity to exercise real responsibility.

A key element of realising our vision was to achieve an acknowledgement by the local community that parents could send their children to Lilian Baylis with confidence. The task of communicating our success beyond the school had seemed daunting. The school had, however, received positive publicity both locally and nationally with respect to my arrival in post and we had established some important relationships with the media who had shown an interest in the school. The local paper, which had previously been damning in reporting the declining fortunes of the school, ran stories of success and achievement. This not only helped to shift local perceptions but was uplifting and inspiring for both teachers and pupils. A national weekly newspaper ran an article describing the school as 'the fastest improving in London' and we were even positively featured in a Norwegian national newspaper.

The press helped us to share our vision with a wider audience and the outcomes were spectacular. We established a police reading scheme with volunteers from the local area working with pupils who needed extra support with literacy skills. Our community mentoring programme expanded until over 30 mentors from local business, services, industry and media were linked with pupils preparing for examinations. Our international evening, which was a celebration of both diversity and unity in our multicultural community, was attended by almost 300 people, a significant difference from the 13 who had attended the last school function.

Our greatest opportunity for sharing our vision and our successes came from the interest of a television company. They spent several days filming in the school and produced a 30-minute documentary which was screened across London.

THE LAST BIT WITH THE HAPPY ENDING

In October 1997 a team of Her Majesty's Inspectors arrived at Lilian Baylis to monitor the progress that had been made since the last visit. They reported favourably on improvements to behaviour, attendance, progress in lessons and described pupils as 'ready and willing to learn'. They also noted the positive ethos of the school. They stated that progress had been made against all the key issues the school was required to address and as a result was ready for a Section 9 inspection with a view to removing the school from special measures. The findings of the report suggested that we were not about to limp out of special measures but to emerge with a flourish without serious weaknesses and with much to celebrate. In January 1998 that final visit took place. Lilian Baylis School was found to be no longer in need of special measures. The press reported that we had leapt from 'named and ashamed' to 'named and acclaimed' in less than 6 months. The powerful, shared vision that had driven our work through intense and difficult times had been realised. We had a school that we could all be justifiably proud of.

We celebrated the achievement of our remarkable teaching staff. We also celebrated the achievement of our children through special awards, both for academic excellence and those which recognised loyalty, leadership and contribution to the success of Lilian Baylis. We thanked our many partners and friends in the community who had shared, and been part of, our vision.

The future of Lilian Baylis now depends upon the formulation of a vision that takes the school further away from special measures and firmly into a bright and ambitious future. The vision of the local authority is an exciting one. It involves, amongst other things, specialist status for Lilian Baylis as a centre of excellence for information and communications technology. The school is also now part of an Education Action Zone which adds a political agenda to the direction in which the school is expected to develop. The opportunities arising from these initiatives have the potential to take the school forward but the vision must belong to the school and to those who will work to realise it. The school will need to formulate a vision which takes account of the external agendas but which builds on the shared values and common philosophy that underpinned the remarkable turnaround of Lilian Baylis School.

REFERENCES

Caldwell, B.J. and Spinks, J.M. (1990) *Leading the Self-Managing School*, London, The Falmer Press.

Fullan, M.G. (1991) *The New Meaning of Educational Change*, London, Cassell.

Jenkins, H.O. (1991) *Getting it Right*, Oxford, Blackwell.

9

The Process of Vision Creation – Intuition and Accountability

JOHN CAIN

The gossip about the school was quite clear – this was not the school to send your child to if you were in a position to exercise a choice – and there was a lot of choice available in the local area both from LEA and independent schools. There were, thankfully, parents loyal to their local school who supported the school against the prevailing wind. There appeared to be some schools that were considered to be more socially and academically acceptable than others for parents to send their children to. The process of taking children past one school to go to another is very damaging particularly when it is being done by influential parents. Of course, their decision to do this would be based on the premise that quite simply some schools were just better than others and their main concern was to give the best education possible to their child. This view deprives schools of access to more able students and the opportunity to break the downwards spiral of either declining student numbers or the ability to improve the overall academic profile of the students on intake. Therefore the issue was one of convincing the local and wider community that the school could deliver high standards to all children.

THE STARTING POINT

Woodhatch School, as it was called in 1993, was, in my view, unjustly labelled as a difficult school. The students were well behaved and because of some outstanding financial control the school was solvent even with a roll of just under 400. There was a surplus of about £50,000 which was available for use.

Therefore, two of the essential conditions for success were already in place, namely, discipline and finance. In my previous post the issue of calming and ordering the school had had to be undertaken and this in itself had taken the best part of two years. It appears that it is often this part of the school improvement process that gets most notice because the results can be relatively rapid and fairly dramatic. However the process of moving on from there to be competitive with the best in terms of academic outcomes is more challenging

96

and more difficult. Also, if my analysis of the school being undervalued was correct, I would also expect to find some high-performing staff and this was to prove true in the senior management team, amongst middle managers and the teaching staff.

In 1993 it was widely felt that closure of schools would come from the implementation of the process of delegated financial management and budgetary problems – OFSTED had yet to cut its teeth. It was assumed that schools would, because of falling numbers, wither on the vine and LEAs would not encounter reorganisational difficulties as the financial imperatives would drive the decision-making. From the outset this was not a pressing problem but I did feel that a secondary school did need to be around 750 to start to be viable.

One of the key activities of governors is to appoint headteachers who can present and deliver a vision of the future. Sometimes that might mean they are keen to preserve the status quo, in other circumstances they might be looking for radical change. Part of the lengthy interview process should enable a candidate to establish just what is required and the degree of freedom which will be allowed to achieve it. It soon became clear in my own case that the school governors would give considerable freedom to the new head to take a new direction. However it was clear that the past history and achievements of the school had still to be respected.

Consequently, the process was to be one of building on what the school had achieved rather than having that rather dubious luxury of being able to say we were starting again and the only way the school could go was up. This was not to be a concept of a phoenix rising from the ashes but rather the development of a school which had a sound, if misunderstood, platform from which to develop. However, the reality of the problem hit very soon. I was appointed to the headship during the week of the open evening for recruiting the next year's intake. This apparently proved too much of a shock for many parents and the intake crashed from around 100 in previous years to 75 first choices against a planned admission number of 150. That was a tremendously hard blow even before I had taken up the post of headteacher in January 1993. As might be expected, the overall academic profile of that year group was not as good as other years within the school.

A PERSONAL VISION

Whatever the external challenges the school faced and whatever its intake was like these factors never influenced what I wanted the school to be. I wanted to be the head of a school which was well respected in the community, had good academic results and was full. I was not at the time contemplating settling for anything less because of the current circumstances of the school. My vision was about what I wanted to achieve for the school. What the school was currently thought capable of would not be good enough. It never crossed my mind that I would not achieve this goal and I would suggest that if any self-doubt is present then the outcome is likely to be failure. This comment is not made out of any sense of arrogance but I just knew it was possible – it is only on reflection, after three or four years that the enormity of the risk of the situation became apparent.

OPPORTUNITIES TO TAKE CONTROL

At that time the school was a 12–16 school although in 1994 Surrey had decided to abandon its middle-school system and the school was to become 11–16 and would take two year groups in 1994. This meant many other local schools had impressive building schemes announced whilst the renamed Reigate School had just under 200 surplus places and no need to add new places or new buildings. Thus the need to increase the intake became the absolute imperative for survival. But the external environment had at the same time given us an extra year group but no extra or new facilities.

At the time examination results were below the national average and the facilities, although well looked after, were old-fashioned and, in the light of what was starting to happen in other schools, uncompetitive. Also, because the school was undersubscribed in all year groups we tended to have to take the exclusions from elsewhere. Overall, it gave the school a 'secondary modern' type of reputation in a system of comprehensive education. This tended to lead to the label of being a 'caring' school – meaning that it was a good school to send children who had special educational needs.

It is an interesting issue as to the extent to which a school should take action to stem this influx. I would very much doubt that there are sufficient children in an area like Surrey to fill a school looking to increase its intake by orientating towards this particular market niche. Therefore there is a careful balancing act between, quite rightly, meeting the needs of such children, and having them in equal proportions with other schools. Certainly, meeting a vision which involves achieving above-average national standards is not achievable if substantial numbers of students come from the least-able cohort.

There was a feeling in the beginning that other schools were the cause of our problems and the LEA had deliberately starved the school of funds. It never seemed worth looking at either issue because it was clear we would stand or fall by what we did and achieved. We could not afford to worry about what others were doing. Fortunately, however, parents of some able and not so able children did live out their principles and sent their children to us, as their local and nearest school. There were 75 new children coming – it could have been worse and the school was solvent with a reserve which was just waiting to be spent!

AVOIDING THE VISION

From the outset I felt there was a need to gain credibility with the staff, students, parents and governors. I deliberately avoided the big 'vision' meeting with any group to say how things would be set right. In terms of delivering the vision it just was not my style and there was always the nagging doubt that if it all goes wrong public pronouncements would come back to haunt me. Also, from this very low intake base of student numbers the leap of faith that would be necessary was so considerable that being visionary might have been construed as living in a fantasy world.

So a written vision was delayed and I was put under no pressure to produce it in any concrete form. Everybody was made aware in conversations and the normal programme of meetings that we just had to recruit bigger numbers otherwise the outlook was very bleak. However, I did need to make an impact in order to prove that change was possible and, in time, any change was possible.

THE QUALITY OF THE SCHOOL ENVIRONMENT

Initially funds went on improving the school environment – I did not consult over this, I just did it, working on the principle that people expected something to happen. This was going to be it because I believed the environment mattered because the investment could be seen. A programme of redecoration was started and noticeboards for displaying students' work were put on every available wall. The message to the students was quite simple – it was that the school will invest in your education to give you the best and your work is important and should be seen. Within a very short time the new carpets we had put down seemed to be known about all over the area and a youth worker whom I had known for some time asked the students about the impact of my arrival and they said 'we've been given carpets'.

It is certain some would argue for books or equipment as the key area of expenditure but the value of getting the environment right is always a high priority for me. Today, the school employs a full-time painter and decorator and it is only recently a governor commented how he was surprised and doubtful about my first actions but now recognised it had had a profound impact. It must have taken considerable nerve on the part of the governors to allow me to proceed in this way. I cannot remember them stopping any one of my expenditure or curriculum proposals. It seems important therefore that not only a shared vision is necessary but there is also the need for schools to have a clear and undisputed way of managing its delivery. I always knew there was not time for a protracted debate about what we were doing.

Next, Surrey provided some funding for building work and because the sports facilities were so poor it was spent on a green porous tarmac play area – again very noticeable. This support from the LEA was invaluable – it gave everyone a sense of confidence and the feeling that the future was more secure. However, the school was still without an art room, this subject being taught in a science laboratory because there were sinks!

Having had a very visual impact there was still a need to convince parents to send their children to the school. I had to get across my vision of the future for the school and I had no direct access to this group. Therefore it was very important that we did all that was possible for our own students because they were the ones taking the messages out into the community every day about what the school was like. This is the area which makes the local gossip about the school and it was very important to make this positive and work in favour of the school.

MOVING TOWARDS A VISION

Broadly, the vision running round in my mind was to increase the intake, raise standards, and to have the students behaving well in good facilities. Daily activity in the school focused around these factors and a fortuitous permanent exclusion in my second week had me labelled as standing no nonsense. I still felt that declaring visions when the school intake had just dropped to 75 would not convince anybody. However, my conversations with staff and governors always focused on the importance of recruitment and I am fairly sure all were aware of what I saw as most important. The open evenings for the double year of intake came with a term of almost unbearable tension and hard work by all concerned with the school.

The vision was conveyed in the most part in my individual meetings with parents. I took each parent on a tour of the school – each took an hour – and more came when they heard this was on offer. The tours took a huge amount of time but eventually they paid off in terms of improving what locals were saying about the school. Invitations to the open evening or a personal tour of the school had been sent to all local primary children – this invitation was a glossy brochure which had a real quality feel about it and no other local school had done this before.

Staff knew the importance of lessons being well ordered and challenging and this contributed greatly to the success of the tours. We had also decided to set students by ability from the very start of Year 7 and use discrete sets for English, mathematics, science, French and history and geography. The reasoning behind this was to be able to say to parents of more able children that their education was secure in such groups but at the same time we had to ensure an equally good deal was given to students in the lower sets. Not surprisingly, timetabling became difficult but the offer clearly worked in terms of recruitment.

The two years of intake were both to be about 140, a considerable success and something of a surprise to observers of the school as generally it was thought that if we could get back to 100 it would have been a good achievement. This improvement was just the platform we needed to set out our stall for the future. We could now start thinking about a vision but in my mind we were still playing catch-up.

Announcing a vision which only matched what other local schools were already achieving could do as much damage as benefit in terms of the recruitment battle. However, external factors now started to take an influence. The LEA was now convinced we could recruit and looked to expand the size of the school to take up to 750 students. They offered an investment of £1 million to improve facilities to enable us to have five year groups of 150. I had always felt that was a challenging target because it meant moving even more children away from other schools, but we accepted the challenge to get the buildings. Around all this activity it was clear the school's reputation was improving.

DECLARING THE VISION

It became clear we could now make a vision statement about our future because we felt that people would believe it was going to happen. So much had happened that this would just be one more target we would reach. Perhaps purists in this field would argue that declaring the vision first might have speeded us up but I would argue that it would have required optimism beyond belief to have arrived at this point.

Numbers had picked up. However the issue of raising standards was more vexed. Value-added analysis indicated good progress was being made but we knew the intake of 75 students when they arrived at GCSE in 1997 would produce an uncomfortable league table outcome and this could be in a range between 32 and 40%, potentially disastrous but it would have to be dealt with. Thus setting a vision about standards with this lurking around was problematic. But we were convinced that raw standards, not value added, were where most credibility lay. Examination of the academic profile of the year groups indicated that as each year group grew in size it improved in quality. Therefore the further in to the future we went the better the results were likely to be even though a certain unevenness in the academic profiles of year groups was developing.

There was now a feeling that the vision statement had to be formulated. I presented one to the senior management meeting, where it got hacked around and became: 'By the year 2001 there would be 850 students, achieving a GCSE pass rate at above the national average in a school which would value and respect all its members.' This was then offered to the staff and governors for discussion and amendment and came through unaltered. It is largely measurable, achievable and realistic and was constructed in 1995. The statement does convey what we are about as a school. It does raise issues of ownership and sharing the vision. I wondered about working groups to come up with a vision but as headteacher the vision has to be what I think is most important and the prospect of consulting then ignoring the results is very damaging. It was my judgement that this action was what was required by this school in this situation. If I had felt pressure to consult more widely then I would have done so.

Perhaps the two years building up to the vision had focused everybody's mind in the same direction – we all knew what we needed to survive and be successful. There was no particular publicity for it because it still says we have work to do to exceed the national average but it is now realistically achievable and we know it is within our capacity to achieve it. This might lay me open to the criticism that it is not a vision that is challenging. I would argue that this statement merely formalises what we have been about and that certainly has been challenging.

I think on reflection that the statement made earlier that 'broadly the vision running round in my mind was to increase the intake, raise standards, and have the students behaving well in good facilities' was what was driving the process. I would regard these values as so obvious that I never thought it necessary to write them down anywhere because I thought they just had to be shared – perhaps somewhere in the process it was apparent that we all knew where we were heading. I could be considered lucky to have got away with it or just reaped the benefits of being driven by a set of core values and a belief that it would happen. Certainly, the way it evolved was not the textbook way of creating and sharing a vision. Although had I tried to manage the vision issue in a less intuitive way I might have been far less successful. In addition, the marketing impact of a very public vision which only aspired to what others had already achieved troubled me although that might well be just an underestimation of the sophistication of the local market.

MOVING THE VISION ON

In 1995 Surrey came back with another offer. Demographic trends indicated rising student numbers in the local area in the future. We were successful, so would we expand the school to 1,000 students with a yearly intake of 200?

The issue of where the school was going was now being driven by external forces. How could we achieve these sorts of numbers without substantial increases in achievement? To some extent, to have that sort of belief put in yourself, your staff, governors, students and parents is very flattering but also quite an awesome prospect. We had made significant progress, we now almost had to add the same number of students again. We knew that the 1996 OFSTED inspection would have a crucial bearing on the future of the school and the report did reflect the progress the school had made and classified Reigate School as a 'good 'school.

Thus taking up the expansion offer of five technology rooms, six classrooms, two new music rooms and a science laboratory was now realistic, although curriculum planning numbers for the 1998 intake year ranged from 150 to 200 – some indication that we felt we might be getting overstretched in terms of our capacity to recruit.

In November 1997 we heard that the intake for 1998 was 200 first choices. This was off a 39% 5 A–C pass rate from that low intake year. Evidence that league tables were not uppermost in parents' minds was being presented but I still found the increase in student numbers quite astonishing. It is interesting to note that after five years in post as headteacher the change was still being regarded as new and recent. I suppose that as each new year group in primary schools looks at secondary school choices they still reflect on what the school used to be like. Parents will now openly say that a number of years ago they would not have considered the school but now they felt very comfortable with it. I always explained the low intake year to prospective parents by describing how I had been appointed during that week five years ago and how I was to blame! The tale, which is quite true, is normally regarded as a very reasonable explanation.

In 1998 the new buildings had been finished, the examination pass rate had improved to above the national average, the intake had incredibly reached 200. Time had now come again to take stock and look at the sort of future we were going to make happen.

I still find it very difficult to take in what has happened to the school. It is immensely satisfying but I realise also that we cannot stop. I know that thinking the problem has been cracked is the most dangerous time in the lifecycle of an organisation. If you look at any schools in an area over a period of 10–15 years all sorts of changes are identifiable – is another school just about to take off and inflict damage on to us?

Also the issue is raised as to the extent to which the five-year period is the maximum for a head to make an impact and that a second renewal is more likely or more easily achieved by a new person. However, my management style is developing into one that is now more strategic and analytical and the school has changed. Reigate School is now a different organisation, being larger, more complex and more successful. Also over the last five years my management knowledge has developed and this gives me a greater range of options, of which intuition still plays a significant part. I now see this as an opportunity for me to take forward a school which is substantially different from the school I became head of in 1993.

THE NEXT VISION

When the next vision is being considered it is now increasingly important to consider the external agenda. The centralisation of education has meant we are all now playing to a common set of rules and standards. Quite simply whatever the government puts up as having to be achieved becomes the vision for the future. We know those not achieving will be dealt with and little time is available for improvement or change. Consequently, for schools operating in difficult conditions visions may start to become increasingly short term because of the annual cycle on which we operate and the way in which deadlines for improvement are set. My experience is that building quality in to a school actually takes some time but our educational system is not currently designed to accept that. Thus we may see headteachers doing one or two years in difficult schools and producing some improvements without giving a commitment to delivering a longer-term vision which a school will need if it is not to be constantly in danger from hit squads, special measures and falling rolls. In my view having a vision for a school involves making a long-term commitment to it.

Many headteachers may see controlling their intake as the surest and quickest way to raise standards. The issue of a diverse range of specialist schools in certain areas will no doubt shape the vision schools have for themselves, although their ability to select a certain percentage of students for their specialisms will further distort the principle of comprehensive education and of comparability between schools. Also it will lead to some children not being wanted by schools.

There has been the significant increase in statistical data used to make comparisons between schools and the publication of data has set an agenda that has put the achievements and reputation of schools into the public domain. We can now see through the mass of data what each year group in the school might achieve over the next five years. For Reigate School the issue must be to improve on what looks to be possible in terms of achievement in absolute and value-added terms. It appears that hitting the right numbers in terms of performance will be the deciding and guiding influence for many schools. We too will have that as a priority.

Reigate School's current vision statement of 'By the year 2001 there would be 850 students, achieving a GCSE pass rate at above the national average in a school which would value and respect all its members' does still seem to carry much of what we would want to retain as the essence of our future thinking. It is perhaps ironic that the aims of the current system which can produce such discomfort for many schools have been at the heart of our efforts for the past few years, although setting it out as an internal goal for yourself is still quite different from having it imposed from elsewhere and also being publicly penalised and humiliated for not achieving it.

It has always been part of my thinking that whatever the rules of the game I will play to win using them. It does not mean I always agree with them or would not seek to change them but it does stop me wasting a lot of time achieving something that the system does not value. Perhaps it might be argued that this is a lack of principles but at the end of the day – a vision of higher standards of education for all students – is difficult to argue with even though the systems and mechanisms for achieving it might be flawed.

However, the accountability model is now quite clear. If you cannot deliver as a headteacher what the government wants for your school, you and your school will not survive. The opportunities for individual and unique expressions of vision may be still available to the highest-performing schools which, having everything else in place, might still have the opportunity to be visionary in methodology, but for many schools delivering higher standards is what it is about. Hopefully, this can still be done in such a way that all students are motivated, challenged, valued and have a concern for others.

10

Leading the Creative School

ELIZABETH DUFFY

In September 1993 I became a headteacher; in September 1998 I took up a second headship. This chapter is my view of my first headship as seen from the threshold of my second. Moving on always provides an opportunity for shaping and 'closing' an episode – a satisfying activity from a psychological, emotional and intellectual point of view, but with the obvious inherent temptations to transform actual experience, in all its messiness and uncontrollability, into tidy cause, effect and, by extension, achievement. In making sense of, and appraising, this period in my career, therefore, I am shaping it into a graspable section of my 'life'. That is the central theme of this chapter – the interaction of my sense of 'myself' as an individual with my sense of 'myself' as professional leader and manager. I need, therefore, to start by briefly touching on the road that led me to my first headship.

I never meant to be a teacher. I fell into it. In late autumn, 1974, I returned to England from a postgraduate fellowship in America with no plans for my next step. My sister-in-law worked in a nine-stream secondary modern school which was desperate for a French teacher, to cover a gap between December and Easter when a new head of department would arrive. My degree was in English, but had included some French for two years. I took the temporary post with no preparation time and no training. I simply accepted the job one afternoon and walked into class the next morning. There was no other French teacher but there was a stock cupboard and a detailed scheme of work. In a state of shock, I did my best, learnt an amazing amount amazingly fast and found that I loved it. I decided to see what it was like teaching my 'own' subject – and took a job elsewhere teaching English from the following September. My career in teaching had begun.

I spent the next seven or eight years making it up as I went along – asking questions, copying others, falling into bad practices, falling back on my own memories of lessons as a pupil – gradually learning how to teach. There was no official support or monitoring of my performance or progress as I stumbled excitedly and enjoyably along. Gradually I got good at it and was enormously stimulated and challenged by an MA at the London Institute of Education. My track record and 'standing' as a teacher were good; my personal life was rich and happy; I was ready for greater responsibility and for new challenges – time for a move. I then worked, with increasing levels of responsibility, at three more schools until, with five very different schools behind me (secondary modern, direct grant, grammar, inner-London comprehensive – girls, boys, mixed) I became a headteacher.

The road to headship, thus summed up, sounds like an orderly progress, gathering breadth of experience along the way, but in reality it was not until I was in my second deputy headship that I felt headship was for me. The stimuli were varied but inter-related. I had begun an MBA at Keele, which provided formal opportunities to crystallise the self-reflectiveness and self-analysis that have been an integral part of my life since I was a child. (You cannot be brought up and educated as a Catholic and not 'check yourself out' regularly!) My professional responsibilities and my senior management perspective necessitated – and of themselves involved me in – focusing on the 'big questions': philosophical ones about the nature and purpose of learning; strategic and analytical ones about structures, processes and developments in a complex organisation, accountable both for its use of public funds and for its effect on young people's lives; practical and administrative ones about the smooth running of the organisation – about communication, about team-working, about systems. Headship felt like a philosophical, analytical and intellectual pursuit – seeing things whole and articulating both the present actuality and the 'vision' for the future. It seemed exciting, challenging – and 'do-able'. It also seemed to me like a natural extension of good, exciting, teaching – what worked in a classroom (motivation, high expectations, pace, passion, clarity) – could work for, and enrich, a whole school.

Running under the intellectual excitement and confidence, then, was a deeper current of personal need – what I believed 'schools' needed was being variously complemented and coloured by what I, personally, needed in order to fulfil myself, to use my talents, to be true to myself, to be happy. I had come to feel that, even though I was in this career by apparent chance, I was a born teacher. Headship had to be an extension, a development, of this 'natural' part of myself or I would lose my way. I wanted the whole school to be vibrant, creative, exciting, fulfilling – constantly experimenting and growing, just as I needed to feel that this particular school needed me (no one else) to make it so, and so this headship had to be the one for me to take. When I took it, I couldn't be sure I was right.

I can articulate much more clearly now than I could then the crucial nature of this double current – the absolute necessity to me of integrating the professional with the personal. The experience of headship – what it really feels like – clarified this point for me in both exhilarating and painful ways.

So, I arrived at headship full of intellectual confidence but with no sense whatsoever of how it would actually feel and not certain if the school and I would match. I discovered quickly that, while I was focusing excitedly and responding personally – as me – I was being perceived as 'The head' – a separate entity from my 'self' – a 'construct'. Every word I uttered seemed to take on a symbolic value – 'The head says'; 'The head's policy is' – instead of being heard as the observations (often exploratory, tentative, unformed, inquiring) of an individual thinking out loud, engaged in a shared and continuous enterprise of growing and developing. My way of thinking – as I saw it, creative and responsive, analysing, appraising, evaluating, reshaping – came up against other people's expectations of 'what a head does' (based largely on their own experience) and some colleagues' preference (need?) for clear parameters, unambiguous rules and instant decisions. My expectation of 'a shared enterprise', trying out new structures and processes for size while expressing expectations of professionalism and involvement, was interacting in a volatile way with others' uncertainty about responsibilities, power and trust. Consultation, openness and clear definition of accountabilities were energising some but destabilising others. A common contradictory desire among colleagues was to be given direction and still to feel free to set their own. Being part of a process which required effort and commitment and which could both empower them and leave them accountable excited some but left others vulnerable, afraid, illequipped or resentful. People were not (surprise, surprise) all like me in attitude, desire, passion, energy or confidence; enthusing and motivating adult professionals seemed not, after all, at this stage, like exciting a class of pupils. Was I getting it wrong? Did I know what I was doing? My professional selfconfidence wobbled as I experienced for the first time that absolute separation between the head and the rest of the professional team. I was more a lightning conductor than the leader of a harmonious orchestra. All very well for Tom Peters (1992, p. 483) to say 'try anything! The more screwups the merrier . . . Recover quickly then try something else'. Yes, my goal was creativity, an essential ingredient of which had to be individuality and, yes, I wanted all those individuals to share in my view that in order to be individuals they had to be professionally confident, willing to take responsibility and to be engaged in continuous development. Otherwise they would merely be shaped by someone else's mould. I hadn't sufficiently grasped what Thomas Jefferson knew – 'Timid men prefer the calm of despotism to the boisterous sea of liberty' (*ibid.*, p. 465). Nor had I yet focused honestly enough on the role played in colleagues' reactions by my own personality. Were those elements of my 'self' which gave me drive and confidence counterproductive in my role as a leader and manager? What, in absolute reality, was the head's role anyway? Could I as a person be getting in the way of my own ability to be a 'good' head (whatever that meant)?

Such reflections and self-analysis can engender paralysing self-consciousness and self-doubt, but can also lead to greater clarity and a restored or reaffirmed sense of direction. Since the issue was, for me, about the inter-relation of 'me' and 'the staff' – especially middle managers – I embarked on a shared action research project into my own headship, with simultaneous and interactive analysis of my own and others' perceptions. I knew that, as head, I couldn't choose but to be in the spotlight, but in choosing to focus on 'What kind of a job am I doing?' I could have been choosing to put myself in my own firing line. Leadership of schools had become, and has remained, a very public issue. The Chief Inspector's OFSTED report in 1995 stated categorically that 'it is . . . the leadership provided by the headteacher which is the critical factor in improving the quality of teaching in today's schools'. I was also naggingly aware that the concept I had accepted of being simultaneously 'leading profes- sional' and 'chief executive' 'ultimately depends for its justification on the extent to which a leadership style is adopted which elicits the co-operation of the professional group' (Hughes, 1985, p. 12). I had done my theoretical homework. I had tried to define roles, responsibilities and expectations. I knew about the varying cultures of organisations and the different styles of leader- ship. I had a vision. I had arrived with enthusiasm and energy, taking the fluid approach, welcoming ideas, inviting co-operation and involvement as essential ingredients of professionalism, hoping (perhaps assuming) that everyone wanted to participate and to develop. Why, then, did it not simply go like clockwork, when I could have ticked off the entire NPQH list? The action research both helped me to answer that question and reminded me to glory in the diversity and uniqueness of individual consciousness.

In my research I aimed to model the risk-taking, reflection and viewpoint- shifting I was identifying (theoretically and through experience) as components of creative activity. I also wanted to keep in mind the phenomenological as- pects of participating colleagues' responses: every individual's view would be different and equally valid. The research itself, I hoped, could prove a catalyst in 'reorienting, focusing and energising participants toward knowing reality in order to transform it', as Comstock suggests (quoted in Lather, 1986, p. 269). I hoped that my 'research into myself' might encourage in my school a climate of trust, a willingness to experiment and review and a preparedness to take risks in order to grow. As Brighouse (1991, p. 24) asserts: 'If they see the leader take risks, they too will be more likely to be innovative and strong-minded and clearly focused', encouraged by example and feeling that they will be backed if they, too, take risks. I wanted them to feel, rather than just to hope or believe, that my 'vision' of a creative school protected and nourished individual experi- mentation rather than subsuming it into 'the leader's sense of mission'. Equally crucial to me were to be true to myself and to ensure that that sense of my self did not compromise or colour colleagues' own sense of themselves. Unless individuality is absolutely protected, I both reasoned and felt, true creativity – individual, unique growth – is impossible (and 'mission' or 'vision' become fascist).

Let me briefly describe the research itself. I inter-related three viewpoints: the personal narrative of my first two years of headship as I experienced it; the middle managers' view through a 'self-review' meeting of a team that I had set up and that I chaired, with feedback to me; the senior managers' view through three SMT meetings, with specific agenda to review the team's role and effect, my role within the team and within the school, and the kind of leadership that might support creativity. The data from these sources included minutes, notes and tapes.

As in all academic research, I went back to the theory, checking out the literature on management and leadership as well as on theories of creativity, which led me by association of ideas and personal interest into philosophy and theology. As well as chaos theory and poststructuralism, Freire, Gutierrez, Bahktin, Descartes and Kierkegaard would figure large. What is individuality and creativity if not growth? What is growth if not the creation of the future? If we all have tomorrow inside us, are we not equally responsible for contributing to the nature of that tomorrow? How could any 'template' leave room for the necessary spontaneity and unpredictability and sheer exuberance of life at its best?

In my narrative and analysis of those two years, and in my interlinking of these with my reading, I found myself constantly asking these sorts of questions. In the earliest days of my new role, a county personnel adviser had visited me and wondered out loud if I was going to prove a 'weak' or a 'strong' head. I was left with mixed feelings that surfaced over the next years – 'I must be a strong head' – 'I must face up to my responsibilities and make others face up to theirs' – 'I must not sway in the wind but behave like a head' – and then repeatedly – 'What does that mean?'. Sometimes, the need (and duty) to emphasise responsibility and accountability, to ensure efficiency in the use of public funds, seemed to go directly against the excitement and fluidity, the energising and 'visioning' of the headship role. In the process of my research I characterised this conflict as an apparent 'crack' between the differing demands of management and of leadership, paralleled by and inter-related with a 'crack' between the 'head' as perceived in the staffroom and the 'person' doing her best. My awareness of this 'crack' sharpened especially when I had done what I believed to be my moral and professional duty with regard to an individual member of staff. Old loyalties divided staff opinion. My strength could attract and alienate. Did 'strong heads' automatically incite animosity? Comfortable practices that challenged nobody would make for a much easier life. This was not a temptation to be resisted; for me, it wasn't even an option. I had to be true to myself or a more damaging fissure would open in me. My self-conscious sensitivity to my effect on others, and my fear, exacerbated by stress, that my vision might be what I needed for my own sense of fulfilment rather than what was right for my school, could instead have led me to decide that I was not, after all, suited either to this headship or to headship *per se* and to look for another job. I had discovered by chance that I was a 'born teacher'; now I had to work out if those same talents and qualities could be truly used in headship. I am writing this because my research led me to conclude that they could.

I was told in the action research feedback that I 'was coming at people like a Gatling gun' – that I was 'knackering people' – that people weren't used to vision, commitment and energy in these large doses – they saw me as someone with a strong sense of direction – 'a sort of zeal'. They wanted to come with me, but were nervous, as if afraid of being left without a safety net, of not really being supported or trusted. My insistence on their responsibilities and accountability seemed at the same time an attractive professional development opportunity and a direct questioning of their present professionalism. I seemed to be demanding too much – couldn't I distil everything so that middle managers didn't have to think so much and could just put my ideas into operation? (This last is a far-from-objective version of middle managers' feedback to me, but it's exactly how I felt it at the time.) My vision relied utterly on individual, whole-hearted, participation. If they wanted to be told what to do, and I could not make them feel this was insulting and damaging to themselves as individuals as well as professionals, then I had failed in my own eyes. I could not operate as the kind of leader who merely wants followers. It would destroy my inner life.

I could see clearly at this point that my personal style and my educational philosophy were inter-related but not necessarily inextricably so. Could I stay true to my course but 'behave' differently so that others were more comfortable about coming with me? Was I still so sure that my course was 'right'? Why should teachers be creative in a climate that seems to demand uniformity, where even the creativity and individuality of leaders are reduced to a list of common competencies? It was the intertwining of my reading and the senior managers' analysis that led me to answers to these questions.

The strand of my reading that was the most profitable for my thinking was not the cultural, managerial or leadership texts but the philosophical. Creativity can be fascinatingly analysed and defined and, some even think, measured, but it is only the philosophical approaches to the concept of creativity itself that lead to educational values – the basic underpinning of any sort of true leadership in schools. Efficiency and effectiveness, smooth-running systems, can certainly contribute to a climate which allows good teaching and learning to happen – but they are neither the cause of the good teaching and learning nor, in themselves, the purpose of a school. To me, as clear as day, the fundamental irreducible purpose of education – of experience – is, in Jungian terms, to enable individuals to fulfil themselves as creative, unique individuals – to become what they, uniquely, may become (see Herzberg, 1966). For individuals to fail in this pursuit could be seen, as Descartes put it, as 'a defect in knowledge or a kind of negation' (1988, p. 122). Even when, to some twentieth-century philosophers, the very notion of the 'self' has been deconstructed, the essential nature of individual consciousness remains, whether or not individuals feel connected to an integrated whole. Education is about growth – about the fundamental stuff of human development – about our individual experience of the human condition and our means of, at the very least, coping with that condition. For many of us, the human condition is a balance (or see-saw!) between an absolute sense of nothingness and mortality and an inspirational, life-giving sense of purpose: creativity. It is from this life-giving sense, perhaps in defiance of the sense of mortality, that passionate commitment comes. 'Spontaneity and inwardness of life' – essentials in Kierkegaard's view of individuality – stem from involvement and integration of the 'whole person', whereas a life characterised by 'objectivity' and analytical observation can transform us into 'such objective observers that we become almost ghosts' (see Warnock, 1970). Indifference is negation, said Descartes. Passion matters.

Teaching should be a creative, passionate profession, not a 'delivery' of a common package of knowledge and skills by teachers who have been passed by, and/or been deformed by, the Teacher Training Agency's quality control bureau or who blindly follow the leader's vision. Time to reach for *A Theology of Liberation* (1973). To Gustavo Gutierrez, growth, development – creativity, – are a moral responsibility as well as a social duty – to intervene personally to break cycles of determinism and move people and societies forward. For what purpose was the Education Act 1944 passed, if not to encourage individuals to become part of that 'human history' which Gutierrez (*ibid.*, p. 10) defines as 'an opening to the future' – we must be 'oriented, definitively and creatively, toward our future, acting in the present for the sake of tomorrow' (p. 32). Paulo Freire (1996, p. 30) said much the same thing in specifically educational terms – we lose our power to 'create and re-create, [our] power to transform the world' if we 'cannot exist authentically'. To be 'whole', to be 'truly human' – to 'live authentically' – we must become more self-aware, accept responsibility for, and take control of, not only our own lives but our contribution to the lives of others. We learn to exercise our creative potential. We become protagonists in our own story, not the passive, 'indifferent' cut-outs in someone else's plot.

I cannot write about such philosophies in a calm and objective tone. They are the stuff of life to me. My reading, self-evidently, strengthened my vision of a creative school. Indeed, you may say, I sought affirmation for it and found it where the vision had originated – in the fundamental values of my life. With Freire and Gutierrez, I believe that the proactive and conscious development of the individual is not only a contribution to the development and well-being of the present and future human community but is that individual's moral responsibility. The cessation of growth is death. None of us has the right to promote death. From Donald Winnicott's (cited in Martin, 1993, pp. 38–9) psychoanalytical viewpoint 'it is creative apperception more than anything else that makes the individual feel that life is worth living. Contrasted with this is a relationship to external reality which is one of compliance'. Compliance is indifference – negation – the opposite of creativity. (Are you listening, TTA?) As headteacher, I need to interconnect individual teachers' need (and, in my terms, responsibility) to be their constantly developing selves with the identical needs and responsibilities of the pupils. Such interconnection is the core of the creative school. And the means? Over to the senior managers' analysis of life with me.

With a lower, or different, emotional stake in the action research than mine, the rest of the SMT could be more analytical. What they laid out for me to see was a historical and interpersonal context into which I had erupted as if from another star system. People liked what I said but needed time to adjust and time to check if I was to be trusted. They also wanted to feel invited to join in but free to decline. (Not everyone was a passionate devotee of Freire!) However, they wanted me to articulate values, set a direction and pace and draw parameters. This was, in their view, the whole purpose of a head. Separate from this was my 'style' which could give the impression of developments happening at breakneck pace even when that perception came only from the speed and volume at which I talked when I was excited!

Most personally significant, in the light of my already articulated values, was the suggestion that not every colleague had to be as openly involved, committed, assertive and energetic as I seemed to want them to be – my wish said more about me than about them. Perhaps some people seemed pedestrian to me merely because they were different from me. I had to learn to cope with them, just as they had to learn to cope with me. I had to go on being 'me' – in my own style because that was part of my psyche and self – but remember how I must seem to the people whom I met at an after-school meeting: 'Wham – bullet-fire – smack – before they've even got into gear!'

The upshot of this highly personal action research was a shared sense that personal relationships based on values and principles (at the very least on mutual respect) were the fillers and combining agents to mend the 'cracks' – between leadership and management; between philosophy and practice; between public persona and personal experience. If we could work together, we could exploit the only 'gap' that ought to remain – between the vision and current reality. It is this gap, says Peter Senge, that truly creative people use to generate energy for change. Principled people, articulating their principles and trying to focus together on the same goal, create a kind of synergy ('creative co-operation' as Stephen Covey, 1992, calls it). The research process itself proved this, and proved that a focus on the development of relationships need not create a cosy culture of complacency or 'group think'. I told the staff that sometimes I had a moral obligation to do things that they wouldn't like (especially in relation to individual colleagues). Focusing on relationships, with a shared sense of values, can build a climate of trust and support in which unpalatable truths can be told without a sense of antagonism and new ideas can be confidently tried out.

Further proof came 18 months after the action research had begun. The SMT invited an external research team to analyse their role – and success – in the relatively new process of development planning. Middle managers were invited to contribute to this appraisal. They said they felt on the sidelines of the process and wanted to be at the heart of it. In discussion with them afterwards, the process was altered and the development planning team – the same people who had wanted merely to put 'my' (i.e. 'the head's') ideas into practice two years before – became the forum in which whole-school priorities were discussed and decided. Both the individuals and the team had grown.

In my last few days of that first headship, the same county personnel adviser who had wondered whether I was going to be a weak or a strong head phoned me to wish me luck. 'Don't forget,' he said. 'The second headship is exactly the same as the first – you can't take the first one with you and begin in a new school by building on the old one. Give yourself four years to judge how you're doing.'

In the significant gap between leaving the one school and joining the next, I reminded myself that, as John Bazalgette (1996) says, 'effective Heads must be able to handle the fact that they are – willy-nilly – the conscious and unconscious focus of all relationships in the school'. I still anticipated the intellectual excitement of analysing a 'new' organisation; I confidently remembered my theoretical background in managerial and leadership issues; I was conscious of my previous experience and how it should help, practically, in dealing with problems or preventing issues from becoming problems.

And how did it begin? In the first weeks of the new term we, as a whole staff, are discussing our fundamental, personal, values and how they link with educational ones. This could be a very creative place . . .

REFERENCES

Bazalgette, J. (1996) Greater than a mere sum of skills, *The Times Educational Supplement*, 31 May.

Brighouse, T. (1991) *What Makes a Good School?* Stafford, Network Educational Press.

Covey, S.R. (1992) *The Seven Habits of Highly Effective People*, London, Simon & Schuster.

Descartes, R. (1988 edition) *Selected Philosophical Writings* (Translated by Cottingham, J. *et al.*), Cambridge, Cambridge University Press.

Freire, P. (1996 edition) *Pedagogy of the Oppressed*, Harmondsworth, Penguin.

Gutierrez, G. (1973) *A Theology of Liberation – History, Politics and Salvation*, New York, Orbis Books.

Herzberg, F. (1966) The motivation-hygiene theory. In Pugh, D.S., ed., (1990) *Organisation Theory*, Harmondsworth, Penguin.

Hughes, M. (1985) Leadership in professionally staffed organisations. In Glatter, R. *et al.*, eds, (1988) *Understanding School Management*, Milton Keynes, Open University Press.

Lather, P. (1986) Research as praxis, *Harvard Educational Review*, Vol. 56, no. 3.

Martin, J.N.T. (1993 edition) Play, reality and creativity. In Henry, J., ed., *Creative Management*, London, Sage (in association with the Open University).

Peters, T. (1992) *Liberation Management – Necessary Disorganisation for the Nanosecond Nineties*, London, Macmillan.

Senge, P.M. (1992) *The Fifth Discipline – The Art and Practice of the Learning Organisation*, London, Random House.

Warnock, M. (1970) *Existentialism*, Oxford, Oxford University Press.

Woodhead, C. (1995) *Chief Inspector's Annual Report for 1993/1994*, London, OFSTED.

11

Modelling Development Alternatives

DAVID GOWER

THE LOGISTICS OF SCHOOL GROWTH

I have been a secondary headteacher for the past nine years. Our school is genuinely comprehensive, serving a well established residential area in the north west where the distribution of pupils, both socially and academically, is broadly representative of the population as a whole. However, we are in competition with other schools in the city and admit a disproportionately large number of pupils whose abilities are less than average. Moreover, our school has three times the national percentage of students with special educational needs. Nevertheless, despite a significantly below-average intake, we expect to achieve national average examination results.

Mine is not a large school but it is a good place in which to work. The comprehensive principle is alive and well, while human values are paramount. This attracted me there in the first place and remains a strong influence on policy and practice. We take genuine pride in the attainments of all students, from those achieving four grade As at A-level to those for whom a single G grade at GCSE represents the summit of intellectual achievement. Moreover, care and concern extend beyond the narrowly academic to meeting the wider needs of the individual.

In the years following my appointment our Year 7 intake began to rise appreciably. Fewer local pupils attended rival schools and market research amongst parents suggested an increasing reputation as a warm-hearted, caring community where most students made good learning progress. LEA forecasts were in line with this upsurge in popularity.

The prospect of such growth was exciting – it meant success! Local management had just been introduced and, to a hard-up school, the additional revenue that extra pupils would bring was more than welcome. Then came second thoughts. As I pondered how to deal with school growth and discussed the questions arising with the senior management team, the situation appeared more complicated than I had at first supposed.

Four issues, in particular, would need to be studied in order to accommodate an expanding roll:

- The LMS formula income.
- The curriculum plan and option structure.
- Teaching group sizes and staffing requirements.
- Teaching accommodation (both specialist and non-specialist).

Some of these issues were complex enough in themselves but they were also interlinked. Take, for example, the connection between our expanding school roll and the consequent staffing requirements and accommodation needs. The relationship is not a simple one since the need for additional staff and class-rooms does not increase directly with student numbers, but changes stepwise (Knight, 1993). In our school (roll somewhat below 600 at that time) each classroom could hold 30 pupils. Some 600 students would therefore require at least 20 teachers and 20 rooms. Yet 601 students would require a minimum of 21 teachers and 21 teaching spaces. The extra pupil, though generating less than 0.2% extra income, would push up associated costs by around 5%. However, the costs of a further 29 pupils would be marginal, since neither extra staff nor accommodation would be needed.

In reality the situation would be further complicated by issues such as the subject specialisms of the staff concerned, the curriculum the extra pupils would study and the need to provide staff with differing numbers of free periods, depend-ing on their out-of-class responsibilities. I began to see that an increasing roll could prove difficult to manage. At various stages, the increases in income generated by additional pupils might not exactly match corresponding expenditure require-ments, particularly those associated with teachers and teaching accommodation. Given generous cash reserves this might not matter, but ours were negligible. The annual school budget was very tight, giving little scope for manoeuvre.

We could see that curriculum issues complicated matters still further. The need for specialist subject teachers (e.g. science) and teaching spaces (e.g. laboratories) would also fluctuate. They depend not only on student numbers but also on the courses taken. Thus National Curriculum regulations, pupils' subject choices at Key Stage 4 and sixth-form staying-on rates would determine teacher require-ments. So might other influences on teaching group sizes, such as workshop safety considerations. Management intervention could include encouraging staff to de-velop new areas of expertise and building or converting teaching accommodation. However, these would be long-term developments. When they came to fruition it would be too late to find that we had made the wrong decisions.

I could see that what the school needed was a forecasting tool; some means of examining the likely consequences of decisions taken on the situation some two to five years later. However, accurate forecasting was likely to prove difficult because demands on schools constantly change. Strategies designed to cope with the problems foreseen in the early 1990s might have been ineffective or worse when they began to take effect in the second half of the decade. There was also a further issue that, at this stage, I could only just begin to perceive. This con-cerned how the character of the school might alter, not directly by having extra pupils but through how I managed the change. Some colleagues argued that by becoming too absorbed in the processes of regulating growth I would have less time for the everyday business of the school. Others envisaged that the management processes would be too mechanistic; systems to be followed in a way that would make the school less accommodating to individuals. Thus I would have less time to give to people or the school ethos would change for the worse.

IN SEARCH OF THE MEANS FOR PLANNING

In the early 1990s I embarked on an education-based MBA. Supposedly a two-year, part-time course, it showed every sign of requiring at least twice that time if it were ever to be completed! However, I persisted because I found it interesting and much of the content proved relevant to the work I was doing at school. Moreover, some 25% of the assessment was based on a research project and I realised that this would provide both the opportunity and the necessary incentive to investigate the issues then confronting my school in a rather more formal and detailed way than I would have done otherwise. I began with a search for an appropriate planning/forecasting method.

Our school was already familiar with development planning as a systematic means of dealing with target-setting and review. In the situation of our growing roll, that technique was relevant, for example, to co-ordinating curriculum plans, teacher recruitment and building projects so that the various aspects would occur at appropriate times. Its limitation, for my new purposes, was that development planning is not a modelling tool. For example, it does not provide a means of calculating the degree to which changes in one variable (like 'school roll') produce changes in another (such as 'teacher requirements'). It cannot evaluate plans to see which maximise educational advantage and minimise expense. It does not facilitate scenario construction, as educational and political parameters change. Such processes require a decision-making/forecasting tool whereas development planning is a scheduling device, designed for action-orientated situations.

My IT skills had developed considerably as a result of local management. In particular I had devised spreadsheets to analyse staffing costs, curriculum plans and to monitor the school budget. However, the number and complexity of the variables in my new problem seemed far beyond any spreadsheet, so I looked to see what solutions were available commercially, but there was no readily available commercial package for my problem.

A search of the research literature was similarly fruitless. There was little contemporary educational research in the UK involving modelling and none that had a school perspective. The dearth of material extended to the USA with the exception of Weissman (1994). However, her work concerned a relatively simple problem with only two variables that she had analysed by using a spreadsheet. It was little help to me in suggesting how to model the complex, multivariate issues facing my school. Perhaps not unsurprisingly, the business literature proved more helpful than did anything I had read in a specifically educational context.

For heads and governors to assume responsibility for their school planning was a consequence that was anticipated by the government consultants who had played a major role in devising LMS (Coopers and Lybrand, 1998). Such multivariate situations are commonplace in the commercial world. For instance, the issues surrounding the launch of a new product are just as complex and inter-related as any I had recognised at school in trying to plan our future. Johnson and Scholes (1989) detail seven issues: 'products', 'research and development', 'manufacturing', 'manpower', 'customers', 'finances' and 'marketing mix'. Their figure, reproduced here as Figure 11.1, sets these out in such a

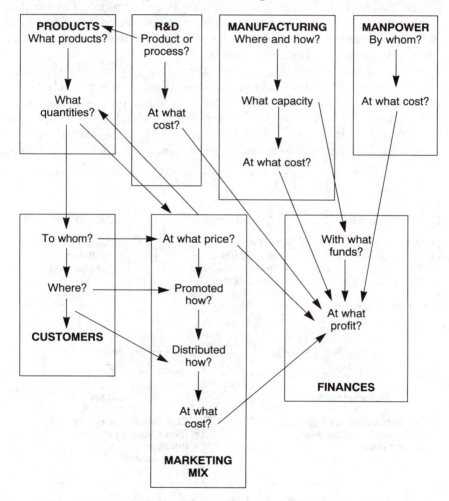

Figure 11.1 Linkages among key business activities in a product launch
Source: Johnson and Scholes, 1989

way as to show key relationships among them. I could envisage a similar diagram using school planning variables such as 'roll' and 'curriculum plan' (see Figure 11.2). I also began to wonder whether the processes used to analyse and manage the business situation might not be applicable to the school one.

In the commercial world the process of setting the broad goals and policies of a business is called 'strategic planning'. A whole literature exists about how to do this and why it is important when a firm is undergoing structural change. A well established argument is that an organisation cannot use its resources efficiently unless its individual activities are closely co-ordinated and in tune with its overall goals. All must be dedicated to the same market strategy, a term used for the pattern that – in successful firms – permeates the whole enterprise, co-ordinating business activities and use of resources with chosen market niches. The outcome is market-place distinctiveness and consequent competitive advantage. Porter (1985) offers considerable evidence for this thesis and for the corollary that lack of strategy is a recipe for business mediocrity.

Porter's argument for the importance of organisational strategy seemed to me to be as relevant to schools as to businesses. The most effective schools are those in which individuals work together for a common purpose. Moreover, I could see the need for this purpose to be tailored to each school's own, particular situation. Thus the picture began to fit together. My school should establish a suitable business strategy to provide a touchstone against which to evaluate

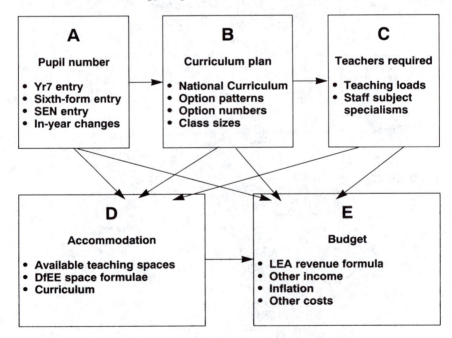

Figure 11.2 Linkages among five key factors in strategic school planning
Source: Johnson and Scholes (1989), *Exploring Corporate Strategy*, Prentice-Hall.

developments as numbers increased. It would also serve to differentiate us from others in a way that would attract pupils.

I could see that a successful strategy for my school would involve careful curriculum planning while setting limits on the school roll in ways that would optimise income, staffing and accommodation use. To determine this, I needed some means of modelling the interaction among those variables. Businesses use bespoke computer models in such situations. Each proposed strategy is tested by assigning appropriate values to the variables and examining the range of possible outcomes. This enables a range of scenarios to be tried until one is found that is robust in a range of likely future operating conditions.

A computer model built on the lines described is the basis of a decision support system (DSS), a term with which I was to become very familiar. Although relative newcomers to IT-based management, DSSs are widely regarded in business as tools for investigating problems by carrying out 'What if?' analyses. They do not automate the actual decision-making process but support personal judgement by providing users with the means to investigate complex situations at will. Outside education their use is widespread: I found examples ranging from the organisation of public libraries to the location of an airport.

As the project advanced, I envisaged a DSS as the means of modelling my school's changing circumstances. However, not all my colleagues were so enthusiastic. Many staff and some governors were suspicious of the consequences of introducing business management techniques into a school. They contended that schools and businesses are essentially chalk and cheese; that management mechanisms designed for profit-orientated institutions inevitably subvert the educational process. This was a challenge to the whole concept of my project.

Such arguments are fairly commonplace in education literature. Simkins (1984) set out the case for regarding school and business management techniques as incompatible. It boils down to the notion that firms are rational and objective institutions, but education is people centred and the appropriate management style is subjective. Using 'rational' techniques in 'people-centred' organisations does violence to them. Simkins (*ibid.*) makes these points using three examples:

• How businesses and schools define their objectives.
• The differing relationships between ends and means.
• Implications of the rational business model for professional autonomy.

By examining the three examples, I came to understand and then to reject the case against using business management techniques in a school.

School objectives include spiritual, mental, moral, cultural and physical dimensions. Reliable indicators of performance for all these are lacking and, despite extensive work in the field of school effectiveness, we know that what makes a good school remains a matter of debate. Businesses, however, set targets in relation to measurable issues such as profitability and market share. Moreover, whereas 'the unintended consequence of grouping large numbers of children together' has social and moral consequences for which schools are held to account (Shipman, 1990, p. 53), similar effects of business activities are widely considered to be merely collateral (Kotler and Armstrong, 1991). No super-market, for example, takes much account of the relations between customers whereas schools are very mindful of the interactions between their pupils.

The idea that business issues are much more clear-cut than educational ones also arises in a comparison of ends and means. Business management is about optimising resource use (means) to achieve company goals (ends). The connections may be direct (for instance, between machine hours and production) or more tenuous (e.g. between advertising and sales) but it is possible to model the linkages mathematically (in a DSS, for example). In schools, however, ends and means are often much less clearly related – e.g. teacher expertise (resource input) and pupils' examination scores (output). In this case no formula exists for estimating how much the latter might be improved by investing in the former, for example through INSET. Such situations are sometimes referred to as 'loosely coupled'. Loose coupling is a key factor in the debate about performance related pay (PRP) for teachers, where immense difficulty is encountered in attributing specific pupils' successes to particular staff. PRP could well be an example of a business management technique that will not work in schools because the context is too different.

Simkins' third issue concerns the workforces. Commercial management needs to be tightly structured in order to ensure the delivery of its objectives. Thus each employee has comparatively little freedom of action. Professionals, on the other hand, cling to a strong sense of the importance of their individual freedom of action. Thus conflict is almost inevitable if school management becomes tightly structured – when, for example, a National Curriculum is imposed. Whereas Simkins calls business organisation 'rational', he urges that a political model would best describe how schools really function. This acknowledges the disparate objectives of the professionals who make up the school community and accepts that goal setting and resource allocation are not objective processes but involve a power struggle among individuals and interest groups.

As I thought about these issues, and read more widely, I realised that the idea that firms are entirely rational, but education is completely people centred, does not hold water. No real business succeeds by pursuing its commercial goals without reference to the needs of its workforce; no school or college will attract students by making their needs entirely subservient to those of the staff. Practical managers take account of both sorts of issues. What matters is that the kind of management tools chosen are those appropriate to the organisation concerned. PRP, for example, works well in sales environments where income can be attributed to particular individuals but is not used in the chemical industry where batch processing is a team responsibility. It seemed to me that 'rational' and 'political' are two ends of a continuum with the culture of most organisations falling somewhere between.

I have illustrated this diagrammatically (see Figure 11.3) using Simkins' three examples of school/business differences. Instead of a clear distinction, each case is better represented by a continuum. In general, the characteristics of commercial firms tend to the left and those of schools to the right, but a spread across both types of organisation probably exists, perhaps with other public sector institutions falling between. I thought that a theatre or church, for example, might consider the association between members of the audience/congregation to be far more important than the casual contact between the customers in a supermarket but less significant than the relationships between pupils in school. Similarly, the goals of a famine relief charity are less clear-cut than those of a cement works but more clearly defined than the long-term aims of a school.

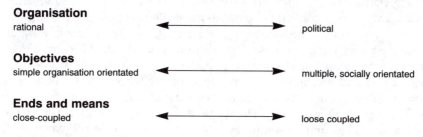

Organisation
rational ⟷ political

Objectives
simple organisation orientated ⟷ multiple, socially orientated

Ends and means
close-coupled ⟷ loose coupled

Figure 11.3   Schools and businesses: three dimensions of difference

Thus I became convinced that the differences between schools and business organisation are a matter of degree. Thus they do not provide sufficient cause for headteachers to reject rational management methods outright. However, any particular technique might not be appropriate across the whole organisational spectrum. Like PRP, some might be inappropriate to schools or need to be tailored specifically to educational circumstances. One needs to adapt the management tool to the situation in which it is to be used.

REDEFINING THE INVESTIGATION

Although I had rejected the case that devising and using a DSS would inevitably corrupt the school ethos, it remained possible that this would happen. The issue had to become part of the project. It was no longer enough to construct and use a DSS; I felt the need to investigate the impact of this process on the school. For example, would the DSS help the school to develop without corrupting its people centredness? Might a DSS make governors too remote from decision-taking? Could the time I devoted, and the resources required for its construction, be better spent?

The original question, with which I had begun the project, also remained: to investigate how best to manage an increasing school roll. I thought it would be possible (though I was not sure how) to construct a decision support system that

- represented the interaction between pupil numbers and other key, quantifiable managerial issues;

- provided a means of forecasting the outcomes of continuous, predictable change, such as transitions of pupils from one year group to the next or the outcomes of current spending decisions; and
- enabled scenarios to be constructed which would indicate the effects of discontinuous change, e.g. LEA budget cuts, sharp changes in school roll.

The notion that a suitable DSS could be constructed seemed quite easy to test, at least in principle, so long as I could find someone with the necessary IT skills or acquire them myself. My DSS could then be checked to see that the required factors associated with the school roll were incorporated, whether the numerical inter-relationships were correct and if appropriate allowances had been made for continuity/discontinuity in the underlying variables. These were essentially logical issues, calling for technical expertise. The other questions that had become part of the investigation stood out in contrast as matters of value. I now had both to construct a DSS and somehow assess its impact on the school ethos. The project had grown alarmingly in scope and various constraints had to be dealt with.

The first constraint was time. There was a degree of synergy between my roles as headteacher and postgraduate student, but most of the work took place out of school during evenings, weekends and 'holidays'. Although, nominally, only 25% of the two-year, part-time MBA is allocated to a research-based dissertation, the actual period required for this particular project was substantially greater. I thought the time spent was justified by the potential utility of the DSS to the school but I was mindful of my critics; there are always people on the staff who think the head has his priorities wrong.

Time was a serious constraint in completing the project within the deadline set by the university. It was clearly impossible to complete and test the DSS, investigate a range of alternative scenarios, devise a school business strategy and investigate the potential impact of such business management procedures on the school. I had to compromise by completing it only sufficiently to demonstrate its potential, but not in every detail.

A second constraint was the ethical issue of asking other people at school to contribute towards the research. The head's authority to direct people is for the express purpose of running the school. I thought it would be unethical to ask staff or pupils to participate directly in the research, for example by attending a meeting or by filling in questionnaire, because some might have found such a request difficult to refuse. Hence I confined my investigations to governors with whom no such authority relationships existed.

The third constraint concerned resources and expertise in IT. DSS construction usually involves collaboration between a manager and an IT specialist. But I had to fulfil both roles, neither time nor funding eventually permitting otherwise. Bespoke decision support software is confined to large budget situations. I looked for computer solutions that would be effective but not necessarily elegant, though my IT skills increased substantially during the project! I was fortunate that Version 5 of Microsoft's 'Excel' spreadsheet software was published shortly before I began this part of the project. Excel 5 was sufficiently sophisticated to meet my IT needs in constructing the DSS.

Limited by the time and resources available, the investigation became a case study based in my school. Investigating the feasibility of the DSS involved extensive IT analysis and the checking of the DSS by experts. This, as far as possible, was an objective process. However, where governors' opinions were sought, my status as researcher could not be that of a detached, scientific observer. Head and governors work closely together at my school, and the former role could not be put aside when it became inconvenient! I designed that part of the project around the classic role of participant observer, taking the appropriate investigatory techniques from the literature on action research.

The DSS was finished in October 1995, governors' opinions were solicited in November and the project was completed in December.

CONSTRUCTING THE DSS

Full details of how I put the DSS together appear in Gower (1996) together with information about how it was checked. There is space here only to mention a few key features. The overall DSS structure is set out in Figure 11.2, where separate boxes represent the school management areas. Excel 5 software enabled me to overcome the problem of having too many variables to represent on one spreadsheet. I set up each one in a separate workbook (i.e. a group of related spreadsheets). Each workbook has the capacity of a large spreadsheet but the individual leaves are readily accessible and can be configured and presented separately.

In Figure 11.2 the bullets indicate specific information required for construction. In addition, data to be transferred among sheets are shown by the network of arrows. I designed each workbook so that it could be stored on a standard floppy disk, making the whole DSS readily portable. Each workbook opened with one or more input sheets for user forecasts, so that scenario construction would require only systematic alteration of the user-defined values and observation of related outputs.

A similarity of layout between related sheets made it easy to transfer information during construction, whilst a common style at the head of each one reinforced the idea that all are part of the same DSS. Since the number of leaves per book is unimportant, I was able to devise layouts that made information easy to interpret without bothering too much about space.

During and after construction of the DSS I talked to senior staff about the issues it raised. We used the parts that I had completed as soon as they became available to inform school planning questions about staffing, curriculum and accommodation that occurred during the year in question. From these discussions I formulated nine management questions. These summed up our expectations: if the DSS helped to answer them, it was potentially a useful tool; if not it was a waste of time. Table 11.1 lists these questions and alongside each one is a response, made with the aid of the DSS.

Table 11.1   Key questions for modelling the school's future: DSS outcomes

1. *General*

a) Can the interaction between the variables that affect revenue (pupil numbers, LEA formula) and those affecting costs (curriculum plan, teacher requirements and accommodation requirements) be modelled in a form that is readily accessible and understandable?

Yes. Such modelling is possible using Excel. However, the DSS required 50 spreadsheets and appears quite complicated. The accessibility of the information to potential users, such as school governors, requires investigation

b) Can the model be used to make predictions about future development in a way that enables alternative scenarios to be examined?

The use of separate input sheets allows data to be mended readily and the interconnected workbooks should readily permit scenario generation

2. *School roll*   If the intake forecasts are projected over, say, five years, how many students can be expected in each year group?

Sheet A4 gives this information

3. *Revenue*

a) What income, according to the LMS formula, will be available each year for, say, the next five?

Sheets E5 and E6 give this information

b) What are the probable effects of LEA reductions/changes in formula funding?

These effects are input through E1 and are included in the projections on E5 and E6

c) What difference would grant-maintained status make?

No attempt was made to compute this. It would require an extra sheet for book E

4. *Curriculum*   How many classes in each subject in each year group will be required, bearing in mind

Numbers of classes per subject for each year group are forecast in curriculum sheets B7–B11

a) student options in KS4 (Key Stage 3) and in the sixth form;

The effects of probable option choice patterns are allowed for in B7–B11

b) changing curriculum patterns, particularly at KS4 post-Dearing; and

Input sheets B3–B5 allow for planned changes in the curriculum structure

c) numbers of students in teaching groups in various subjects?

Input sheets B3–B5 allow the user to specify class maxima and minima by curriculum area

5. *Teachers*   How many teachers of each subject will be required in the future as the roll grows and the curriculum changes?

Sheet C7 provides this information for each curriculum area, given a target contact ratio that is set by the user via input sheet C1

6. *Accommodation*

a) How many students can the school accommodate at present?

The existing capacity (808 pupils) is calculated by sheet D5 using standard DFE formulae

b) Could the buildings readily be adapted/extended?

Adaptation seems the best strategy, given the area surpluses indicated on sheet D11

c) What accommodation will be required in the future, by way of classrooms and specialist facilities such as laboratories and workshops?

D13/14 show that graphically. Moreover, the sheets would be automatically updated following any change in curriculum structure (book B)

7. *Budget* If spending patterns continue unchanged, what are the forecast outcomes for the next five years of the difference between income and expenditure?

This information is not currently available because book E is unfinished. Following its completion a graph showing both projected income and projected expenditure on the same axes could be provided

8. *Costs*
a) How are costs influenced by factors such as curriculum plan, class sizes, teacher contact time and accommodation use?

Analysis of costs is beyond the scope of the DSS until book E is completed. Such a detailed analysis might require an extra workbook

b) As the school grows, what will happen to unit costs?

9. *Management issues*
a) Is there an optimum size for the school that maximises educational considerations and minimises costs?

'Educational considerations' are for the user to define. The DSS shows maximum school capacity if additional space was adapted for teaching use

b) Would it be feasible, rather than to increase the numbers of teachers in line with growth in pupils numbers, to pursue an alternative such as employing more classroom assistants, more support staff or utilizing more IT equipment?

Such a question requires scenario analysis, but should be within the scope of the DSS once book E is completed together with an analysis of unit costs

The precise responses obtained from the DSS would depend on the input data which, in turn, would depend on the judgement of the user. However, it was evident to colleagues that the DSS could answer the management questions posed, though with certain exceptions. For example, the incomplete budget analysis (book E) was a shortcoming resulting from the restricted time available for the study. Nevertheless, within the limitations of the project, the DSS was conspicuously successful.

IMPACT ON SCHOOL ETHOS

The construction of the DSS had become only a part of my project. I saw its potential impact on the school ethos as, in many ways, a more significant issue. It was also much harder to investigate because of the subjective nature of the questions concerned. I turned, at this stage, to the techniques of action research, a well documented process for formalising a case study. Typically a group of teachers plan together and monitor their results with a view to improving their professional practice. Success is assessed subjectively in terms, for example, of pupil reaction. Thus action research is collaborative and self-evaluated, with the research problem at the focus.

My first degree is in chemistry, and I had subsequently completed two research degrees utilising the classic social science research paradigm, characterised by control of variables, careful sampling and inferential statistics. Thus I expected any researcher to be objective and to stand outside the phenomena he or she was investigating. When I read Marris and Rein's (1967) contention that 'even the term "Action Research" is an oxymoron' I chuckled in response. However, I could see that the action research process could provide precise, useful information, albeit about a specific situation as opposed to generalised scientific knowledge.

Within these limitations, action research appeared to have its own rigour. Techniques exist to compensate for its potential weaknesses, in particular the issues of reliability and validity. Reliability is improved by 'triangulation' – i.e. corroboration among three or more different sets of data. I could understand this process as analogous to other evidence-based situations, such as teacher appraisal, where more than one witness's view will usually be sought and the appraiser is a participant observer. The literature attaches particular importance to triangulation, both between kinds of evidence (e.g. written reports, interviews, participant observation) and sources (e.g. governors with business associations, parent governors, teacher governors).

The issue of the validity of action research was more difficult. Does the evidence really mean what it appears to mean? It is hard for practitioners to stand back from the action and describe events clearly: they are biased towards its success. Moreover, collaboration does not encourage cool objectivity. If the researcher is well known to colleagues he or she may be inclined to give the responses that they think he or she wants and wrong conclusions will be inevitable. Such situations would seem more likely when a team that includes the researcher has invested itself heavily in the outcome of a piece of research. Clearly these conditions obtained at school, where governors actively supported me, for example by allowing a month's study leave and devoting meeting time to discussing the DSS and its outcomes.

Governors participated in the project in a number of ways:

- A seminar for all governors, where I introduced the DSS and then acted as participant observer while two governors took notes.
- Participant observation of a subsequent resources subcommittee meeting and a curriculum subcommittee meeting when the sections of the DSS dealing with accommodation/budgeting and curriculum/timetable were respectively explained and discussed.
- Structured, individual interviews with three governors (a business person, a teacher and a parent). I thought tape recording would be too intrusive. Instead I verified what had been said by employing a range of interview techniques, such as reflection, in-filling, playing devil's advocate, etc. Because I was well known to the interviewees, it was easy to sustain a comfortable atmosphere, but the colleague governor may have been less inclined to say anything disparaging about the research.

From my reading it was apparent that concern about the applicability of business techniques to schools centred around their potential impact on the school ethos. This was evident, too, in my informal conversations with colleagues. Our school aims and values are set out in publications such as the prospectus and the policy handbook. I compared these with reports of governors' and school management meetings, regarding the views expressed and actions recommended there as indicators of people's implicit values. Three areas stood out. They were prominent in the school literature and illustrated aspects of the ethos that, according to the literature search, would be most vulnerable to damage through the introduction of business methodologies. As such, I thought they would be effective barometers of change. They were

- consultation and openness
- concern for staff welfare
- the equal value of all students within the school community.

The governors held a special meeting to examine the DSS. In addition, I interviewed three governors separately to provide feedback on my impressions from the seminar. The composition of the final trio was largely determined by who was available, but included at least one representative from each seminar group and fortuitously comprised a parent, a teacher and a co-opted governor. However, all were male and in that respect unrepresentative of the governing body, which was gender balanced. As far as possible the interviews followed the normal pattern of headteacher/governor meetings – i.e. two colleagues getting together to discuss matters of mutual concern, although the conversation was carefully structured. I gave each interviewee every opportunity to put forward their views and develop ideas, whilst checking progress:

> What you seem to be saying is . . .
> Can you tell me if what I've written down here is correct . . .? etc.

Finally I discussed the main points noted with the interviewee in a way that made it easy for them to suggest changes. Later they were given a copy of the printed report of the discussion and, again, asked to suggest alterations.

Although individuals expressed their views in different ways, the points they made were similar. There were no factions. Those who attended the seminar may have been self-selecting, but their unanimity of outlook extended to the subcommittees, to conversations with others who missed the seminar and to the interviews. Interviewees resoundingly rejected the idea that commitment to the research or loyalty to the researcher might have influenced what they said.

Governors' opinions were the more credible for being balanced and reflective. For example:

> It provides information that can have advantages and disadvantages.
> [Avoid] over-reliance on a computer-based system and its forecasts.

Overwhelmingly they supported the DSS as a step forward from existing planning procedures because 'It centralises planning and information, providing an early-warning system of problems and opportunities'. The modelling capabilities were widely appreciated:

The model takes the information we already use together a big step forward, allowing 'what-if?' questions.

If you decide to change one variable it can show consequences or benefits.

Some governors went further, basing their comments on business notions of strategic planning. They saw the utility of the model as a tool in devising a strategy: 'Ability to respond to events earlier and plan better [are an important advantage]. It will make the school more proactive and give us an edge in attracting pupils.' This was not simply adoption of the researcher's terminology. The group concerned went on to provide two examples of their own, relating to governors' discussions in the past few months but not mentioned at the seminar:

Useful as a 'what-if'? to see what could happen if we become a technology school.

Changing the teaching/non-teaching balance: . . . Feed in the criteria and see what comes out.

Governors clearly did not stand in awe of the DSS. Many had IT experience and laughingly cautioned against reliance on computer forecasts. They understood the dangers of becoming wedded to a single scenario but would have considered it naive to adopt such a position. There was a strong consensus among governors that employing the DSS as a tool would enhance the quality of decision-making. However, they were clear that they would not allow the model in any sense to control them. The notion of a decision support system as opposed to a decision-taking system was also well appreciated:

[It needs to be] part of an open system involving people.

The model makes sense so long as you're in the driving seat, but don't let the model take over.

The reasons for reluctance to be sidelined by an expert system were also made clear:

Don't over-rely on tools: people don't always understand the assumptions on which they're based or the strengths and weaknesses of the inherent assumptions.

We need to understand the how and the why – not just to understand the solution.

Governors themselves introduced the issue of not concentrating power in the hands of an in-group:

If not used properly, and only one person uses it, knowledge brings power.

If people take part it produces an open planning system.

Governors were clear both in their understanding of the existing school ethos and their determination that the DSS should not undermine it:

The model must not be a hard-nosed management tool leading to decisions against the school ethos.

Don't shift the focus to the measurable. The model is a pure numbers game and there's a lot more to the school.

Beware not to argue 'X must go because it's not cost-effective' when X is the whole point of the school.

However, governors were equally clear that the DSS had a proper place: 'It doesn't hurt to be hard-edged and technical as a separate management tool.' The importance of not excluding people was again conspicuous: 'It's only part of a system involving people. The tool is neutral, the use you make of it is critical.' One final comment sums it up: 'It's the use that's made of it that matters. It could improve things, but not necessarily. If misused, it were better it had not existed.'

Thus governors specifically stated that they saw the DSS as a self-improvement tool that could be used to enhance achievement of the school aims and mission. Moreover there was no indication that any of the three ethos barometers would suffer in the process while the notion that business methodologies are inherently inimical to schools was implicitly rejected in favour of the argument 'it depends how you use them'.

CONCLUSIONS

My study began with a broad vision, arising from the circumstances of one particular high school. My original aim was to computer model changes in pupil numbers, to forecast their effects on key management variables and thereby to deduce optimum resource patterns for school development. Finally, by systematically altering the future values of variables, I planned to generate a range of possible scenarios that could assist governors in strategy formulation. The importance of keeping development firmly focused on the school mission was acknowledged from the outset. I readily conceded that modelling was a management tool that should be abandoned immediately if it began to subvert the school's educational aims.

The scope of the project was necessarily limited compared with the original vision. Time and resources restricted what could be achieved. Even now, the DSS remains incomplete. Thus no scenarios have been generated nor has any strategic plan been tested. However, each of the books of spreadsheets for analysing staffing, accommodation, etc., is in use in an updated version and the insights it has given into the whole picture of strategic development have remained useful. Thus, limited though the findings were, the notions with which I began the project received much support. It appears that the original aims were worth pursuing. It proved possible to construct a DSS which could represent the interaction of the variables envisaged in a manner that governors could understand. The model appears to provide a means of forecasting the outcomes of continuous, predictable change and there seems to be no reason why, by changing input values, a range of alternative scenarios could not be constructed once the DSS is completed.

My governors argued that the DSS could be operated in a way that would enable the whole governing body to participate effectively in decision-making.

They believed that it could enhance achievement of the school's aims and give a sharper, better defined mission. With regard to the impact of business methodologies on the school ethos, they could see no reason why key people-centred aspects of the school ethos should be disrupted: it would depend on how the DSS was used.

Thus I concluded that the time on the project had been well spent. However, I would like to reiterate a cautionary note from a study by Thomas and Bullock (1994). Their three-year investigation into the impact of LMS found that not everyone was convinced that children's learning had improved. It seems to me that it is learning – in its broadest sense – that must be the touchstone. If the DSS – or any management tool – can help to produce the right information to make the right decisions to create the sort of school in which children thrive and the school community believes, only then it is a worthwhile tool.

One of my governors put it this way: 'Beware the OFSTED culture, valuing only the measurable. However, it doesn't hurt to be hard-edged and technical as a separate management tool.'

REFERENCES

Coopers and Lybrand (1998) *Local Management of Schools*, London, HMSO.

Gower, D. (1996) Modelling developmental alternatives, MBA dissertation, University of Keele.

Houlden, B. (1990) *Understanding Company Strategy*, Oxford, Blackwell.

Johnson, J. and Scholes, K. (1989) *Exploring Corporate Strategy*, London, Prentice-Hall.

Knight, B. (1993) Of inputs and outputs, *The Times Educational Supplement*, 1 October.

Kotler, P. and Armstrong, G. (1991) *Principles of Marketing*, Englewood Cliffs, NJ, Prentice-Hall.

Marris, P. and Rein, M. (1967) Dilemmas of social reform: poverty and community action in the United States. In Bell, *et al.*, eds, *Conducting Small-Scale Investigations in Educational Management*, London, PCP.

Porter, M. (1985) *Competitive Advantage: Creating and Sustaining Superior Performance*, New York, Free Press.

Shipman, M. (1990) *In Search of Learning*, Oxford, Blackwell.

Simkins, T. (1984) Budgeting as a political and organisational process in educational institutions. In Levacic, R., ed., (1989) *Financial Management in Schools*, Milton Keynes, Open University Press.

SIMS (1995) *Managing Secondary Schools*, London, Self-published leaflet.

Thody, A. (1991) Strategic planning and school management, *School Organization*, Vol. 2, no. 1.

Thomas, H. and Bullock, A. (1994) In search of quality time, *The Times Educational Supplement*, 20 May.

Weissman, J. (1994) Enrolment projections: combining statistics and gut feelings, *Journal of Applied Research in the Community College*, Vol. 1, no. 2, pp. 143–52.

12

Sustaining the Vision: Quality Management and School Effectiveness

ERIC TOPE

INTRODUCTION

The increasing amount and pace of global change have forced a radical rethink by all of us in the field of education. Today's successful organisations have had to reflect and redesign their practices in order to survive. Schools are now in the competitive arena and even those carefully protected by local authorities will need to change substantially if they wish pupils to enrol and thus maintain survival (Bowring Carr, 1997).

The need for change in our schools is not disputed but whether the changes are intended or needed depends on careful informing and reflecting followed by sensitive planning and implementation. Change does certainly not take place simply because leaders issue instructions or raise its profile within or without an institution. Moreover change is very often more apparent than real with well intentioned development plans not coming to fruition. Comparative studies by Rutter *et al.* (1979) and Mortimore *et al.* (1988) have shown the importance of institutional culture for successful change to occur. All schools possess a culture. Whether or not it provides the conditions to overcome entrenched attitudes and improve the quality of learning is a question that needs to be explored.

Schools are now, more than ever, under real pressure to improve and for some that will provide challenge and fulfilment, others will struggle even to survive. Wherever teachers work real transformations in the culture of class-room practice and pupil learning are needed. Teacher-leaders need to create, establish and maintain cultures where traditional practices are increasingly seen as out-moded, and teachers, both new and experienced, really desire innovation and change.

Our current inspection system, whilst encouraging self-evaluation and often stimulating much-needed change, does not encourage innovative culture and modes of learning. Too often schools are highly praised for their outcomes whilst their classrooms have teachers who are the sole source of information

131

and the sole focus for learning. Enlightened practitioners are realising that increasingly their role is to facilitate individual learning by helping pupils to define problems, pose questions and seek information. Such a fundamental change of learning style will not take place without shared vision and a culture of readiness which desires change in teaching styles.

This piece of work is about reality and is written by a committed practitioner working in a south London Catholic boys' 11–16 comprehensive. I make no apologies for writing about our culture, our visions, our needs, our energy, our strengths, our criteria for success, our improvement and where we want to go next. Hopefully our experience of change and improvement over the past five years will complement the contributions of my co-writers and play a part in defining the practitioner's understanding of vision and in how to maintain the momentum of growth and sustain improvement.

Where we have used research and literature to inform and enlighten I shall endeavour to acknowledge so. Aligning theory and practice is not easy but it can be done. Our journey has considered vision and values, change and feelings, quality and improvement and the maturing of a learning community.

VISION, VALUES AND LEADERSHIP

> A Shared Vision is not an idea. It is not even an important idea such as freedom. It is, rather a force in people's hearts, a force of impressive power. It may be inspired by an idea, but once it goes further – if it is compelling enough to acquire the support of one person – then it is no longer an abstraction. It is palpable. People begin to see it as though it exists. Few, if any, forces in human affairs are as powerful as shared vision.
>
> (Senge, 1990, p. 206)

In the early 1980s the then Inner London Education Authority ran an excellent leadership course. Amongst the many areas covered was the all-important, pre-National Curriculum challenge of designing a curriculum for one's ideal school. As a starting point each team of four or five was encouraged to share their individual personal philosophies of education. What did we stand for? What was important to us? What should be the priorities for the children in our care? This sharing of thoughts, beliefs and values synthesised into the aims and objectives of our fictional school. This exercise of sharing and focusing enabled us to see clearly where we wanted to go and thus decide on what curriculum offer would enable us to get there.

In the late 1980s local education authorities started to formalise the concept of a school development plan. Heads, deputies and governors were dragged off to training days to learn of the cycle of audit, planning, implementation and evaluation. Very quickly schools were asking the why and the what of development planning and statements of mission started to appear. Mission statement training days involved staff, governors, parents and pupils to varying degrees, values were reflected on, articulated and shared. The final products no doubt exist today, examples of shared values, intentions and sometimes aspirations.

In the 1990s we have had vision. Am I wrong or is this word in danger of overexposure, overuse and going over the top? I recently addressed a large group of National Professional Qualification for Headteachers (NPQH) candidates and deliberately teased them by asking the question: 'Have you been asked to articulate your vision recently?', knowing full well that they had just been assessed. Their responses were a mix of laughter and groans, they had of course been trying to conjure up and then articulate their 'visions' (over a period of weeks) in order to be assessed as suitable for headship. How many chairs of governors open up headship interviews with a request for the candidate's vision for the school? More recently a ten-minute presentation has become *de rigueur*. A neighbouring head who is a close colleague recently informed me that she considered the concept of vision to be fashionable nonsense. When asked why, she referred me to any member of staff below her senior management team adding that anyone teaching 5C on a Friday afternoon would give a suitable short sharp answer.

What, then, do we mean by vision at our school? I tend to agree with Senge in that if it is felt rather than described something significant can happen. In our case events, survival, culture and ambition somehow combined to create a bonding, a feeling of a shared determination to demonstrate to the world that we were a school with much to commend it and with enormous potential to achieve.

Long before we thought about vision we had to survive. Our school had opened in the 1960s as a new four-form entry comprehensive for catholic boys in south London. It very quickly expanded to six forms of entry. A dwindling urban population in the late 1970s forced many closures in inner London and boys' schools were particularly vulnerable for a variety of reasons including the popular opinion that girls achieved well in girls-only schools and boys in mixed schools. Catholic schools in south London were reorganised in the mid-1980s and we became a four-form entry 11–16 comprehensive with an intake at that time of 90 boys.

Events then continued to pull us together as a school. We were new, with 50% new staff and a fresh faculty structure linked to a different pastoral system. There was a naive feeling abroad of cheerful optimism and a blind faith in the future – a group of talented teachers and pupils with a variety of personal skills who were able to face ignorance with confidence (Senge, 1990). All schools are unique and our culture was, indeed is, one of south London street wisdom, outrageous nerve, shared pride in ourselves, joy in one another's success and enormous pastoral care rooted firmly in our Catholic ethos. These qualities enabled us to survive with a tremendous amount of hard work by everyone and a great deal of fun by our chair of governors, boys and staff shared by immensely loyal parents. Stoll and Fink (1996) write of vision helping schools to define their own direction and have an attitude of being in charge of change. Vision or not, certainly having a clear sense of direction provided by an identified goal and followed by a community with a shared sense of purpose bound together by a common culture undoubtedly creates a moving as opposed to a cruising, strolling or sinking school (Stoll and Fink, 1996).

We arrived back to a new academic year in 1993 to our first OFSTED inspection. Survival had been attained with a roll back up to 600, rising popularity and in retrospect a fresh sense of direction needed. Our report was 'satisfactory', a little-used word up to then, but not glowing and we received it with a touch of annoyance and sense of 'could do better'. After sulking for the remainder of the year we returned in 1994 with a fresh mission, namely, we can, we will, do much, much better. Once more, in retrospect, we were focused by external events, grant-maintained status and the ever-popular league tables. Our new status freed us up and suited our south London entrepreneurial culture. The money was in our hands and we could put it towards our priorities and our new governors were as excited as the rest of us.

Townsend (1995) writing on the characteristics of effective schools includes clear school goals centred on learning and achievement together with a positive climate of pride. His research concludes that a school with staff, parents and pupils working together towards common goals is truly effective. The introduction of league tables gave us the perfect opportunity to be effective and improve our school. Unlike our competitors, I use that word intentionally, we were battle hardened by our fight for survival. We had blended our cultures into one, we had experienced working together in the same direction, we had experienced our success. Improving schools need to set their own criteria for success (Stoll and Fink, 1996), and we moved into a fresh direction to improve our league table scores. Whitely (1991) describes a school vision as a vivid picture of a challenging yet desirable state which is clearly seen by all as a magnificent improvement on the present. All our stakeholders and potential stakeholders viewed improved results as that desirable state, it merely needed a clear commitment from all our leaders, including myself, to produce what Caldwell and Spinks (1992) refer to as transformational leadership. Clarke (1994) points out that everyone in an organisation should be excited by the future and want to play a part to achieve success. She talks of vision and leadership harmonising the energy and resources of colleagues. In our case we have had both in abundance and the merest touch on the tiller, to set the direction, was all that has been required. Once the goals had been set and staff reflected on the direction of their energies and ways of improving our performance, we discovered a more enlightened atmosphere where we worked not harder but certainly a whole lot smarter.

QUALITY IMPROVEMENT

I have already said that aligning theory and practice is not easy; conversely, one needs to acknowledge that good theory and good practice are intertwined and in reality one does not exist without the other. Much has been written by academics, researchers and even practitioners on the quality of effective schools, management and school improvement. There is little point in producing a review of the relevant literature for the purposes of this chapter. However, it is important to acknowledge the part played by academic reflection and rigour in our work at the St Thomas the Apostle College. It is common to hear practitioners bemoaning the situation where their daily routines leave little or no time for reading and discussion and certainly individual formal learning is just a dream. As a long-time practitioner I grow more convinced that such 'luxury' activities are at the heart of real leadership with the majority of daily management routines at the periphery of what successful moving schools are all about.

In the 1980s our global, national and local environments changed; in the 1990s the bright crisp light of reality has gradually removed the mists of conservation and it is clearly there for all to see. We know that our society is now client orientated, we know that survival means improvement, we are increasingly obliged systematically to evaluate and report; over-riding these imperatives is the moral obligation to ensure that our cherished values are implemented. To release the learning potential of the members of our school community, pupils and staff, a look at some aspects of quality management proved to be a worthwhile start.

Murgatroyd and Morgan (1992) describe a quality organisation in terms of culture, commitment and communication. We were confidently aware of the first two and realised that the third demanded simplicity and clarity. The work of Myer and Zucher (1989) produced the well-known five features which described a so-called TQM (total quality management) organisation. Whilst not aiming for a particular label I did feel that for ease of empowerment and communication these features would provide us with a good working framework for improvement and they sat quite naturally on the culture we had developed, namely, shared vision, customer-driven provision, team performance, challenging goals and the systematic recording of performance and feedback.

A reminder, then, of the reasons why a change of direction or renewal of vision was needed in 1994:

1) A one-year recovery period following our OFSTED inspection and acquisition of grant-maintained status provided a 'readiness' to move on.
2) The demands for quality provision from parents and prospective parents were increasing and better informed.
3) The inspection report had identified a need for systematic use of data to monitor pupil performance and evaluate planning.

Any new initiative must be given a high profile from the start with active leadership, concentrated energy and unstinted resource support. The simple message of quality improvement was quickly conveyed through senior management meetings and a whole–staff training day. The improvement of GCSE

5 A/C passes was assumed by the staff to remain as an area for everyone to work on. An additional area put forward by several subject teachers was the raising of literacy levels in our first year (Year 7).

The first formal part of our quality process was the SMT meeting which planned our way forward. The following key decisions were taken:

1) Rename SMT as the Quality Management Team.
2) Signpost our mission with a statement of intent, 'Achieving Excellence with Care', using three key easily remembered concepts to keep the vision 'alive' for pupils, parents and staff in our daily work.
3) Use the assistant head as quality co-ordinator to inform and facilitate teams.

The subsequent heads of departments meeting reinforced our agreed features of vision, customer, teams, goals and systematic recording and linked them to the work of the previous year. All were agreed that the careful identification of key borderline pupils and individual action planning had produced an excellent seven-point improvement in our GCSE league table results moving from a 22 to 29% 5 A/C pass rate. Building on this success with a formal system for further improvement seemed to be a natural next step towards ambitious departmental team targets. All departments vigorously reflected the views of their members that a literacy programme was urgently required for Year 7 to address the low mean reading age of 9.6 across the cohort on entry.

The third stage of our launch into a new direction was the staff training day early in the autumn term. Briefly the aforementioned areas were reinforced, clarified and discussed with a high-profile input from an outside agency. Departments produced their own action plan for quality improvement in the two areas outlined and these were displayed for all to see at the end of the day.

I am aware that the reader might regard the above description as needlessly parochial and possibly simplistic. Remember I write about our school and the reality of a process of change can appear uninteresting until the concepts involved are transferred to your own unique organisation. All schools are different and it is most important for each to set its own agenda with relevant goals and culture-based processes. Significantly our results the following year leapt to 41% 5 A/C passes and 98% A/G passes, which encouraged us all to look for further improvements and vindicated our strategies. Departments have linked improved literacy levels to future GCSE performance and this has strengthened our shared commitment to raise levels across the whole curriculum. Each subject area produced its key-word list for Year 7 and a high-quality booklet containing these has been produced. Every pupil in the year carried the booklet and it was used at the start of every lesson and at home. Pupils were regularly tested on pronunciation, spelling, meaning and context use. Reading ages were monitored and recorded through the year.

At the time of writing every boy in Years 7 and 8 is experiencing a culture of basic skills improvement. He brings his key-word book to every lesson throughout the week; he expects to be tested and encouraged in all his subject areas. In addition he is challenged on a daily basis to test his knowledge of multiplication tables in English, French and RE lessons as well as in technology, mathematics and science. Very quickly this 'new' culture has become the norm for our typical student and he will relate his improvement of basic skills to our current 5 A/C pass rate of 53%. He will also acknowledge that there are gaps in his knowledge and weaknesses in his learning and he expects to be encouraged and supported to fill these gaps.

PLANNING AND CHANGE

Once a school is on the move and not merely cruising it is important to maintain momentum (Stoll and Fink, 1996). The majority of schools now produce excellent development plans with contributions from all areas of the curriculum. Why is it then that many schools are *not* on the move, not sinking but certainly strolling? Bell and Harrison (1995) point out the semantic confusion that often exists between leadership, management and administration. To maintain momentum, to enable growth and change to become part of the culture, real leadership is required from all involved. Middle and senior managers often run very efficient teams, teachers can run very efficient classrooms, bursars run excellent administrations, and yet change and growth are lacking. It is very tempting to allow complacency to reign if the level of achievement is satisfactory or better and there is general agreement among stakeholders that a reasonable level of teaching and learning is taking place. To get moving and then maintain momentum requires everyone to gain insight of the current reality (Senge, 1990).

Our use of quality management techniques for 1994–95 has been maintained through our development planning for the years following. The 1995–96 plan emphasised a look to the future to encourage a strategic view to the year 2000. Our planning to that date had become efficient because we had honed our skills of evaluating, planning and implementing over the previous six years. Complacency was knocking on our door and their was a danger of incremental drift in our planning cycles. Looking five years ahead to our ideal scenarios and then planning the necessary steps to reach these made us look at where we were strolling and perhaps losing momentum. In 1996–97 slower-moving departments were supported by the prescription of ten development areas by our planning team and the provision of a monitor for each subject area to evaluate progress throughout the year. To sustain the vision, keep on course and maintain momentum the listening leader must be sensitive to the rate of change and growth and use development planning as a vehicle to regulate their pace.

Occasionally schools need a little more than a touch on the tiller, a more fundamental change of direction is embarked on and sensitive care is required from the head and the change leaders to support other colleagues. Any planned change that starts at the top (and not all do) must recognise that the process can ignore the feelings of some staff and is over-reliant on the logic and argument of others. Plant (1987) and Clarke (1994) both point out that resistance to any change is *not* a rational process but is perfectly natural in the face of the unknown. The two areas worth reflecting on for any successful change are culture and energy. Evolutionary, persistent, steady-change cultures produce minimal resistance. A sudden announcement of a change decision by the head will produce a sudden non-reflective shock reaction. A school with high levels of excitement and energy can allow people to articulate their fears, reducing resistance and creating energy sources for successful implementation.

SCHOOL IMPROVEMENT AND TEACHING

It is most unlikely that any member of the profession would disagree with the importance of classroom practice. How many of us would seriously question our own practice? The newly qualified or struggling teacher might well be ready to listen to advice, to change his or her style, to learn from more experienced colleagues. The same would not be true of our successful colleagues with high institutional reputations that are often enhanced by less successful colleagues.

In our 1996–97 development year our culture had evolved to encourage informal discussion of teaching styles and even the occasional unofficial observation of lessons or parts of lessons were taking place between close-working colleagues. In addition to the appraisal process teachers were asking senior colleagues to watch them in action with a particular class or when teaching a particular topic. In anticipation of our next inspection I and a senior colleague trained as OFSTED inspectors and this encouraged others to invite us to evaluate their work. It was clear that we were ready for some form of classroom observation to be established, but how ready were we?

Early in the year a timetable of visits to lessons was compiled. Every member of staff would be seen for one lesson as a part of our development of quality in the classroom and to identify key components of high-quality teaching. Copies of the OFSTED style form were supplied for information and an in-house form was designed for use by the OFSTED-trained observers. Areas covered by our in-house form were targets, preparation, pace, pitch, participation, progress, style, homework and resource use. Teachers all treated the visits seriously and prepared well, having been notified in advance. At the end of the observation there was a brief informal oral feedback but no return of the completed forms. The plan was to use the forms as part of the feedback to each department, but this was resisted by the first department in the schedule. Surprisingly the strongest resistance was presented by the two most senior teachers who were acknowledged in the school to be high-quality practitioners. At that stage it was agreed that feedback be deferred until the whole-school exercise was complete and that it would be presented through heads of faculty at a QMT meeting.

Following completion of the observations the observers invited two heads of faculty to join them to plan for our next stage. At the report back to the QMT it was agreed to move forward with a training day for all staff in the summer term prepared by the team. A basic concern was the need to know how staff felt about observing and being observed and what training would be required. A move to a culture where formal observations become the norm was recognised as fundamental and the team needed information on feelings, readiness and resistance. After much discussion it was agreed to survey the staff by means of a questionnaire and a task-based interview technique based on their single observed lesson.

THE SURVEY

We used our 1997 summer term training day to gather our evidence. The questionnaires were anonymously completed at the start of the day by everyone whilst we were all together. Our formal input focused on collegiate approaches to the improvement of teaching and learning styles and was followed by separate group discussions led by members of the planning team. Useful points raised by the groups included feedback, training needs and observing within departmental teams.

The remainder of the day was dedicated to other areas for development and departmental planning. During this time 36 teachers completed the interview task individually with their respective facilitators. The task which was based on the work of Ainslow *et al.* (1995) was designed to measure the feelings of individuals towards a particular change, in this case classroom observation.

It is not my intention to give detailed results and analysis of our survey but rather to give an overview of our findings and our conclusions. Teachers were asked to rate 11 areas in the questionnaire on levels of significance from 0 to 3 ranging across high, moderate, low and none. Overwhelmingly 84% rated 'feedback' as being highly significant with 68% rating 'preparation' as such. When high and moderate responses were taken together 95% of the responses indicated feedback. Interestingly only 26% and 24% rated concerns prior and during the observation as highly significant.

The interview task, when teachers were asked to indicate 'often felt' feelings presented by the facilitators, produced a very high positive to negative ratio of 206:37. Over half the staff felt committed, enthusiastic, optimistic, stimulated and interested by the proposed change of observations. Only five indicated feelings of anxiety and disappointment and these *could* have been related to the feedback response in the questionnaire.

The process of the above survey exercise undoubtedly renewed our shared sense of direction or vision and raised our awareness of our existing culture. The major conclusion made was the existence of a readiness to move to a formal system of observation and how little resistance appeared to exist to its implementation. The resulting key recommendation of the planning team was to involve team leaders and their practitioners in planning for observations during our current academic year (1997–98). Several members of staff have expressed an unsolicited desire to join a working group to form a code of practice.

A LEARNING COMMUNITY

At the beginning of this chapter I talked of our journey. We have considered direction, vision and values; we have introduced quality management to improve our school; we have measured feelings and prepared for change; we are now nurturing a learning community.

Our journey over the past five years and beyond has made us realise that there was, and indeed is, much for us as teachers to learn. Continuing professional development in its various forms is at the heart of our strategic development planning. We are just beginning to reflect, share and articulate our needs as individuals and as a collegiate body.

In September 1996 we opened our Centre for Research, Development and Teacher Training, the Uden Centre, named after our founding head. It is a practical symbol of our commitment to professional growth and self-improvement, it is at the heart of our culture as a developing learning community. In its first year it has provided a physical base for our planning and most importantly our reflective discussion. A growing number of our teachers have been involved in providing training for practitioners both locally and nationally. An increasing number of outside agencies value its use to provide teaching and learning for colleagues from near and indeed far away.

Throughout the year 1996–97 close links were forged with the University of Greenwich, School of Education. Since September 1997 an ambitious programme of school-based initial teacher training has been developed. This programme has involved over half of our staff as mentors and senior mentors. Throughout the present year our first cohort of MA students has been based in our centre. We are delighted that 12 members of our staff and 4 from neighbouring schools have committed themselves to formal learning as part of their personal and professional development. Our teacher students are each working on an area of our development plan as part of their study for this degree, a practical example of school and teacher development progressing together. Other activities have included work as OFSTED inspectors and NPQH trainers along with pre- and post-inspection consultancies and no doubt fresh work is on the horizon.

We face our future with increasing confidence supported by systematic self-development. Senge (1990) refers to personal mastery as being formed by such self-development, which means that we as teachers should never cease to learn and nurture our individual personal growth. Our centre for research, development and teacher training will help us to be a place where teachers never stop thinking about their own teaching and daily renew their views of what it means to learn. Above all we are establishing a culture where learning is a shared endeavour between pupils, teachers and parents as separate and as interacting groups. Our culture has preserved what Stoll and Fink (1996) refer to as the magic ingredient for successful change, that of care for one another. As a truly learning community we care not just about each other's pastoral and spiritual welfare but about the quality of learning enjoyed by every member of our school.

REFERENCES

Ainscow, M., Hargreaves, D. and Hopkins, D. (1994) *Mapping Change in Schools*, University of Cambridge, Institute of Education.

Bell, J. and Harrison, B.T. (1995) *Vision and Values in Managing Education*, David Fulton.

Bowring-Carr, C. (1997) The Anachionistic School, *Headlines – The Journal of the Secondary Heads Association*, Vol. 21, pp. 29–31.

Caldwell, B. and Spinks, J. (1992) *Leading the Self-Managing School*. The Falmer Press.

Clarke, L. (1994) *The Essence of Change*. Prentice Hall International.

Mortimore, P. *et al.* (1988) *School Matters: the junior years*. Sommerset, United Kingdom, Open Books.

Murrgatroyd, S. and Morgan, C. (1992) *Total Quality Management and the School*. Open University Press.

Myer, M. and Zucher, L.G. (1989) *Permanently Failing Organisations*. Beverley Hills CA, Sage.

Plant, R. (1987) *Managing Change and Making It Stick*. Harper-Collins.

Rutter, M. *et al.* (1979) *Fifteen Thousand Hours: Secondary Schools and their effects on children*. London, Open Books.

Senge, P. (1990) *The Fifth Discipline: The Art and Practice of the Learning Organisation*. New York, Doubleday.

Stoll, P. and Fink, (1996) *Changing our Schools*. Open University Press.

Townsend, T. (1995) Community Perceptions of What Makes Schools Effective: Implications for Leaders of Tomorrow's Schools, *Leading and Managing*, Vol. 1, no. 2, pp. 111 – 36.

Whitely, R. (1991) *The Customer Driven Company: Moving from Talk to Action*. The Forum Cooperation. Addison-Wesley.

13

Teacher Participation in Decision-making

TONY TUCKWELL

INTRODUCTION

At a time when teachers are reacting against work overload, including the number of meetings they attend, it is perhaps appropriate to question the efficacy of participation as a means of improving teaching and learning.

A considerable amount of literature which deals directly or indirectly with this issue has emerged as school self-management has spread in the English-speaking world. This chapter analyses some of the main themes of the literature, my own research into middle managers' attitudes towards participative decision-making and the lessons that may come from it in defining my own vision of effective leadership, namely, that school management skills do not differ from the skills of a good teacher – establishing quality and respectful relationships, understanding the people with whom one works, ensuring clarity of purpose and providing sufficient information so that participation can focus on learning rather than on unravelling confusion. This agenda would develop both teacher and pupil as independent learners. It is just the context that is different.

RATIONALE FOR PARTICIPATION IN DECISION-MAKING AND ITS INNER CONTRADICTIONS

In the literature the participation of teachers in the shaping and implementation of policy would appear to be the very essence of good management theory. It is one of the characteristics associated with an effective school (Reid *et al.*, 1987). The advocates of total quality management (West Burnham, 1992) consider it to be one of the fundamental quality processes. Those who are attracted by successful commercial experience go for the Peters and Waterman (1982) model with decisions being made close to the point of production, although many of Peters and Waterman's top companies have since disappeared from the scene, which demonstrates that the process of decision-making may not be the panacea for all ills. For others participation is an ethical entitlement (Bottery, 1992; White, 1997). They advocate a transformational or moral model of leadership: 'All members of an institution should participate in

142

its decision-making processes, since in that way they can bear the moral responsibility for institutional arrangements and policies' (White, 1987, p. 87). This view is not far removed from the Australian experiment in community democracy based on the belief that widespread consultation, with teachers involved in community discussions on their schools' aims and objectives, will produce common values and purpose. In the USA Moss (1991, p. 65) sees the process as the most important aspect: 'It is through participation in interactive planning that members of an organisation can develop . . . Participation enables them to acquire an understanding of the organisation and makes it possible for them to serve organisational ends more effectively.'

So most authors for different reasons see participation as a good thing. But all deal in generalisations and look at the problem from the overarching viewpoint of the well meaning manager rather than of the hard-pressed classroom teacher.

For this reason I have long been fascinated by the apparent contradictions of school management. On the one hand we have the need for senior management to ensure unity of purpose and a holistic curriculum experience for the pupils. Yet improving teachers need the freedom of action which enables them to be inspirational and follow their own creative instincts. In other words, they have a significant need to define their own work patterns and participative groupings. This rather risky element of freedom does not sit easily with the concept of public accountability and value for money which is about control rather than empowerment. Schools are under pressure from media league tables, OFSTED, the Qualifications and Curriculum Authority (QCA), government 'naming and shaming' and, every now and then, the National Audit Office, to ensure that there are verifiable outcomes which satisfy the current checklist of success criteria. Caught up in this whirlpool are the varied pressures from governing bodies. Overwhelmingly the danger is that teachers are pressurised into a management agenda to produce conformity to that which others expect rather than to produce personal and professional growth.

THE PURPOSE OF PARTICIPATION: CONTROL OF TEACHERS OR IMPROVEMENT OF LEARNING?

Is there any evidence that widespread teacher participation in decision-making actually makes a difference to pupils? Or is it just a kind of health and safety educational audit, to make sure that preordained systems are secure but not challenged? In my own experience, I was most effective as a curriculum innovator in the 1970s when given free rein to develop my own ideas backed by a trusting head with a cheque book. Similarly the major educational leaps made in my own school have emerged by backing teams running with an idea and sharing the outcomes rather than imposing systems.

At the most basic level no one would disagree with John Donne that 'no man is an island' and that there is a limit to what we can learn by keeping ourselves to ourselves. One cannot have a learning institution for pupils without a learning institution for adults, though that does not necessarily require bureaucratic meeting structures to achieve the four pillars of a successful institution described by Fullan (1993) – shared vision, inquiry, mastery and collaboration. Collaboration in particular evolves its own agenda. It cannot be superimposed. To support his point Fullan quotes Taylor and Teddie's (1992) study of 33 schools, 16 with site-based management and a higher level of teacher participation, 17 without. Despite all the meetings in the former group there was no change in teaching strategies upon which learning improvements depend. In other words teacher participation in decision-making can, like any process, be used to ensure efficiency in the wrong things and lack of effectiveness in the things that matter.

The art of participatory systems is to focus on the core function of curriculum and learning. Even that may be easier said than done. Apparently participatory systems, where values are not shared, can be subverted by negative group think and can limit themselves to seeking the safest compromise so that the lowest common denominator teacher solution triumphs over the best solution for the pupils. Senge (1993, p. 277) points out that productive participation requires a culture change:

> Participative openness may lead to more 'buy-in' on certain decisions, but by itself will rarely lead to better quality decisions because it does not influence the thinking behind people's positions . . . It focuses purely on the 'means' or the process of interacting, not on the 'results' of that interaction . . . While participative openness leads to people speaking out, 'reflective openness' leads to people looking inward . . . to challenge our own thinking.

If Senge is right then much participation in so-called decision-making, as currently practised, is overtly manipulated by managers to secure compliance or twisted by subgroups to pursue their own agendas. Smyth (1993, p. 5) sceptically characterises participation as 'an extremely deft slip of the hand . . . These ideas, while they are dressed up to look democratic, are basically being pushed around by the New Right largely as a way of enabling central educational authorities to increase rather than decrease their control over schools'.

THE ART OF MANAGEMENT: SHARED VALUES AND UNDERSTANDING OF INDIVIDUALS

Handy (1993) gets to the heart of the matter. He develops the concept of the 'psychological contract' whereby the individual has voluntarily identified with the goals of the organisation and will become creative in pursuit of them. Management will be able to relinquish detailed control but retain ultimate control by the right selection of people. Participative decision-making becomes a possibility and creates a virtuous circle whereby a more supportive style of leadership creates greater subordinate satisfaction. How to get there and how to determine when such a degree of participative agreement is leading to sufficient growth for the pupils rather than cosy comradeship for the teachers is the crux.

Fiedler's contingency theory (1965) takes us a step further. He says that when the task is clearly defined and the leader strong and well respected he or she is expected to get on with the job and be fairly directive (e.g. creating a school budget). When the task is ambiguous (e.g. differentiated learning strategies) and the leader is in a weak position *vis-à-vis* the group (for instance, they do not respect him or her or have superior expert knowledge) then the best strategy is still to be directive to avoid the appearance of abdication. But an ambiguous task confronted by a respected leader calls for a more supportive approach if he or she is to draw out from the group all the contributions they can make.

Handy (1993) goes on to formulate his own 'best fit' approach. Like Fiedler, he believes that there are horses for courses. It all depends on the way that the leader (his or her preferred style of operating and personal characteristics), the subordinates (their preferred style of leadership in the light of the circumstances) and the task interact with the environment. Thus, the leader's tight or flexible approach will be influenced by his or her value system, confidence in his or her subordinates, habitual style, assessment of the importance of his or her own personal contribution, need for certainty, degree of stress (more leads to tighter control) and age (older people seem to need more structuring). The subordinates' preference will be influenced by their estimate of their own intelligence and competence, psychological contracts with the group and the leader, interest in the problem and view of its importance, tolerance for ambiguity, past experience and cultural factors such as age and education. The task will influence the decision – an open-ended or technically complex problem will tend towards a flexible approach, the need for absolute precision will lead to a controlled decision, unimportant tasks would not merit the time spent on consultation. Finally the environment introduces six variables – the power position of the leader, the relationship of the leader to the group, the organisational norms, the structure and technology of the organisation, the variety of tasks and the variety of subordinates. All these will influence the way a leader takes a decision or arranges for it to be taken and may operate in quite a different way for the next decision five minutes later. However the more constant the environment and the more predictable the subordinates, the more consistent the leader can be in his or her *modus operandi* in decision-making.

Yet if the 'psychological contract' is important how do we distinguish mirage from reality? Cowan and Wright (1989) analysed the use of directed time. Of senior management team members in the schools they studied, 57% saw directed time meetings as truly consultative, 28% as a vehicle for promulgation, 15% did not know. Heads of department in the same institutions split 36% : 38% : 26% and main-scale teachers 23% : 55% : 22%. Perception of participation as genuine appears to invert as one descends the power scale.

A further complication arises. Individual teachers not only have a variety of attitudes but they will vary during the course of a career. Floden and

Huberman (1989) observe that teachers' beliefs and commitments swing as the years pass, even in schools spared the intrusion of abrupt changes in policy and practice. They tentatively divide teachers' lives into periods of stabilisation up to 35, stock-taking 35–50 and disengagement over 50, with the most activist at 40 (my date of appointment to headship) tending to be the most disengaged at 55 (my age now!). Poppleton and Riseborough (1990) show similar findings in their research on the centrality of work in teachers' lives, dividing 686 South Wales teachers into restricted professionals, extended professionals, coasters and no hopers, strongly correlated to promoted position and career. In Switzerland Huberman's own research (1989, p. 463) showed that

> male secondary teachers lead more saw-toothed careers, with alternating periods of manic over-investment and angry disengagement whereas women report fewer highs and lows and attribute this to their engagements outside school . . . This brings us to the disquieting inference that higher levels of satisfaction with the teaching career are found among those who do not have full-time responsibilities or, if they do, reserve important sums of time and energy for interests lying outside their work.

This uneven engagement of teachers places a significant question-mark against the assumption that participation will be welcome or of beneficial effect for all teachers all the time. As to participation's responsibility for improved outcomes we are still faced with the impossibility of disentangling cause and effect. As Handy (1993, p. 13) says, 'the multiplicity of variables impinging on any one organisational situation is so great [he suggests over 60] that data on all of them sufficient to predict the outcome of that multiple inter-relationship would never in practice be forthcoming'.

HOW MIDDLE MANAGERS ASSESS THE QUALITATIVE VALUE OF PARTICIPATION

The volume of specifically English research on this issue is quite small. Paisey (1982) concludes that it is the quality and not just the quantity of participation that is important. He suggests that the costs of participation should be evaluated. The expenditure of time, money, energy and morale may not be warranted. Nor may the process produce a rapid enough decision to solve the problem in time, e.g. if the school is losing pupils. He concludes that (*ibid*., p. 34) 'participation . . . is . . . essentially a variable phenomenon and, therefore, its presence and manifestation are subject to judgement. It presumably can be used both correctly and in error – a view that should be compared with the assumption of participation as an invariable good.'

Davies (1983) provides an early piece of quantitative research analysing 51 heads of department (HODs) in three schools in three LEAs. He asked HODs to rate their level of actual and desired participation in eight key areas: 1) decisions on resource allocation; 2) use of the school fund; 3) appointments and promotions within the department; 4) use of community-based funds; 5) curriculum design for the whole school; 6) stock ordering and equipment; 7) curriculum design for the department and; 8) allocation of staff to classes. HODs were asked to rate their actual level and their desired levels of participation on a seven-point scale (from seven = saturation to one = no involvement). The deficit between actual and desired levels of participation in the first five, principally whole-school issues, was about –4.0 points, in the others –2.0. Spence (1988) administered a similar questionnaire to 22 heads of science in two LEAs and added pupil allocation, decisions about pastoral care and contact with parents to Davies' categories. HODs showed a deprivation of about –3.0 points on whole-school issues. However neither piece of research discovered why HODs felt deprived. HODs may equally have been expressing dissatisfaction with management *per se* rather than seeking a radical change in the management structure. What is it that they did not like? Chater (1985) was perhaps getting closer to an answer in his analysis of seven schools' methods of distributing capitation. Staff in six of them wanted more involvement. They did not understand the process due to lack of information. So is a desire to be involved merely a quest for information rather than power? Hamlin (1990) seemed to verify this. He asked over 200 West Midlands HODs to analyse those management characteristics which were most effective. Control of resources was cited by over 60% only as a negative factor which, where badly done, caused concern.

When all is said and done all that we have learned so far is that good management lies in ensuring that teacher and institutional agendas overlap in a mutual psychological contract, in so far as one can demonstrate that this exists. There is circumstantial evidence but no actual proof that teacher participation in whole-school decision-making improves schools. Moreover, individuals and circumstances are infinitely varied. In the end it is in understanding the institution's circumstances and then securing coherence around agreed values and aims that the real art of management lies. And that requires an understanding of one's own teachers and the variety of perceptions and attitudes they import into the equation.

FUSING THE DIFFERENT STRANDS OF RESEARCH IN A CASE STUDY

From my own point of view the accumulative research posed a tantalising possibility. Davies (1983) and Spence (1988) examined middle managers' perceptions to decision-making, Chater (1985) the impact of internal communications on teachers' desire to be involved in decision-making, Floden and Huberman (1989) teachers' enthusiasm for involvement that may vary with age and gender (and, perhaps, perceptions of stress), and Poppleton and Risborough (1990) the influence on teachers' thinking of their perception of the all-importance or otherwise of their job. Could this not all be brought together to see the extent to which the various components influenced each other?

In research conducted in my own school (Tuckwell, 1995) this attempt was made. Using Davies' (1983) seven-point scale, 18 managers were asked to assess their actual and desired level of participation in decision-making in 20 areas relevant to a grant-maintained school. They were by and large the same as those of Davies and Spence plus the use of support staff, premises, whole-school facilities (e.g. IT), staff development, school development planning and monitoring and evaluation, all representing the new thrusts of 1990s' self-management. Middle managers were also asked to evaluate on the same seven-point scale how adequate the provision of information was in each of these areas; the centrality of work in their lives; and the contribution of 20 named factors to levels of unacceptable stress. It would be interesting to see the extent to which these three new factors explained why middle managers reached their more or less satisfied conclusions about participation. Knowing what their views are is not so important as knowing why.

The findings were interesting. Middle managers experienced a marginal overall level of deprivation in decision-making of –0.93, significantly down on Davies and Spence's. Four areas of traditionally department-based decision-making (books and equipment, allocation of staff to classes, curriculum design at departmental level, allocation of staff development resources at departmental level) were at near saturation level of actual participation (i.e. point 7) with negligible feelings of deprivation. Seven whole-school decision-making areas (e.g. use of support staff, allocation of private funds and capitation) had a low level of actual participation (between 1 and 3 on the seven-point scale) but also a low level of desired participation. In other words HODs were not involved too much and were satisfied with the situation.

The appearance of finance in this group of low deprivation and low import-ance issues is a very interesting contrast with Davies, Spence and Chater. But the level of information provided for all staff is rated as being high in these areas, more so with capitation (rated at over 6.0) compared to private funds (rated at over 4.0). This might reflect an open practice of publishing details of where the money had come from, to whom it had gone and why. In general the 10 decision-making areas where information provision was greatest had a lower average decision-making deprivation level of –0.7 while the 10 areas in the bottom half of the order for provision of information had a higher average decision-making deprivation level of –1.2. So the more information one has, the less one feels the need to be involved in decision-making.

But overall averages hide a variation of response. The individual 'psycholog-ical contract' may vary considerably from one to another. One HOD particip-ated more than he would have wished (actual 6.2, desired 5.7), was sated with information (6.8) and felt a considerable amount of unacceptable stress. A second HOD had a low level of deprivation (–0.5) from a perceived low level of actual involvement (3.6) but said he experienced a high level of unaccept-able stress and rated workload as the chief culprit. This HOD seemed to want to rein in because he was finding it difficult to handle work. On the other hand a third HOD also indicated that he was experiencing a great deal of unaccept-able stress, had an overwhelming desire to be further involved in decision-making (actual level 3.8, desired level 6.0) and seemed to see the way out of the impasse as doing even more work. Fourth and fifth HODs were very satisfied with the provision of information (5.4 and 5.8 compared to the average 5.1), experienced very low levels of unacceptable stress and had relatively high levels of decision deprivation (−1.2 and −1.6). These almost certainly believed they had much more capacity to be tapped.

If one takes stress factors as the main guideline other associations are clearly established. High-stress middle managers (one third of the total) showed a higher than average desire to participate in decision-making and a very high commitment to participation in whole-school planning (perhaps as a means of protecting themselves and reducing stress?). Yet they felt saturated by workload and their work was very important to them, occupying their thoughts more outside working hours than any other group. They felt more insecure in their relations with those immediately above and below them in line management. A degree of isolation is suggested. They appeared to be in a Protestant work ethic vortex where they believed work stress could only be resolved by more work. But interpersonal relations may have been an unrecognised problem.

Low-stress middle managers (just over one third of the total) also had a relatively high desire to participate. They too wanted to be involved at a high level in school planning. They showed near maximum scores for involvement in monitoring and evaluation. This activity, as a stress factor, caused them virtually no worry, although it was the issue where middle managers as a whole felt the greatest sense of deprivation in decision-making. The low-stress middle managers had virtually no unacceptable stress caused by those immediately above and below them in line management. They were clearly content with themselves and their areas of expertise.

On its own this case study was a valuable in-house tool. Direct comparisons with previous research should be cautiously made. The whole climate and structure of management in schools had changed since the 1980s with devolution to site-based management. Inferences need to be carefully drawn. A teacher who believes there is a healthy equilibrium between actual and desired involvement in decision-making might be professionally satisfied but might not be fully satisfying pupils' needs. A teacher who wants to be involved more might be right where decision-making participation centres on the work and resources of the classroom. Beyond that it might signify personal ambition more than dedication to pupils' progress. Or as this study has confirmed, a teacher's apparent desire to be involved more in decision-making may be a cry for more information rather than more democracy, or a well intentioned but ill-advised response to stress.

WHAT EFFECT DID MY RESEARCH HAVE ON MY OWN PRACTICE?

First, it reinforced an intuitive feel about the way teachers should be managed. There is no substitute for reacting to teachers in the same way as pupils, knowing and understanding them individually. Those who are essentially controllers of pupils and think in terms of power will find it difficult to do otherwise with teachers. In such circumstances management may be coercive rather than developmental, controlling rather than influencing. History shows that those with power have no constructive long-term impact, those with influence determine events. In schools the withholding of information is an ultimate form of control. It creates mysteries and gives the opportunity to manipulate. My own policy of minimal confidentiality and maximum divulging of information enhances understanding. It provides at most a healthy basis for dialogue and perception of opportunity and at least evidence that management can be trusted. But the fundamental reason why I manage in this way is not influenced by the pragmatic outcomes of research but by who I am, my own personality and value system as defined by my own happy upbringing. Values and interpersonal skills are well embedded even before one starts teaching. Personal and observational experience may make me better at implementation but will not change the belief system on which my practice is founded. That is why managers who come and go with fads or are predominantly reactive in their responses smother their own values and appear inconsistent.

Secondly, it seems to me to reinforce doubts about the simplistic use of performance-related pay or appraisal linked to outcomes as mechanisms for securing improved educational standards. If the oft-repeated cliché that teachers are our greatest resource is to have any meaning, then one needs to start with the internal motivation of teachers and see the universe from their individual viewpoints. This research points in that direction and will inform our reassessment of teacher appraisal. With pupils, one starts by knowing and understanding the individual. Why treat teachers differently?

Thirdly, the research confirmed, as Fiedler suggests, that a respected leader faced with an ambiguous task (and surely defining learning is just that) should adopt a supportive rather than a controlling role. And if a headteacher or a senior management team cannot achieve respect in this most fundamental of activities then all is lost. The blind will be leading the sighted. Only when there is unity of learning purpose can the vision of the school be clarified and extended.

But what is that vision? I have heard the term used so frequently as a management cliché in anodyne mission statements as though its mere utterance will open Aladdin's cave.

The first problem is that vision is often seen as a future state. Yet the most important vision is a vision for pupils now. Future scenarios are of marginal significance for them except in so far as teachers who are not capable of thinking about future developments will probably provide a meagre diet for the present. The excitement of learning today and the vibrant experience of the school as a living community have to be the prime vision.

Therefore, the second, and most important aspect of vision, which is central to this chapter, concerns itself with the manager's capacity to liberate the internal visions that dance within each teacher's head. Just as able pupils, when given their head in a creative project, will come up with a sophisticated and exciting result that one would not have been capable of predicting, so with able teachers. To help teachers articulate their aspirations and then to provide the resource and staff development base so that they can be achieved enables a school to make quantum leaps in pupil development defying anything that top-down management can manufacture. The intermeshing of these teacher visions also creates an excitingly unpredictable dynamic that informs the other two aspects of the vision, the learning process now and in the future. It builds a vision from bottom-up which has roots and a life beyond the contract of the current headteacher so that the school, rather like a church, has a meaning which is the expression of its members rather than representing the passing cult of an individual. It provides consenting growth and a decision-making process that evolves rather than compliant obeisance and a cosmetic form of participation that is imposed. It is also the only answer to the prolonged spells in office which most headteachers will experience (in my case 15 years). It ensures that their own personal visions become subsumed by the collective vision of the institution. It gives headteachers constant renewal rather than premature exhaustion.

Thirdly there is the vision of where the school might be in five years' time or whatever is the fashionable time span of the moment. This is attractive because it is finite and tangible. It is usually concerned with curriculum or physical structures such as the development of new buildings to fulfil currently frustrated curriculum aspirations, expanded learning processes through the expansion of IT, the introduction of non-European languages or whatever seems most appropriate for the institution under scrutiny. The wealthier the institution the more the vision may get stuck in this groove. Yet without the buzz of ideas released from within teachers these concrete and electronic visions will remain just a glossy marketing concept.

I think it is because I have been able to get inside teachers' heads that we have such little sense of decision deprivation. We do not have a centrally imposed staff development programme. HODs are canvassed for the issues that they and their departments would want to concentrate on for the forthcoming year. They always include the issues that, as senior managers, we would have chosen, and they never lose track of statutory imperatives, but their ideas have a discrete identity and their own nuances. Departmental development plans link into these issues and drive the school budget enabling us to meet requests, even if not all have been immediate. Teachers will tell you that there is something particularly exciting about meeting a need which has been part of a long-term vision and is ultimately realised. This has created a can-do mindset in which success breeds confidence and a desire to taste more.

And we have now gone a stage further. We have decided that the number of examination options on offer is an expensive red herring. Rather than spend the equivalent of a full-time teacher's salary on two minority subjects, we are to divert it to bolstering the staffing of departments that have bid successfully to the governors' learning strategies committee to undertake action research, for example in liaison with university institutes of education, other schools in this country or abroad or new technologies in industry and higher education, which will feed back into all the pupils' learning experience. Providing time through enhanced staffing (a kind of in-house TVEI) for teachers to develop their own ideas is, to me, the ultimate participation in decision-making. It gives an added curriculum edge to financial planning. We as senior managers provide the support and resources, the teachers take the lead and formulate the agenda in making the ideas work. Accountability to external stakeholders is subsumed within a wider process in which the teachers share control. And ultimately it makes the question of how much or how little participation is desirable purely academic. Handy's psychological contract has been struck and one is working with professional volunteers.

Thus in the end statistical analyses of teachers' attitudes to decision-making are interesting but not the solution. They are useful in dispelling or confirming assumptions that one may make about teachers' attitudes but they cannot be a practical way to manage. Their only value lies in prompting the observant senior manager to ask the right questions and get inside people's minds to understand what makes them tick. In my case 46 teachers will inevitably be more productive than one headteacher.

The headteacher's skill should be that of the artistic director with talented actors improvising a play – to brainstorm for ideas, work out how to script them, provide the set and the props, pull all the parts together in a unique drama and, every now and then, provide a shaft of insight that lights the way to implementing a shared ideal. That is real participation where all can be kings.

REFERENCES

Bottery, M. (1992) *The Ethics of Educational Management*, London, Cassell.

Chater, R. (1985) Aspects of decision-making in secondary schools, *Educational Management and Administration*, Vol. 13, pp. 207–14.

Cowan, B.J. and Wright, N. (1989) Directed time, a year on: staff perspectives, *School Organisation*, Vol. 9, no. 3, pp. 375–89.

Davies, B. (1983) HOD involvement in decisions, *Educational Management and Administration*, Vol. 11 no. 3, pp. 173–6.

Fiedler, F.E. (1965) Engineer the job to fit the manager, *Harvard Business Review*, Vol. 43.

Floden, R.E. and Huberman, M. (1989) Research on teachers' life cycles is a late addition to research in teaching, *Journal of Educational Research*, Vol. 13 no. 4, pp. 445–65.

Fullan, M.G. (1993) *Change Forces*, Lewes, Falmer.

Hamlin, B. (1990) The competent manager in secondary schools, *Educational Management and Administration*, Vol. 18, no. 3, pp. 3–10.

Handy, C. (1993) *Understanding Organisations*, Harmondsworth, Penguin Books.

Moss, G. (1991) Restructuring public schools for internal democratic governance : a circular approach, *School Organisation*, Vol. 11, no. 1, pp. 71–85.

Paisey, A. (1982) Participation in school organisation, *Educational Management and Administration*, Vol. 10, no. 1, pp. 31–5.

Peters, T. and Waterman, R. (1982) *In search of excellence*, Harper & Row.

Poppleton, P. and Riseborough, G. (1990) Teaching in the mid 1980s: the centrality of work in secondary teacher's lives, *British Educational Research Journal*, Vol. 16, no. 2, pp. 105–24.

Reid, K., Hopkins, D. and Holly, P. (1987) *Towards the effective school*, Oxford, Blackwell.

Senge, P.M. (1993) *The Fifth Discipline: The Art and Practice of the Learning Organisation*, London, Century Business.

Smyth, J. (ed.) (1993) *A Socially Critical View of the Self-Managing School*, Lewes, Falmer.

Spence, B. (1988) Decisional deprivation among senior staff in secondary schools, *School Organisation*, Vol. 8, no. 3, pp. 331–7.

Taylor, D. and Teddie, C. (1992) Restructuring and the classroom: a view from a reform district. Paper presented at the annual meeting of the American Educational Research Association, San Francisco.

Tuckwell, A.D. (1995) Middle management participation in decision-making: a case study of King Edward VI Grammar School, Chelmsford. MBA thesis, Leeds Metropolitan University.

West-Burnham, J. (1992) *Managing Quality in Schools*, Harlow, Longman.

White, P. (1987) Self-respect, self-esteem and the management of educational institutions: a question of values, *Educational Management and Administration*, Vol. 15, no. 2, pp. 85–91.

14

Creating the Vision and Making it Happen

MARK WASSERBERG

This chapter considers the period from September 1993 to December 1997, when I was headteacher of Dane Valley High School, an 11–18 mixed comprehensive school in Congleton, Cheshire.

BACKGROUND

Dane Valley was during this period the smallest of the three secondary schools in Congleton. For demographic reasons it also experienced falling rolls, leading to a compulsory redundancy, the implementation of a flatter management structure, and a reduction from two deputies to one. Numbers at the end of this period were 620 on roll, of whom just over 100 were post-sixteen students. For many years, the Congleton secondary schools had co-operated in the teaching of minority A-levels and the introduction of vocational qualifications. The period 1993–97 saw a rapid extension of co-operation, leading to the launch of the Congleton Sixth Form in 1995. An interesting dimension to the strategic vision discussed in this chapter was that running parallel to it was a growing awareness that the future of secondary education in the town would be better served by two schools of approximately six-form entry than its current structure. Such was the work that went on at all levels, including governors, that when I left to take up a second headship in December 1997, I was not replaced and plans for reorganisation were invited by the three governing bodies of the town's secondary schools.

Dane Valley has a mixed catchment of urban and rural areas and of different kinds of housing. It has very few pupils who are not white. The numbers having free school meals is low. The ability profile of the school reveals a perfect bell curve distribution, with a higher than average percentage of able children. It has excellent relationships with its feeder primary schools.

A CONSIDERATION OF VISION

Vision starts from core values: the deeply held convictions about the way schools should be. For me they are

- schools are concerned with learning and all members of the school community are learners;
- every member of the school community is valued as an individual;
- the school exists to serve its pupils and the local community;
- learning is about the development of the whole person and happens in and out of classrooms; and
- people prosper with trust, encouragement and praise.

All good noble stuff! However, there are problems with this 'vision thing'. How are these core values shared with everybody in the school community? How do they become part of the way in which people think and feel about the school? How do the routines and systems of the school reflect these values? In the day-to-day confusion of school life, how is it possible to keep them to the fore as a shaper of the school's culture?

One thing is for sure, it does not happen as the result of a nice logical sequence of actions. Because schools are about people, they are messy places. Just as in politics, 'events' can play havoc with plans. People may purport to hold the same values, but actually mean quite different things when they espouse them. Habit can play at least as big a part in determining how things actually work as values. And, as my own understanding as a new headteacher was changing and developing, my ideas of how to make progress changed and developed too.

Some key events helped develop the vision of the school as a learning community. The first was our preparation for, experience of and response to an OFSTED inspection in November 1995. I was the only member of staff who had experience of an inspection under the new framework. (As a deputy I had been involved in one of the pilot inspections for the New Framework.) Indeed, most of the staff had never undergone an inspection of any kind.

From my arrival, we had OFSTED in mind. I saw it as an important part of my job to help prepare the staff. There was amongst the staff a degree of anxiety about inspection which helped us move with a pace and energy which may otherwise have been impossible. Although I have misgivings about aspects of the inspection process, the framework's emphasis on the quality of teaching and the quality of learning is surely right. With the senior management team of the school we used the 'threat' of the approaching inspection to make progress in key areas. These were

- increasing the focus on quality in the classroom;
- developing and updating policy statements and departmental documentation; and
- boosting the school community's belief in the quality of its work.

When the inspection did come, its timing was almost ideal. I had been in the school for just over two years and it was a good time to see what progress we had made. We used a training day at the start of the term in which the inspection was to take place to pull together our preparation. The key message we aimed to share was that the heart of the inspection would be an examination of the quality of work in classrooms. By the training day, the senior management team, which included all heads of faculty, had agreed the documentation preparation would be completed to allow the proper focus on teaching and learning. We used OFSTED's lesson observation form to explore aspects of quality in classroom work. The other key message of the training day was that we had much to be proud of in the quality of our teaching and learning. We were approaching the inspection from a position of strength.

The inspection itself was conducted by a highly skilled LEA team and in a very professional manner. At the end of the week we had a party in a local pub owned by parents of students in the school and I was able to give a very positive account of the verbal feedback my deputy and I had received. This was important. We had asked a huge amount of staff and they had responded with tremendous energy and professionalism. A good report provided a proper reward for that commitment. It was very important for us that the quality of our work was acknowledged. We made sure the report was well publicised and celebrated. It was also good for our students who responded magnificently during the week and fully shared in the outcome.

In terms of clarifying our vision for the school, we had concentrated on the quality of learning and teaching in our preparation and those aspects of our work had been highly praised in the report. The inspection had helped to bind us together as a staff and in doing so had encouraged us to develop a shared language for talking about learning and teaching. Finally, our approach and emphasis had been vindicated by the very positive outcome.

A second key to the development of our vision was an increasing understanding of how people learn and a corresponding concentration on learning and teaching styles. I am not sure exactly how this started. As so often, a mixture of factors came together over a period of time and gradually coalesced. We were concerned about the relative underperformance of boys in the school. This was particularly true in the third and fourth quartiles of the ability range. We were first alerted to the problem by trends in GCSE performance and by the increasing sophistication of data provided by Cheshire LEA, which showed that our gap between girls' and boys' performance was larger than the average in the county. One of the outcomes of this concern was to send a variety of staff on relevant courses. Through these we encountered the work of Geoff Hannen, Tony Buzan, Paul Dickinson and Howard Gardner. The Deputy Headteacher, had a long-standing interest in thinking and study skills. The Head of the Pastoral Faculty, was leading work on target-setting and self-evaluation, with emphasis on the teacher as mentor. Post-sixteen, there was concern that the transition from GCSE to A-level was proving very difficult for some students who did not have the repertoire of learning skills necessary to deal with the challenge.

All these factors contributed to a changed understanding in the school, helping to move us from a culture devoted to quality of teaching, to an increasing awareness of the primacy of learning.

A third key was my personal professional development. I started the Open University MA with a module on 'Leadership and management in education'. I felt the need to place my practical experience of headship into a theoretical framework, which I hoped would help me reflect more critically on my work. The course proved an excellent medium for that process. Also, much of the reading was of value to colleagues. I felt a new excitement at many of the ideas I was encountering. They helped me understand more about how schools and people change and develop and about the different dimensions to leadership and management. They made me re-evaluate my leadership style and recognise the need to develop a greater responsiveness to the needs of others. Some of this was painful stuff, but it was personal and professional development of the best kind because it changed the way I work and think.

TURNING THE VISION INTO PRACTICE – SHAPING THE CULTURE

Schein (1985) argues that leadership is centrally about changing culture. How does an institution develop its culture? I tried to concentrate on a few integrating principles which were consistently followed:

- Keep a persistent focus on the quality of learning.
- Build positive relationships throughout the school.
- Aim for professional openness and honesty.
- Enjoy our work.

I believed that if these were right in the school and explicitly underpinning how we worked, then the culture would become increasingly positive, coherent and committed to improvement.

How did this work in practice? One example is the work we did on opening classrooms to shared observation. A blockage to a culture of professional openness and focus on learning was that the staff were not used to or confident about the mutual observation of lessons for the purpose of discussing and improving learning. We had not had a very successful appraisal scheme and it had only had a marginal effect on whole-school thinking. Early in my headship I made it a priority to visit classrooms and see colleagues teach. I arranged faculty visits, in which I saw all members of a faculty teach and then wrote up my observations for discussion at a faculty meeting. I consistently made the point that watching colleagues teach was the best professional development available and something I regarded as a privilege. I also ensured that I made much in my reports of the good practice that was going on and raised concerns at a general faculty level rather than individually.

I suggested that we use a percentage of our professional development budget to free teachers to allow mutual observation, either within faculties or across them. This was not initially seized upon as a wonderful opportunity! Staff were in the middle of coping with radical changes in GCSE and A-level syllabuses and there was heavy demand for external courses and time to help aid these developments. I thought this was an interesting example of how the culture was more geared to teaching than it was to learning. So, as a freeing mechanism I offered faculties the opportunity to undertake mutual observation and I would be the cover teacher. Mathematics and modern foreign languages took up the offer. They found it a valuable experience leading to real discussion of good practice and sharing of teaching and learning styles. Formal discussion of what had happened at senior management team and informal talk in the staffroom helped to change people's perceptions and gradually shift the culture.

The staff of the school had a long-standing friendliness and commitment to each other. Despite the increasing pressures of the job, people did find time to show interest and concern for each other and to have fun. I underlined my own commitment to this dimension of school life by participating fully in staff activities and those occasions when the whole-school community came together. Every two years, the school holds a fun-day to raise money for the school. The timetable is collapsed and a range of fun activities are held instead. The staff responsible for organising this give a huge amount of time and energy to its success. I made sure I sang in the karioke, took my turn in the stocks and got round to all the activities which were taking place. Such days did as much as anything to develop relationships between staff and students and to create the right culture of co-operation and shared endeavour, which is at the heart of the school.

Similarly, I played in the school band, refereed the occasional football match and helped with a wonderful production of *A Midsummer Night's Dream*. I am sounding too much as though I am blowing my own trumpet here but the reality is quite different. If colleagues were willing to give so much of themselves for the benefit of students, the least I could do was show that I valued what they were doing by offering some support by my personal involvement. All these activities were also hugely enjoyable and excellent opportunities for me to get to know students better. There are dangers I think in forgetting that what really constitutes a school is the totality of the contacts between people that happen every day. Our business is utterly about people and the way we treat each other.

Leadership

I am sure John West-Burnham (1998) is right when he says leadership happens in the swamp rather than on the high ground looking down. In such a messy environment, you have to make what you do as telling as possible. I see the primary role of any leader to be the unification of people around key values. I spend a lot of time as a headteacher talking to people about what we believe and trying to exemplify those values in my working life – in other words, 'walking the talk'.

Christopher Bowring-Carr and John West-Burnham (1997) write about 'loose-tight' organisations: loose in their bureaucratic organisation giving people freedom of action, but tight in adherence to the central values. If we are serious about seeing leadership as a quality to be encouraged and exercised in the many rather than the few, then we have to take on the challenge of the 'loose-tight' organisation.

Walking the talk meant being on the corridors a lot, talking to students, being in the staffroom at breaks and lunchtimes, talking with staff, doing a fair share of cover, meeting with school council to hear the views of students first hand, getting involved in school life as fully as possible. It also meant (one of the real luxuries of leading a small school) knowing almost every student by name, getting to know lots of parents and playing an active role in the local community. I regard every conversation I have with students, in terms of the way I talk to them and listen to their views, as being as significant an aspect of leadership as the most strategic thinking about the school's future direction or budgetary difficulties. It matters enormously, I think, that people see you living out what you say you believe. That integrity underpins everything else that you try to do.

From that position of integrity it is then the role of leadership to enthuse others, to support them in their work and to challenge them always to believe they can do better. That mixture of support and challenge is vital. Teaching and learning are hugely demanding. Teachers and students need to feel supported in what they are trying to do. They need to feel that it is all right to experiment and take risks, and that failure *en route* to real learning is OK. Equally, challenge is crucial to help people develop the skills of being reflective learners, prepared to question what they do and how they do it.

Being open and honest with people makes it possible to achieve the balance between challenge and support. One of the core values I tried to espouse in the school was that you should never lie to a student. This applied equally to my dealings with colleagues. This is not an easy position to sustain because it depends on students and colleagues also being honest with you, even if some of the messages are not ones you really wish to hear! Paul Clarke (1998), in discussing how to manage change successfully, considers how to uncover the cultural assumptions that may be blocking change. He suggests asking two questions in pursuit of 'naming the elephants – publicly talking out issues':

- What don't we talk about here?
- Why don't we talk about not talking about it?

In my leadership, I try to create a climate in which all things can be talked about. It is possible to challenge someone's views and ways of working without that being confused with a personal attack on his or her value as a person. This is what I understand by professionalism.

An important element of this was my willingness to acknowledge my own mistakes. I have always enjoyed the pastoral work of a school. At the end of my first year at Dane Valley, the head of the pastoral faculty raised an issue through the faculty review. The heads of year were concerned that I was becoming too involved in pastoral and behaviour incidents at too early a stage. They felt this removed one of the tiers of authority to which a student could be passed if necessary. They were right and I made sure I responded positively to their concerns and changed my behaviour. I was, incidentally, pleased they felt able to raise their concerns in such a professional way.

At all levels of the school, and in my own dealing with students and parents, I tried to encourage honesty. Where we had made mistakes I said so and then suggested we look at ways of putting right what had gone wrong. Equally, where I felt parents or students had not played their part in putting things right I said so. Occasionally individual teachers found this difficult, because they felt they were not getting the support from me they should, but the benefit in terms of trust from the community for the work of the school was huge. I hasten to add that I did not 'drop colleagues in it', but that I took responsibility on behalf of the school for things which had not gone as they should and then pursued them internally to see what we could do to ensure they did not happen again.

The last quality of leadership I want to mention is the encouragement of others to see themselves as leaders. The hierarchical nature of schools can easily create a dependency culture or a hugely regulated organisation in which no one can do anything without permission. Part of my learning as a head-teacher, helped enormously by the OU MA work on leadership and management, has been to try to curb my desire to run everything. Giving people the genuine responsibility for their own work and for leading whole-school developments is essential if schools are to harness the enormous potential for creativity contained in the people who work there. An example of this in practice followed the appointment of a colleague as IT co-ordinator in only his second year of teaching. We negotiated how to help him develop the skills necessary to lead such an important aspect of school life. This involved me initially chairing the IT Development Group, which brought together people with expertise from different curriculum areas, allowing the new co-ordinator to concentrate on leading the discussion and shaping the school's policy in IT. I also worked with my colleague to agree an action plan for his first year in post. My role emerged as a questioning one, trying to ensure that he did not become solely focused on task completion, but was able to recognise the importance of using the right processes to involve others in reaching his goals. Once the action plan was agreed, he knew that others were available to help if he required it, but that he had full responsibility to take the work forward.

The deputy headteacher of the school also encouraged staff to become involved in the excellent middle management courses run by Cheshire County Council. We wanted the staff to see themselves as learners and as leaders.

Management

Underpinning the work we were doing on trying to shape the culture was a series of steps to make the organisation and processes of the school less bureaucratic, more efficient and more in keeping with the core values we were espousing.

Senior management team

When I arrived at the school the senior management team consisted of the head, two deputies and three senior teachers. By common agreement the team was not functioning well, partly because many departments not represented on the SMT felt their views were not properly represented. I was concerned to create a senior management structure which was flatter and which gave equal representation and voice to all. We took the risk of creating a senior management team of 12 – larger than we would have wanted in terms of operating as an effective team – but which had the benefit of including the heads of all faculties. At the same time we created a pastoral 'faculty' so that the views of the pastoral team could also be represented. So the SMT consisted of head, two deputies and nine heads of faculty. When we reduced to one deputy in response to our falling roll, the head of sixth form joined the team reflecting the growing importance of the Congleton Sixth Form in our work. Because of the size of the team we agreed that meetings would need to have very tight agendas and clear operating procedures.

The team met once a fortnight. In the intervening week, faculty meetings were held. This meant that communication was vastly improved. A discussion could take place at SMT on one week, faculties could discuss the issues the following week and the week after that responses could be fed back to SMT. Everybody's views were represented. This meant decision-making became very open and earned a high level of commitment. For example, all capitation bids were shared at SMT, leading to open debate as to which developments could be supported from the limited funds available. After an open debate, decisions were taken and even those who led faculties which lost out accepted the process had been completely fair. Similarly issues such as numbers of groups to be run in Years 10 and 11, the nature of the Key Stage 3 and 4 curriculum, building developments all came before SMT for full and open debate. This proved a healthy and progressive forum. Its main weakness was that the creation of the agendas for meetings and the impetus for initiating developments tended to come from myself and the deputy. We tried various ways to change this, but there remained an underlying belief that the SMT meeting was for everyone to debate issues which had been brought forward by the head and deputy. The only occasions when this was not true was when a member of SMT felt strongly that the head and deputy had got something badly wrong.

Nevertheless, the advantages outweighed the problems. One advantage was that the pay structure of the staff became transparently clear and fair. All heads of faculty were on the same number of responsibility points and the staffing structure reflected a similar pattern in all faculties. It also provided a forum for professional development for heads of faculty. For example, as we prepared for our OFSTED inspection, we used several SMT meetings to share progress on departmental documentation, working to a format agreed in SMT.

School development planning

We introduced four key changes to the school development planning process. First we agreed a shared process for arriving at whole-school priorities. This included governors, SMT, faculty teams and whole-staff meetings. The idea was for all staff and governors to have the opportunity to identify areas for development. Secondly we brought the school development planning cycle in line with financial planning. Whole-school priorities for the following academic year were agreed in November of the previous year. This meant that in planning the budget from January to May full account could be taken of the school's priorities. The impact of this can be seen in the development of IT facilities, in which ambitious school development plans required considerable investment, without which implementation was impossible.

Thirdly, faculty development plans and professional development strategy reflected whole-school priorities as they were developed during the summer term for the following year. This was a good example of our efforts to develop a 'loose-tight' organisation, although we did not know that is what it was called at the time! Faculties had to reflect whole-school priorities, but also had their own priorities which they pursued and which reflected their own professional needs and ambitions.

Fourthly, as we became clearer about our focus on improving the quality of students' learning, we were able to use school development planning to ensure we kept our eye on the ball. All priorities were measured against the contribution they were intended to make to improving the quality of learning. This was a very practical step in shaping the culture and realising our vision of a learning school.

Staff development

Having established a system whereby whole-school priorities were measured against our core values of developing quality learning, we worked hard to ensure that professional development also promoted our core values. I have already described how we have promoted mutual observation of lessons by teachers. We were anxious to get away from the long-standing problem of individuals attending courses and there being no real benefit to the school. We identified courses which we felt would contribute to our understanding of how to improve the quality of students' learning and then arranged for two staff to attend the course together. In order to increase the likelihood of new learning being shared in the school we created two fora for communication. One was an in-house INSET newsletter produced termly, which contained information from all courses attended with a whole-school dimension. We also established a series of staff meetings and after-school sessions at which colleagues who had attended courses made presentations. Hearing colleagues, who worked in the same context, explain what they had gained from an outside course was powerful.

Faculty reviews

A system of faculty reviews was already in place before my appointment. It had been a means by which the head of faculty had reflected with the head on what had been achieved in the previous year. I felt that an opportunity was being missed, however, to involve all teachers in that discussion. Our core values of seeing everyone as learners, of trusting each other and of being open with each other would be better served by a more open process. Faculty reviews came to be shared by the whole faculty and the deputy headteacher, who had responsibility for the curriculum, also participated in the process. I attended full faculty meetings to discuss issues raised. There was still a meeting between the head of faculty, the head and the deputy, but this became an opportunity to discuss personnel issues, the work of the head of faculty and the quality of support which the deputy and I had provided.

The reviews dovetailed with the school development planning process described earlier. The reviews reflected on progress made with the previous year's faculty development plan and finished with the targets for the following year's plan. We wanted all staff to be involved in this process. We believed it played an important part in helping us all become more reflective about our professional work.

Use of support staff

We wanted teachers to become increasingly focused on the quality of students' learning. Part of the journey was to employ support staff to do those things teachers did which others could do better and which were distractions. I have always felt that senior staff and particularly deputy headteachers get involved in all kinds of work which would be much better done by support staff. The reduction from two deputies to one and the early retirement of a senior teacher provided opportunities to address the issue.

We made two appointments in the area of IT. The first was a data-processing appointment to support the administrative Sims system. The second was a network manager who took responsibility for the health and development of the educational network. We also enhanced the role of the school's registrar, to include responsibility for the buildings.

These may not seem very significant in terms of 'creating the vision and making it happen'. But actually, they made a lot of difference. They were part of a cultural shift saying that teachers' professional work and time should be respected. At the same time, we were enhancing the importance and status of support staff.

Raising achievement

As we became more focused on students' learning, raising achievement became a means of pulling together many of the threads discussed in this chapter. Brought together in the school development plan were a series of practical strategies combining ideas from the school improvement and school effectiveness movements. They were:

- Individual mentoring of students in Years 10 and 11 (first of all at the GCSE C/D borderline but later more widely).
- Use of value-added data to provide individual targets for all students.
- Creating opportunities and time for form tutors to counsel pupils one-to-one or observe their tutor groups in lessons.
- Mutual observation of lessons for professional development.
- The development of student planners to help students organise their study.
- Study skills course by outside providers for Years 10 and 12.

What is heartening is that these ideas came from the full staff consultation process for creating the school development plan. They indicate, I think, the journey we were all embarked upon in changing the culture from one where teaching was the primary focus of our work, to one where learning is at the heart.

CONCLUSION

The key factor in turning a vision into reality is getting the culture right. This is an endless and complicated process. However, change which does not address the issue of school culture is unlikely to bring lasting success.

The key elements for shaping the culture are

- the quality of relationships at all levels of the school;
- a clear focus on the quality of learning;
- the personal involvement and example of senior staff; and
- seeing leadership and management as organisational qualities to be encouraged in all members of the school (Ogawa and Bossert, 1995).

I moved on from Dane Valley at the point when much of our work was beginning to come to fruition. The reorganisation proposals for Congleton have placed an extra burden on the school, bringing concerns about jobs and identity in the future. It is clear, however, that the acting headteacher is continuing to take forward the work we began together in an atmosphere of professional trust and confidence. Creating the right culture is, I believe, the only way in which a school community can deal effectively with the external demands for change which all of us face. It is the foundation on which everything else is built.

REFERENCES

Bowring-Carr, C. and West-Burnham, J. (1997) *Effective Learning in Schools*, London, Pitman.

Clarke, P. (1998) Lecture given to the Cheshire Association of Secondary Heads.

Ogawa, R.T. and Bossert, S.T. (1995) Leadership as an organisational quality. In Crawford, M. *et al.*, eds, (1997) *Leadership and Teams in Educational Management*, Buckingham, The Open University.

Schein, E. (1985) *Organizational Culture and Leadership*, San Francisco, Jossey-Bass.

West-Burnham, J. (1998) Lecture given to the Cheshire Association of Secondary Heads.

Index